MW00898656

DIABETIC AIR FRYER COOKBOOK

1200-Days of Crispy and Healthy Recipes to Take Care of Your Well-Being without Sacrificing Taste | Flavorful Dishes from Breakfast to Dinner

Allison Lawrence

Table of Contents

Breakfast

1. Air Fried Eggs

Preparation Time: 15 minutes **Cooking Time: 15 minutes**
Servings: 4

Ingredients:
- 4 eggs
- 2 cups baby spinach, rinsed
- 1 tbsp. extra-virgin olive oil
- ½ cup cheddar cheese, reduced-fat, shredded, divided
- Bacon, sliced
- Pinch salt
- Pinch pepper

Directions: Preheat the Air Fryer to 350°F.
Warm oil in a pan over medium-high flame. Cook the spinach until wilted. Drain the excess liquid. Put the cooked spinach into four greased ramekins.
Add a slice of bacon to each ramekin, crack an egg, and put cheese on top. Season with salt and pepper.
Put the ramekins inside the cooking basket of the Air Fryer. Cook for 15 minutes.

Nutrition: Calories: 105.5, Carbs: 9.5g, Fat: 3g, Protein: 9.5g, Fiber: 1.2g

2. Cinnamon Pancake

Preparation Time: 15 minutes **Cooking Time: 16 minutes**
Servings: 4

Ingredients:
- 2 eggs
- 2 cups cream cheese, reduced-fat
- ½ tsp. cinnamon
- 1 pack Stevia

Directions: Preheat Air Fryer to 330°F.
Combine cream cheese, cinnamon, eggs, and stevia in a blender. Pour ¼ of the mixture in the air fryer basket. Cook for 2 minutes on each side. Repeat the process with the rest of the mixture. Serve.

Nutrition: Calories: 105.7, Carbs: 9.5g, Fat: 3.2g, Fiber: 1.2g, Protein: 9.5g

3. Spinach and Mushrooms Omelet

Preparation Time: 15 minutes **Cooking Time: 6 minutes**
Servings: 4

Ingredients:
- ½ cup spinach leaves
- 1 cup mushrooms
- 3 green onions
- 1 cup water
- ½ tsp. turmeric
- ½ red bell pepper
- 2 tbsp. butter, low fat
- 1 cup almond flour
- ½ tsp. onion powder
- ½ tsp. garlic powder
- ½ tsp. fresh ground black pepper
- ¼ tsp. ground thyme
- 2 tbsp. extra-virgin olive oil
- 1 tsp. black salt
- Salsa, store-bought

Directions: Preheat the Air Fryer to 300°F. Rinse spinach leaves over tap water. Set aside.
In a mixing bowl, combine green onions, onion powder, garlic powder, red bell pepper, mushrooms, turmeric, thyme, olive oil, salt, and pepper. Mix well.
In another bowl, combine water and flour to form a smooth paste.
In a pan, heat olive oil. Sauté peppers and mushrooms for 3 minutes. Tip in spinach and cook for 3 minutes. Set aside. Put in the air fryer basket our omelet batter. Cook for 3 minutes before flipping. Place vegetables on top. Season with salt. Serve with salsa on the side.

Nutrition: Calories: 108.5, Carbs: 8.4g, Fat: 1.1g, Fiber: 1.0g, Protein: 5.9g

4. All Berries Pancakes

Preparation Time: 15 minutes **Cooking Time: 10 minutes**
Servings: 4

Ingredients:
- ½ cup frozen blueberries, thawed
- ½ cup frozen cranberries, thawed
- 1 cup coconut milk
- 2 tbsp. coconut oil, for greasing
- 2 tbsp. stevia
- 1 cup whole wheat flour, finely milled
- 1 tbsp. baking powder
- 1 tsp. vanilla extract
- ¼ tsp. salt

Directions: Preheat Air Fryer to 330°F. In a mixing bowl, combine coconut oil, coconut milk, flour, stevia, baking powder, vanilla extract, and salt. Gently fold in berries.
Divide batter into equal portions. Pour into the Air fryer basket. Flip once the edges are set. Do not press down on pancakes. Transfer to a plate. Sprinkle with palm sugar. Serve.

Nutrition: Calories: 57, Carbs: 13.6g, Fat: 0.5g, Protein: 0.9g, Fiber: 2.4g

5. Scrambled Eggs

Preparation Time: 5 minutes   **Cooking Time: 5 minutes**
Servings: 2

Ingredients:
- 4 large eggs.
- ½ cup shredded sharp Cheddar cheese.
- 2 tbsp. unsalted butter; melted.

Directions: Crack eggs into a 2-cup round baking dish and whisk. Place dish into the air fryer basket.
Set the temperature to 400 Degrees F and set the timer for 10 minutes.
After 5 minutes, stir the eggs and add the butter and cheese. Let cook for 3 minutes and stir again.
Allow eggs to finish cooking an additional 2 minutes or remove if they are to your desired liking.
Use a fork to fluff. Serve warm.

Nutrition: Calories: 358.3, Protein: 19.8g, Fiber: 0g, Fat: 27.2g, Carbs: 0.9g

6. Fennel Frittata

Preparation Time: 5 minutes   **Cooking Time: 15 minutes**
Servings: 6

Ingredients:
- 1 fennel bulb; shredded
- 6 eggs; whisked
- 2 tsp. cilantro; chopped.
- 1 tsp. sweet paprika
- Cooking spray
- A pinch of salt and black pepper

Directions: Take a bowl and mix all the ingredients except the cooking spray and stir well.
Grease a baking pan with the cooking spray, pour the frittata mix and spread well.
Put the pan in the Air Fryer and cook at 370°F for 15 minutes. Divide between plates and serve them for breakfast.

Nutrition: Calories: 199.2, Fat: 11.4g, Fiber: 1g, Carbs: 4.7g, Protein: 8.4g

7. Strawberries Oatmeal

Preparation Time: 5 minutes   **Cooking Time: 15 minutes**
Servings: 4

Ingredients:
- ½ cup coconut; shredded
- ¼ cup strawberries
- Cooking spray
- 2 cups coconut milk
- ¼ tsp. vanilla extract
- 2 tsp. stevia

Directions: Grease the Air Fryer's pan with the cooking spray, add all the ingredients inside, and toss.
Cook at 365°F for 15 minutes, divide into bowls, and serve.

Nutrition: Calories: 141.3, Fat: 6.4g, Fiber: 2g, Carbs: 2.8g, Protein: 5.4g

8. Mushroom and Cheese Frittata

Preparation Time: 20 minutes
Servings: 4

Cooking Time: 20 minutes

Ingredients:
- 6 eggs
- 6 cups button mushrooms, sliced thinly
- 1 red onion, sliced into thin rounds
- 6 tbsp. Feta cheese, reduced fat, crumbled
- Pinch salt
- 2 tbsp. olive oil

Directions: Preheat Air Fryer to 330°F.
Sauté onions and mushrooms. Transfer to a plate with a paper towel. Meanwhile, beat the eggs in a bowl.
Season with salt. Coat a baking dish with cooking spray. Pour egg mixture.
Add in mushrooms and onions. Top with crumbled feta cheese.
Place baking dish in the Air fryer basket. Cook for 20 minutes. Serve.

Nutrition: Calorie: 139.2, Carbs: 5.6g, Fat: 10.4g, Protein: 22.9g, Fiber: 1.2g

9. Cinnamon and Cheese Pancake

Preparation Time: 5–7 minutes
Servings: 4

Cooking Time: 16 minutes

Ingredients:
- 2 eggs
- 2 cups cream cheese, reduced-fat
- ½ tsp. cinnamon
- 1 pack Stevia

Directions: Preheat Air Fryer to 330°F.
Meanwhile, combine cream cheese, cinnamon, eggs, and stevia in a blender.
Pour ¼ of the mixture in the air fryer basket. Cook for 2 minutes on each side. Repeat the process with the rest of the mix. Serve.

Nutrition: Calories: 139.2, Carbs: 5.2g, Fat: 10.4g, Protein: 22.9g, Fiber: 1.2g

10. Hard-Boiled Eggs

Preparation Time: 2 minutes
Servings: 6 eggs

Cooking Time: 15 minutes

Ingredients:
- 6 pieces eggs

Directions: Arrange raw eggs on the rack of your air fryer, giving at least enough space to circulate the surrounding air. Cook the eggs for 15 minutes in the fryer at 260°F.
Remove the boiled eggs from the fryer and submerge them in a bowl with an ice-water bath for 10 minutes.

Nutrition: Calories: 61.8, Fat: 3.8g, Protein: 6.3g

11. Low-Carb White Egg and Spinach Frittata

Preparation Time: 12-15 minutes
Servings: 4

Cooking Time: 12 minutes

Ingredients:
- 8 egg whites
- 2 cups fresh spinach
- 2 tbsp. olive oil
- 1 green pepper, chopped
- 1 red pepper, chopped
- ½ cup feta cheese, reduced fat, crumbled
- ¼ yellow onion, chopped
- 1 tsp. salt
- 1 tsp. pepper

Directions: Warm the Air Fryer to 330°F.
Meanwhile, place red and green peppers and onions in the Air Fryer basket, and cook for 3 minutes. Season with salt and pepper. Pour egg whites and cook for 4 minutes. Add in the spinach and feta cheese on top.
Cook for 5 minutes. Transfer to a plate, slice, and service.

Nutrition: Calories: 119.5, Carbs: 12.4g, Fat: 4.2g, Protein: 10.2g, Fiber: 1.2g

12. Scallion Sandwich

Preparation Time: 10 minutes
Servings: 1

Cooking Time: 10 minutes

Ingredients:

- 2 slices wheat bread
- 2 tsp. butter, low fat
- 2 scallions, sliced thinly
- 1 tbsp. parmesan cheese, grated
- ¾ cup cheddar cheese, reduced-fat, grated

Directions: Preheat the Air fryer to 356°F.
Spread butter on a slice of bread. Place inside the cooking basket with the butter side facing down.
Place cheese and scallions on top. Spread the rest of the butter on the other slice of bread, put it on top of the sandwich, and sprinkle with parmesan cheese. Cook for 10 minutes.

Nutrition: Calories: 153.5, Carbs: 8.7g, Fat: 2.3g, Protein: 8.9g, Fiber: 2.4g

13. Monkey Bread

Preparation Time: 2 minutes
Servings: 8

Cooking Time: 7 minutes

Ingredients:

- 1 cup non-fat Greek yogurt
- 1 cup self-rising flour
- 1 tsp. sugar
- ½ tsp. cinnamon

Directions: Combine in a medium bowl the self-rising flour and yogurt; mix well to form into dough.
Custom the dough into a large ball and cut into fourths.
Remove each dough wedge to shape into a flattened circular disc, and then cut into eight pieces, similar to a pizza. Remove each wedge from the disc and roll it to form into balls.
Combine cinnamon and sugar in a Ziploc or resealable plastic bag. Add the dough balls and seal the bag; shake to coat the balls well. Prepare a mini loaf pan by lightly misting it with non-stick spray.
Arrange the dough balls in the pan and sprinkle lightly with the sugar-cinnamon mix.
Put the loaf pan inside the air fryer. Bake the bread for 7 minutes, at 375°F. Let cool.

Nutrition: Calories: 72.4, Carbs: 14.1g, Fiber: 0.5g, Sugar: 2.2g, Protein: 3.3g

14. Air Fryer Bacon

Preparation Time: 2 minutes
Servings: 5

Cooking Time: 10 minutes

Ingredients:

- 5 slices (thick-cut) bacon

Directions: Lay the bacon slices into your air fryer basket, at least 1 inch apart, to cook. Heat the air fryer at 390°F. Cook bacon for 10 minutes until crispy.
Drain on a kitchen napkin before serving.

Nutrition: Calories: 102.7, Fat: 2.5g, Carbs: 0.4g, Fiber: 0g, Sugar: 0g, Protein: 8.3g

15. Grilled Cheese Sandwiches

Preparation Time: 2 minutes
Servings: 2 sandwiches

Cooking Time: 7 minutes

Ingredients:

- 4 slices American cheese
- 4 slices sandwich bread
- Pat Butter

Directions: Warm your air fryer to 360°F. Fill the center of 2 bread slices with two slices of American cheese.
Binge an even layer of butter on each side of the sandwich and position it in the hamper of your air fryer in a single layer. Insert toothpicks on the corners of each sandwich to seal.
Air-fries the sandwiches for 4 minutes, flipping once, and cook for another 3 minutes until toasted.

Nutrition: Calories: 296.8, Fat: 14.4g, Carbs: 30.7g, Fiber: 1g, Sugar: 6.8g, Protein: 12.1g

16. Asparagus Omelet

Preparation Time: 10 minutes
Servings: 2

Cooking Time: 8 minutes

Ingredients:
- 3 eggs
- 5 steamed asparagus tips
- 2 tbsp. of warm milk
- 1 tbsp. parmesan cheese, grated
- Salt and pepper, to taste
- Non-stick cooking spray

Directions: Mix in a large bowl, eggs, cheese, milk, salt, and pepper, then blend them.
Spray a baking pan with non-stick cooking spray.
Transfer the mixture into the pan and add the asparagus, then place the pan inside the baking basket.
Set the air fryer to 320°F for 8 minutes. Serve warm.

Nutrition: Calories: 230.2, Fat: 9g, Carbs: 7.8g, Protein: 12.4g

17. Pumpkin Pie French Toast

Preparation Time: 10 minutes
Servings: 4

Cooking Time: 20 minutes

Ingredients:
- 2 larges, beaten eggs
- 4 slices cinnamon swirl bread
- ¼ cup milk
- ¼ cup pumpkin puree
- ¼ tsp. pumpkin spices
- ¼ cup butter

Directions: In a large mixing bowl, mix pumpkin puree, milk, eggs, and pie spice. Whisk until the mixture is smooth. In the egg mixture, dip the bread on both sides.
Place the rack inside of the air fryer's cooking basket. Place 2 slices of bread onto the rack. Set the temperature to 340°F for 10 minutes. Serve pumpkin pie toast with butter.

Nutrition: Calories: 211.5, Fat: 7.8g, Carbs: 6.7g, Protein: 11.6g

18. Breakfast Cheese Bread Cups

Preparation Time: 10 minutes
Servings: 2

Cooking Time: 15 minutes

Ingredients:
- 2 eggs
- 2 tbsp. cheddar cheese, grated
- Salt and pepper, to taste
- 1 ham slice, cut into 2 pieces
- 4 bread slices, flatten with a rolling pin

Directions: Spray the inside of 2 ramekins with cooking spray.
Place 2 flat pieces of bread into each ramekin. Add the ham slice pieces into each ramekin.
Crack an egg in each ramekin, then sprinkle with cheese. Season with salt and pepper.
Place the ramekins into the air fryer at 300°F for 15 minutes. Serve warm.

Nutrition: Calories: 161.2, Fat: 7.8g, Carbs: 9.6g, Protein: 12.1g

19. Breakfast Cod Nuggets

Preparation Time: 10 minutes
Servings: 4

Cooking Time: 10 minutes

Ingredients:
- 1 lb. cod

For breading:
- 2 eggs, beaten
- 2 tbsp. olive oil
- 1 cup almond flour
- ¾ cup breadcrumbs
- 1 tsp. dried parsley
- Pinch sea salt
- ½ tsp. black pepper

Directions: Preheat the air fryer to 390°F.
Cut the cod into strips about 1-inch by 2-inches. Blend breadcrumbs, olive oil, salt, parsley, and pepper in a food processor.

In 3 separate bowls, add breadcrumbs, eggs, and flour. Place each piece of fish into flour, then the eggs, and the breadcrumbs. Add pieces of cod to the air fryer basket and cook for 10 minutes. Serve warm.

Nutrition: Calories: 212.5, Fat: 12.2g, Carbs: 8.8g, Protein: 13.6g

20. <u>Vegetable Egg Pancake</u>

Preparation Time: 10 minutes   **Cooking Time: 15 minutes**
Servings: 2

Ingredients:
- *1 cup almond flour*
- *½ cup milk*
- *1 tbsp. parmesan cheese, grated*
- *3 eggs*
- *1 potato, grated*
- *1 beet, peeled and grated*
- *1 carrot, grated*
- *1 zucchini, grated*
- *1 tbsp. olive oil*
- *¼ tsp. nutmeg*
- *1 tsp. onion powder*
- *1 tsp. garlic powder*
- *½ tsp. black pepper*

Directions: Preheat your air fryer to 390°F.
Mix the zucchini, potato, beet, carrot, eggs, milk, almond flour, and parmesan in a bowl. Place olive oil into an oven-safe dish. Form patties with the vegetable mix and flatten them to form patties.
Place patties into an oven-safe dish and cook in the air fryer for 15 minutes.
Serve with sliced tomatoes, sour cream, and toast.

Nutrition: Calories: 222.8, Fat: 10.8g, Carbs: 10.1g, Proteins: 13.8g

21. <u>Oriental Omelet</u>

Preparation Time: 10 minutes   **Cooking Time: 24 minutes**
Servings: 1

Ingredients:
- *½ cup fresh Shimeji mushrooms, sliced*
- *2 eggs, whisked*
- *Salt and pepper, to taste*
- *1 clove garlic, minced*
- *A handful of sliced tofu*
- *2 tbsp. onion, finely chopped*
- *Cooking spray*

Directions: Spray the baking dish with cooking spray. Add onions and garlic. Air fry in the preheated air fryer at 355°F for 4 minutes. Place the tofu and mushrooms over the onions and add salt and pepper to taste.
Whisk the eggs and pour them over tofu and mushrooms. Air fry again for 20 minutes. Serve warm.

Nutrition: Calories: 209.5, Fat: 10.5g, Carbs: 8.4g, Protein: 12.9g

22. <u>Crispy Breakfast Avocado Fries</u>

Preparation Time: 10 minutes   **Cooking Time: 6 minutes**
Servings: 2

Ingredients:
- *2 eggs, beaten*
- *2 large avocados, peeled, pitted, cut into 8 slices each*
- *¼ tsp. pepper*
- *½ tsp. cayenne pepper*
- *Salt, to taste*
- *½ a lemon, Juice*
- *½ cup whole-wheat flour*
- *1 cup whole-wheat breadcrumbs*
- *Greek yogurt to serve*

Directions: Add flour, salt, pepper, and cayenne pepper to bowl and mix. Add bread crumbs into another bowl. Beat eggs in a third bowl.
First, dredge the avocado slices in the flour mixture. Next, dip them into the egg mixture, and finally dredge them in the breadcrumbs. Place avocado fries into the air fryer basket. Preheat the air fryer to 390°F.
Place the air fryer basket into the air fryer and cook for 6 minutes.
When Cooking Time is completed, transfer the avocado fries onto a serving platter.
Sprinkle with lemon juice and serve with Greek yogurt.

Nutrition: Calories: 271.5, Fat: 12.9g, Carbs: 10.8g, Protein: 15.9g

23. Cheese and Egg Breakfast Sandwich

Preparation Time: 10 minutes
Servings: 1

Cooking Time: 6 minutes

Ingredients:
- 1–2 eggs
- 1–2 slices cheddar or Swiss cheese
- A bit butters
- 1 roll sliced in half (your choice, Kaiser Bun, English muffin, etc.)

Directions: Butter your sliced roll on both sides.
Place the eggs in an oven-safe dish and whisk. Add seasoning if you wish, such as dill, chives, oregano, and salt.
Place the egg dish, roll, and cheese into the air fryer.
Make assured the buttered sides of the roll are in front of upwards. Set the air fryer to 390°F with a Cooking Time of 6 minutes. Remove the ingredients when Cooking Time is completed by the air fryer.
Place the egg and cheese between the pieces of roll and serve warm.
You might like to try adding slices of avocado and tomatoes to this breakfast sandwich!

Nutrition: Calories: 211.5, Fat: 10.7g, Carbs: 9.1g, Protein: 12.8g

24. Baked Mini Quiche

Preparation Time: 10 minutes
Servings: 2

Cooking Time: 15 minutes

Ingredients:
- 2 eggs
- 1 large yellow onion, diced
- 1 ¾ cups whole-wheat flour
- 1 ½ cups spinach, chopped
- ¾ cup cottage cheese
- Salt and black pepper, to taste
- 2 tbsp. olive oil
- ¾ cup butter
- ¼ cup milk

Directions: Preheat the air fryer to 355°F. Add the flour, butter, salt, and milk to the bowl and knead the dough until smooth and refrigerate for 15 minutes. Abode a frying pan over medium heat and add the oil to it.
When the oil is heated, add the onions into the pan and sauté them. Introduce spinach to the pan and cook until it wilts. Drain the excess moisture from spinach. Whisk the eggs together and add cheese to the bowl, and mix.
Take the dough out of the fridge and divide it into eight equal parts. Roll the dough into a ball that will fit into the bottom of the quiche mound. Place the rolled dough into molds. Place the spinach filling over the dough.
Place molds into air fryer basket and place basket inside of air fryer and cook for 15 minutes.
Remove quiche from molds and serve warm or cold.

Nutrition: Calories: 261.4, Fat: 7.8g, Carbs: 7.1g, Protein: 9.9g

25. Peanut Butter and Banana Breakfast Sandwich

Preparation Time: 10 minutes
Servings: 1

Cooking Time: 6 minutes

Ingredients:
- 2 slices whole-wheat bread
- 1 tsp. sugar-free maple syrup
- 1 sliced banana
- 2 tbsp. peanut butter

Directions: Evenly coat both sides of the slices of bread with peanut butter.
Add the sliced banana and drizzle with some sugar-free maple syrup.
Heat in the air fryer to 330°F for 6 minutes. Serve warm.

Nutrition: Calories: 210.7, Fat: 7.7g, Carbs: 6.1g, Protein: 10.7g

26. Eggs and Cocotte on Toast

Preparation Time: 10 minutes
Servings: 2

Cooking Time: 10 minutes

Ingredients:
- ⅛ tsp. black pepper
- ¼ tsp. salt
- ½ tsp. Italian seasoning
- ¼ tsp. balsamic vinegar
- ¼ tsp. sugar-free maple syrup

- 1 cup sausages, chopped into small pieces
- 2 eggs
- 2 slices whole-wheat toast
- 3 tbsp. cheddar cheese, shredded
- 6 slices tomatoes
- Cooking spray
- A little mayonnaise to serve

Directions: Spray a baking dish with cooking spray. Place the bread slices at the bottom of the dish. Sprinkle the sausages over the bread. Lay the tomatoes over it. Sprinkle the top with cheese.
Beat the eggs, and then pour over the top of bread slices. Drizzle vinegar and maple syrup over eggs.
Flavor with Italian seasoning, salt, and pepper, then sprinkle some more cheese on top.
Place the baking dish in the air fryer basket that should be preheated at 320°F and cooked for 10 minutes.
Remove from the air fryer and add a touch of mayonnaise and serve.

Nutrition: Calories 230.5, Fat: 7.1g, Carbs: 5.8g, Protein: 14.8g

27. Breakfast Frittata

Preparation Time: 10 minutes
Servings: 3

Cooking Time: 10 minutes

Ingredients:
- 6 eggs
- 8 cherry tomatoes, halved
- 2 tbsp. parmesan cheese, shredded
- 1 Italian sausage, diced
- Salt and pepper, to taste

Directions: Preheat your air fryer to 355°F.
Add the tomatoes and sausage to the baking dish. Place the baking dish into the air fryer and cook for 5 minutes.
Meanwhile, add eggs, salt, pepper, cheese, and oil into a mixing bowl, and whisk well.
Remove the baking dish from the air fryer and pour the egg mixture on top, spreading evenly.
Place the dish back into the air fryer and bake for additional 5 minutes. Remove from the air fryer and slice into wedges and serve.

Nutrition: Calories: 271.8, Fat: 7.8g, Carbs: 6.7g, Protein: 13.8g

28. Morning Mini Cheeseburger Sliders

Preparation Time: 10 minutes
Servings: 6

Cooking Time: 10 minutes

Ingredients:
- 1 lb. ground beef
- 6 slices cheddar cheese
- 6 dinner rolls
- Salt and black pepper, to taste

Directions: Preheat your air fryer to 390°F.
Form 6 beef patties, and season with salt and black pepper.
Add the burger patties to the cooking basket and cook them for 10 minutes. Remove the burger patties from the air fryer, place the cheese on top of burgers, and return to the air fryer and cook for another minute.
Remove and put burgers on dinner rolls and serve warm.

Nutrition: Calories: 261.7, Fat: 9.2g, Carbs: 7.8g, Protein: 16.8g

29. Avocado and Blueberry Muffins

Preparation Time: 10 minutes
Servings: 12

Cooking Time: 10 minutes

Ingredients:
- 2 eggs
- 1 cup blueberries
- 2 cups almond flour
- 1 tsp. baking soda
- ⅛ tsp. salt
- 2 ripe avocados, peeled, pitted, mashed
- 2 tbsp. liquid Stevia
- 1 cup plain Greek yogurt
- 1 tsp. vanilla extract

For the streusel topping:
- 2 tbsp. Truvia sweetener
- 4 tbsp. butter, softened
- 4 tbsp. almond flour

Directions: Make the streusel topping by mixing Truvia, flour, and butter until you form a crumbly mixture. Place it in the freezer for a while.

23

Meanwhile, make the muffins by sifting together flour, baking powder, baking soda, and salt, and set aside. Add avocados and liquid Stevia to a bowl and mix well. Adding in one egg at a time, continue to beat. Add the vanilla extract and yogurt and beat again.

Add in flour mixture a bit at a time and mix well. Add the blueberries into the mixture and gently fold them in. Pour the batter into greased muffin cups, then add the mixture until they are half-full.

Sprinkle the streusel topping mixture on top of the muffin mixture and place muffin cups in the air fryer basket. Bake in the preheated air fryer at 355°F for 10 minutes. Remove the muffin cups from the air fryer and allow them to cool. Cool completely, then serve.

Nutrition: Calories: 201.5, Fat: 8.7g, Carbs: 6.8g, Protein: 5.7g

30. Cheese Omelet

Preparation Time: 10 minutes   **Cooking Time: 15 minutes**
Servings: 2

Ingredients:
- 3 eggs
- 1 large yellow onion, diced
- 2 tbsp. cheddar cheese, shredded
- ½ tsp. soy sauce
- Salt and pepper, to taste
- Olive oil cooking spray

Directions: In a container, whisk together eggs, soy sauce, pepper, and salt. Spray with olive oil cooking spray a small pan that will fit inside of your air fryer.

Transfer onions to the pan and spread them around. Air fry onions for 7 minutes.

Pour the beaten egg mixture over the cooked onions and sprinkle the top with shredded cheese.

Take back into the air fryer and cook for 6 minutes more.

Remove from the air fryer and serve omelet with toasted multi-grain bread.

Nutrition: Calories: 231.4, Fat: 7.7g, Carbs: 5.7g, Protein: 12.8g

31. Cheese and Mushroom Frittata

Preparation Time: 8–10 minutes   **Cooking Time: 25 minutes**
Servings: 4

Ingredients:
- 4 cups button mushrooms, cut into ¼-inch slices
- 1 large red onion, cut into ¼-inch slices
- 2 tbsp. olive oil
- 1 tsp. garlic, minced
- 6 eggs
- Salt, to taste
- Ground black pepper, to taste
- 6 tbsp. feta cheese

Directions: Put the button mushrooms, onions, and garlic in a pan with a tbsp. of olive oil, and sauté over medium heat for 5 minutes. Transfer to a kitchen towel to dry and cool. Warm up the Air Fryer to 330°F.

Place eggs in a bowl and whisk lightly. Flavor with salt and pepper, and then whisk well.

Brush the baking accessory with olive oil.

Place sautéed onions and mushrooms in the baking accessory, crumble the feta cheese over it, and then pour the eggs on top.

Cook for 20 minutes and serve warm.

Nutrition: Calories: 230.4, Fat: 7.8g, Carbs: 5.8g, Protein: 11.8g

32. Bagels

Preparation Time: 20 minutes   **Cooking Time: 20 minutes**
Servings: 12

Ingredients:
- ½ lb. flour
- 1 tsp. active dry yeast
- 1 tsp. brown sugar
- ½ cup lukewarm water
- 2 tbsp. butter softened
- 1 tsp. salt
- 1 large egg

Directions: Liquefy the yeast and sugar in the warm water. Let rest for 5 minutes.

Add the remaining ingredients and mix until sticky dough forms. Cover and let rest for 40 minutes.

Massage the dough on a lightly floured surface and divide it into 5 large balls. Let rest for 4 minutes.

Preheat air fryer to 360°F.
Flatted the dough balls and make a hole in the center of each. Arrange the bagels on a baking sheet lined with parchment paper. Bake for 20 minutes.

Nutrition: Calories: 231.5, Fat: 7.7g, Carbs: 5.9g, Protein: 12.8g

33. Vegetarian Omelet

Preparation Time: 16 minutes   **Cooking Time: 12 minutes**
Servings: 2

Ingredients:
- 8 oz. spinach leaves
- 3 spring onions, cut into 1-inch slices
- ½ red bell pepper, cut into 1-inch cubes
- 1 cup button mushrooms, cut into ¼-inch slices
- ½ tsp. ground turmeric
- 1 tsp. thyme
- 1 tsp. Kala Namak salt
- ½ tsp. ground black pepper
- 1 tsp. minced garlic
- 3 tbsp. olive oil (extra virgin
- 2 tbsp. butter
- 1 cup chickpea flour
- 1 cup water

Directions: In a bowl, place spring onions, bell peppers, mushrooms, turmeric, thyme, Kala Namak salt, ground black pepper, minced garlic, and 2 tbsp. of olive oil. Toss well to combine. Heat a sauté pan over medium-high heat and tip in the vegetable mixture. Sauté for 3 minutes, frequently tossing.
Add spinach and butter to the pan, and sauté for another 3 minutes, frequently tossing.
Remove from the heat and set aside until needed. Place the chickpea flour and water in a bowl, and whisk to smooth batter. Grease the Air Fryer accessory with olive oil and pour in the batter.
Cook for 3 minutes at 390°F. Flip and cook for another 3 minutes.
Transfer fried Omelet on a serving plate and top with sautéed vegetables. Serve with salsa on the side.

Nutrition: Calories 231.4, Fat 7.7g, Carbs 5.8g, Protein 12.8g

34. Bacon and Cheese Rolls

Preparation Time: 8–10 minutes   **Cooking Time: 10 minutes**
Servings: 4

Ingredients:
- 1 lb. cheddar cheese, grated
- 1 lb. bacon rashers
- 1 8 oz. can Pillsbury Crescent dough

Directions: Warm up the Air Fryer to 330°F.
Cut the bacon rashers across into ¼ inch strips and mix with the cheddar cheese. Set aside.
Cut the dough sheet to 1 by 1.5 inches pieces. Place an equal amount of bacon and cheese mixture on the center of the dough pieces and pinch corners together to enclose stuffing.
Transfer the parcels in the Air Fry basket and bake for 7 minutes at 330°F.
Increase the temperature to 390°F and bake for another 3 minutes. Serve warm.

Nutrition: Calories 231.3, Fat 7.4 g, Carbs: 5.5 g, Protein 13.3 g

Snacks and Appetizers

35. Air Fryer Squash

Preparation Time: 5 minutes   **Cooking Time: 10 minutes**
Servings: 4

Ingredients:
- Olive oil: 1/2 Tablespoon
- One squash
- Salt: 1/2 teaspoon
- Rosemary: 1/2 teaspoon

Directions: Chop the squash in slices of 1/4 thickness. Discard the seeds.
In a bowl, add olive oil, salt, rosemary with squash slices. Mix well.
Cook the squash for ten minutes at 400 ° F. Flip the squash halfway through. Make sure it is cooked completely.

Nutrition: Calories: 67.4, Protein: 1.4g, Carbs: 8.4g, Fat: 3.7g

36. Air Fried Sweet Potatoes

Preparation Time: 5 minutes   **Cooking Time: 5 minutes**
Servings: 2

Ingredients:
- One sweet potato
- A pinch of salt and black pepper
- 1 tsp olive oil

Directions: Cut the peeled potato in French fries. Coat with salt, pepper, and oil.
Cook in the air fryer for 5 minutes, at 400 degrees F.
Cook potatoes in batches, in single layers and shake the basket once or twice.

Nutrition: Calories: 60.7, Protein: 1.5g, Carbs: 10.7g, Fat: 4.5g

37. Air Fried Kale Chips

Preparation Time: 5 minutes   **Cooking Time: 5 minutes**
Servings: 2

Ingredients:
- One bunch of kale
- Half tsp. of garlic powder
- One tsp. of olive oil
- Half tsp. of salt

Directions: Let the air fryer preheat to 370 degrees F. Cut the kale into small pieces and add it in a bowl, with all other ingredients. Put kale to the air fryer and cook for three minutes. Toss it and cook for two minutes more.

Nutrition: Calories: 35.7, Protein: 3.3g, Carbs: 5.1g, Fat: 0.8g

38. Vegetable Rolls

Preparation Time: 10 minutes   **Cooking Time: 8 minutes**
Servings: 4

Ingredients:
- Toasted sesame seeds
- 2 carrots, grated
- Spring roll wrappers
- One egg white
- A dash gluten-free soy sauce
- Half cabbage, sliced
- Olive oil: 2 tbsp.

Directions: In a pan over high flame heat, 2 tbsp. of oil and sauté the chopped vegetables. Add soy sauce, turn off the heat, and add toasted sesame seeds. Lay rolls on a surface and spread egg white with a brush.
Add some vegetable mix in the wrapper and fold.
Spray the rolls with oil spray and cook in the Air Fryer for 8 minutes at 380°F.

Nutrition: Calories: 125.4, Protein: 12.4g, Carbs: 7.6g, Fat: 14.6g

39. Air Fried Bacon-Wrapped Jalapeno Poppers

Preparation Time: 10 minutes   **Cooking Time: 8 minutes**
Servings: 10

Ingredients:
- Cream cheese: 1/3 cup
- Ten jalapenos
- Bacon: 5 strips

Directions: Let the air fryer preheat to 370 °F.
Wash and pat dry the jalapenos. Cut in half and take out the seeds. Spread the cream cheese. Cut the bacon strips in half. Wrap the cream cheese filled jalapenos with slices of bacon. Secure with a toothpick.
Place the jalapenos in the air fryer, cook at 370 °F for 6-8 minutes.

Nutrition: Calories: 74.7, Protein: 3.5g, Carbs: 1.4g, Fat: 6.3g

40. Air Fried Zucchini Chips

Preparation Time: 10 minutes   **Cooking Time: 10 minutes**
Servings: 2

Ingredients:
- Parmesan Cheese: 3 Tbsp.
- Garlic Powder: 1/4 tsp
- Thin sliced zucchini: 1 Cup
- Corn Starch: 1/4 Cup
- Onion Powder: 1/4 tsp
- Salt: 1/4 tsp
- Whole wheat Bread Crumbs: 1/2 Cup
- Olive oil

Directions: Let the Air Fryer preheat to 390 ° F.
In a food processor, blend into finer pieces garlic powder, salt, bread crumbs, parmesan cheese, and onion powder.
In 2 separate bowls, add corn starch in one, and whole wheat breadcrumb in the other. Coat zucchini chips into corn starch, then coat in bread crumbs.
Spray the air fryer basket with olive oil. Add breaded zucchini chips in a single layer in the air fryer and spray with olive oil.
Air fry for six minutes at preheated temperature. Cook for another four minutes after turning zucchini chips.

Nutrition: Calories: 217.6, Protein: 12.4g, Carbs: 10.4g, Fat: 20.5g

41. Crisp Egg Cups

Preparation Time: 10 minutes   **Cooking Time: 10 minutes**
Servings: 4

Ingredients:
- Toasted whole-wheat bread: 4 slices
- Cooking spray
- 4 eggs
- 1 and a half tbsp. butter (trans-fat free)
- Ham: 1 thick slice
- Salt: 1/8 tsp
- Black pepper: 1/8 tsp

Directions: Let the air fryer Preheat to 375 ° F. Take four ramekins, and spray with cooking spray.
Trim off the crusts from bread, and add butter to one side. Put the bread down into a ramekin, with butter-side in.
Cut the ham in strips, half-inch thick, and add on top of the bread.
Add one egg to each ramekin. Add salt and pepper.
Put the custard cups in the air fryer at 375 °F for 10–13 minutes.

Nutrition: Calories: 148.5, Protein: 11.5g, Carbs: 4.7g, Fat: 7.7g

42. Lemon-Garlic Tofu with Quinoa

Preparation Time: 20 minutes   **Cooking Time: 15 minutes**
Servings: 2

Ingredients:
- Cooked quinoa: 2 cups
- Lemons: two zest and juice
- Sea salt & white pepper to taste
- Tofu: one block - pressed and sliced into half pieces
- Garlic – minced: 2 cloves

Directions: Add the tofu into a deep dish.

In another bowl, add the garlic, lemon juice, lemon zest, salt, pepper.
Pour this marinade over tofu. Let it marinate for 15 minutes.
Add the tofu to the air fryer basket. Let it air fry at 370°F for 15 minutes. Shake the basket after 8 minutes of cooking. In a big deep bowl, add the cooked quinoa with the lemon-garlic Tofu, and serve.

Nutrition: Calories: 185.6, Protein: 21.5g, Carbs: 7.1g, Fat: 8.1g

43. Vegan Mashed Potato

Preparation Time: 10 minutes   **Cooking Time: 10 minutes**
Servings: 4

Ingredients:

For mashed potatoes:
- Olive oil
- Red potatoes cooked with the skin on, cut into one-inch pieces

For the Tofu:
- One teaspoon of garlic powder

- 1/4 tsp of salt
- Sea salt and black pepper - to taste

- One block of extra firm tofu: pressed, cut into one-inch pieces

- Half cup of unsweetened soy milk or vegan milk

- Light soy sauce:2 tablespoons

Directions: Add the red cooked potatoes to a large bowl, mash with masher with olive oil. Then add milk and mix well.
Cover the bowl with plastic wrap, so it will keep warm and let it rest.
Meanwhile, add the tofu in one even layer in the air fryer, add the garlic and soy sauce, and make sure to cover all the tofu. Let it cook for ten minutes at 400°F. In the bowls, add the mashed potatoes, and cover with tofu.

Nutrition: Calories: 250.6, Protein: 19.5g, Carbs: 10.6g, Fat: 14.7g

44. Vegan Sandwich

Preparation Time: 10 minutes   **Cooking Time: 10 minutes**
Servings: 4

Ingredients:

For Tofu:
- Garlic powder: 1 teaspoon
- Light soy sauce: 1/4 cup

For sandwich:
- 4 English vegan muffins
- Avocado: one cut into slices

- Turmeric: 1/2 teaspoon

- 4 tomato slices
- Vegan cheese: 4 slices

- 1 block extra firm pressed tofu: cut into 4 round slices

- 1 sliced onion
- Vegan mayonnaise

Directions: In a deep dish, add the tofu circles with turmeric, soy sauce, and garlic powder. Let it for 10 minutes.
Put the marinated tofu in an air fryer. Cook for ten minutes at 400 ° F and shake the basket after 5 minutes.
Add vegan mayonnaise to the English muffins. Add vegan cheese, avocado slices, tomato, onion, and marinated, cooked tofu. Top with the other half of the muffins.

Nutrition: Calories: 196.7, Protein: 19.5g, Carbs: 11.6g, Fat: 8.7g

45. Crispy Potatoes

Preparation Time: 10 minutes   **Cooking Time: 15 minutes**
Servings: 3

Ingredients:
- Red potatoes: 1 and 1/2 pounds
- Aquafaba: 1 tablespoon
- Tomato paste: 1 teaspoon

- Sea salt: 1 teaspoon
- Brown rice flour: half tablespoon
- Garlic powder: half teaspoon

- Sweet smoked paprika: 3/4 tsp.

Directions: Cut the potatoes into small quarters, making sure they are the same sized. The maximum thickness of potatoes should be one and a half-inch thick.

Boil the potatoes, drain and add them in a large bowl. In another bowl, add tomato paste and aquafaba.
In a third bowl, mix the remaining ingredients with flour.
Now add the last two bowls to the potatoes, and coat every piece.
Preheat the air fryer to 360°F for 3 minutes, then place the potatoes in the basket and cook for 12 minutes.
Shake the basket every six minutes, making sure no potatoes get stuck on the bottom.

Nutrition: Calories: 170.5, Protein: 5.5g, Carbs: 21.6g, Fat: 4.8g

46. <u>Veggie Air Fryer Eggs</u>

Preparation Time: 10 minutes   **Cooking Time: 14 minutes**
Servings: 4

Ingredients:
- *Shredded cheese: 1 cup*
- *Non-stick cooking spray*
- *Vegetables of your choice: 1 cup diced*
- *Chopped cilantro: 1 Tbsp.*
- *Four eggs*
- *Salt and Pepper to taste*

Directions: Take four ramekins, grease them with oil.
In a bowl, crack the eggs with half the cheese, cilantro, salt, diced vegetables, and pepper. Pour in the ramekins.
Put in the air-fryer basket and cook for 12 minutes, at 300 ° F. Then add the cheese to the cups.
Set the air-fryer at 400 degrees F and continue to cook for two minutes, until cheese is lightly browned and melted.

Nutrition: Calories: 193.7, Protein: 15.5g, Carbs: 6.1g, Fat: 10.5g

47. <u>Low Carb Baked Eggs</u>

Preparation Time: 10 minutes   **Cooking Time: 15 minutes**
Servings: 4

Ingredients:
- *Cooking Spray*
- *Grated cheese: 1-2 teaspoons*
- *One egg*
- *Fresh sautéed spinach: 1 tablespoon*
- *Salt to taste*
- *Soy milk: 1 tablespoon*
- *Black pepper to taste*

Directions: Take ramekins and spray them with cooking spray. Add milk, spinach, egg, and cheese.
Add salt and pepper. Stir everything but do not break the yolk.
Let it air fry for 6-12 minutes at 330 ° F. If you want runny yolks, cook for less time.

Nutrition: Calories: 113.9, Protein: 11.5g, Carbs: 1g, Fat: 5.7g

48. <u>Air Fryer Omelet</u>

Preparation Time: 10 minutes   **Cooking Time: 6 minutes**
Servings: 2

Ingredients:
- *Breakfast Seasoning: 1 teaspoon*
- *Two eggs*
- *A pinch of salt*
- *Milk: 1/4 cup*
- *Shredded cheese: 1/4 cup*
- *Diced veggies: green onions, red bell pepper, and mushrooms*

Directions: In a bowl, mix the milk and eggs, combine them well. Season with a pinch of salt. Add the chopped vegetables. Add the egg mixture to a 6"x3" baking pan. Make sure it is well greased.
Put the pan in the air fryer basket. Air fry for 8-10 minutes at 350º F.
After 5 minutes, add the breakfast seasoning and top with shredded cheese.
Take out from the air fryer, and transfer to the plate.

Nutrition: Calories: 225.7, Protein: 14.5g, Carbs: 7.2g, Fat: 11.6g

49. <u>Appetizer Bombs</u>

Preparation Time: 10 minutes   **Cooking Time: 15 minutes**

Servings: 3

Ingredients:
- Three eggs, lightly whisked
- Low-fat cream cheese: two tbsp. Softened
- Chopped chives: 1 tablespoon
- Freshly prepared whole-wheat pizza dough: 4 ounces
- Cooking spray
- 3 pieces of bacon

Directions: In a skillet, cook the bacon slices for about ten minutes. Crumble them. Add the eggs to the skillet and cook for almost one minute. In a bowl, mix chives, cheese, and bacon.

Cut the dough into four pieces. Make it into a five-inch circle. Add 1/4 of egg mixture in the center of each dough circle pieces. Seal the dough seams with water and pinch.

Add dough pockets in one single layer in the air fryer. Spray with cooking oil.

Cook for 5-6 minutes, at 350°F or until light golden brown.

Nutrition: Calories: 294.6, Protein: 19.5g, Carbs: 23.6g, Fat: 13.7g

50. Air Fryer Ham Tarts

Preparation Time: 5 minutes
Servings: 4

Cooking Time: 20 minutes

Ingredients:
- Chopped fresh chives: one tbsp.
- Frozen puff pastry: one sheet, thawed
- Eggs: four large
- 4 tbsp. cooked ham, chopped
- 4 tbsp. of Cheddar cheese, shredded

Directions: Let the air fryer preheat to 400 °F. Lay puff pastry on a surface and slice into four squares.

Add two squares of puff pastry in the air fryer and cook for 8 minutes.

Take out from the air fryer and make an indentation in the dough's center. Add one tbsp. Of ham and one tbsp. of cheddar cheese in every hole. Add one egg to it. Add on the other two squares of pastry. Seal the dough seams with water and pinch.

Return the basket to the air fryer. Let it cook for about six minutes.

Take out from the basket of the air fryer and cool for 5 minutes.

Top with chives and serve hot.

Nutrition: Calories: 152.6, Protein: 10.4g, Carbs: 6.8g, Fat: 6.8g

51. Cheesy Chicken Omelet

Preparation Time: 5 minutes
Servings: 2

Cooking Time: 18 minutes

Ingredients:
- Cooked Chicken Breast: half cup (diced)
- Four eggs
- Onion powder: 1/4 tsp
- Salt: 1/2 tsp.
- Pepper: 1/4 tsp.
- Shredded cheese: 2 tbsp.
- Garlic powder: 1/4 tsp.

Directions: Take two ramekins, grease with olive oil. Divided all ingredients in 2 portions.

Add two eggs to each ramekin. Add cheese, onion powder, salt, pepper, garlic and blend to combine. Add 1/4 cup of cooked chicken on top.

Cook at 330 °F for 14-18 minutes in the air fryer.

Nutrition: Calories: 184.6, Protein: 19.5g, Carbs: 8.7g, Fat: 4.7g

52. Green Onions and Parmesan Tomatoes

Preparation Time: 7 minutes
Servings: 4

Cooking Time: 15 minutes

Ingredients:
- 4 large tomatoes, cut into slices
- 1 tbsp. olive oil
- Salt and pepper to taste
- 1/2 tsp. thyme, dried
- 2 garlic cloves, minced
- 2 green onions, finely chopped
- 1/2 cup Parmesan cheese, freshly grated

Directions: Preheat your air fryer to 390ºF.

Coat the tomato slices with olive oil and season with garlic, thyme, salt, and pepper.
Top with Parmesan and chopped green onions.
Place the tomatoes in the air fryer and cook for 15 minutes.
Serve on top of crostini or any meat, poultry, or fish.

Nutrition: Calories: 68.7, Fat: 3.3g, Carbs: 64.9g, Protein: 1.9g

53. <u>Green Bell Peppers With Cauliflower Stuffing</u>

Preparation Time: 7 minutes   **Cooking Time: 10 minutes**
Servings: 4

Ingredients:
- *4 green bell peppers, top cut, deseeded*
- *1 tsp. lemon juice*
- *2 tbsp. coriander leaves, finely chopped*
- *2 green chilies, finely chopped*
- *2 cups cauliflower, cooked and mashed*
- *2 onions, finely chopped*
- *1 tsp. cumin seeds*
- *1/4 tsp. turmeric powder*
- *1/4 tsp. chili powder*
- *1/4 tsp. garam masala*
- *Salt to taste*
- *Olive oil as needed*

Directions: In a saucepan, warm the oil and sauté the chilies, onion, and cumin seeds. Swell the rest of the ingredients except the bell peppers and mix well.
Preheat the air fryer to 390ºF for 10 minutes.
Brush the green bell peppers with olive oil inside and out and stuff each pepper with cauliflower mixture.
Place them into the air fryer and grill for 10 minutes.

Nutrition: Calories: 256.8, Fat: 3.7g, Carbs: 44.1g, Protein: 12.7g

54. <u>Cheesy Chickpea and Zucchini Burgers</u>

Preparation Time: 7 minutes   **Cooking Time: 15 minutes**
Servings: 4

Ingredients:
- *1 can chickpeas, drained*
- *3 tbsp. coriander*
- *1 oz. cheddar cheese, shredded*
- *2 eggs, beaten*
- *1 tsp. garlic puree*
- *1 zucchini spiralized*
- *1 red onion, diced*
- *1 tsp. chili powder*
- *1 tsp. mixed spice*
- *Salt and pepper to taste*
- *1 tsp. cumin*

Directions: Mix all the ingredients in a mixing bowl.
Shape portions of the mixture into burgers. Place in the air fryer at 300ºF for 15 minutes.

Nutrition: Calories: 184.1, Fat: 9.7g, Carbs: 18.1g, Protein: 12.8g

55. <u>Spicy Sweet Potatoes</u>

Preparation Time: 7 minutes   **Cooking Time: 23 minutes**
Servings: 4

Ingredients:
- *3 sweet potatoes, peeled and chopped into chips*
- *1 tsp. chili powder*
- *1 tsp. paprika*
- *2 tbsp. olive oil*
- *1 tbsp. red wine vinegar*
- *1 tomato, thinly sliced*
- *1/2 cup tomato sauce*
- *1 onion, peeled and diced*
- *Salt and pepper to taste*
- *1 tsp. rosemary*
- *1 tsp. oregano*
- *1 tsp. mixed spice*
- *2 tsp. thyme*
- *2 tsp. coriander*

Directions: Toss the chips in a bowl with olive oil. Add to the air fryer and cook for 15 minutes at 360ºF.
Mix the remaining ingredients in a baking dish. Place the sauce in the air fryer for 8 minutes.
Toss the potatoes in the sauce and serve warmly.

Nutrition: Calories: 302.5, Fat: 4.6g, Carbs: 56.5g, Protein: 8.7g

56. Olive, Cheese, and Broccoli

Preparation Time: 7 minutes
Servings: 4
Cooking Time: 15 minutes

Ingredients:
- 2 lbs. broccoli florets
- 2 tbsp. olive oil
- 1/4 cup Parmesan cheese shaved
- 2 tsp. lemon zest, grated
- 1/3 cup Kalamata olives (halved, pitted
- 1/2 tsp. ground black pepper
- 1 tsp. sea salt
- Water

Directions: Boil the water in a pan over medium heat and cook the broccoli for about 4 minutes. Drain. Add the broccoli with salt, pepper, and olive oil in a bowl.
Place in the air fryer and cook at 400ºF for 15 minutes.
Stir twice during the Cooking Time. Place on a plate and toss with lemon zest, cheese, and olives.

Nutrition: Calories: 213.5, Fat: 13.2g, Carbs: 12.8g, Protein: 12.9g

57. Veggie Mix

Preparation Time: 7 minutes
Servings: 4
Cooking Time: 35 minutes

Ingredients:
- 1/2 lb. carrots, peeled, cubed
- 6 tsp. olive oil
- 1/2 tsp. tarragon leaves
- 1/2 tsp. white pepper
- Salt to taste
- 1 lb. yellow squash, chopped into wedges
- 1 lb. zucchini, chopped into wedges

Directions: Toss the carrots with 2 tsp. of olive oil in your air fryer basket. Cook at 400ºF for 5 minutes.
Pour the squash and zucchini along with the remaining oil, salt, and pepper into the air fryer. Cook for 30 more minutes, stirring twice during the Cooking Time. Toss with tarragon and serve.

Nutrition: Calories: 161.5, Fat: 1g, Carbs: 29.7g, Protein: 7.1g

58. Garlic Potatoes

Preparation Time: 7 minutes
Servings: 2
Cooking Time: 10 minutes

Ingredients:
- 8 oz. boiled baby potatoes
- 1/2 tsp. sesame seeds
- Red chili powder to taste
- Salt and pepper to taste
- 1/2 tsp. garlic paste
- 1/4 tsp. coriander seeds, dry roasted
- 1/4 tsp. cumin seeds, dry roasted
- 1/2 cup fresh cream

Directions: Grind the coriander and cumin seeds to form a powder. Toss all the ingredients in a baking dish except the cream.
Preheat your air fryer for 5 minutes at 360ºF. Cook the potatoes for 5 minutes.
Mix with the cream and air fry for 5 extra minutes. Garnish with sesame seeds.

Nutrition: Calories: 497.8, Fat: 18.8g, Carbs: 66.7g, Protein: 16.8g

59. Red Cabbage and Mushroom Stickers

Preparation Time: 12 minutes
Servings: 12 potstickers
Cooking Time: 15 minutes

Ingredients:
- 1 cup red cabbage, shredded
- 1/4 cup button mushrooms, chopped
- 1/4 cup carrot, grated
- 2 tbsp. onion, minced
- 2 garlic cloves, minced
- 2 tsp. fresh ginger, grated
- 12 Gyoza potsticker wrappers
- 2 1/2 tsp. olive oil, divided
- 1 tbsp. water

Directions: Combine the red cabbage, mushrooms, carrot, onion, garlic, and ginger in a baking pan. Add 1 tbsp. of water. Place in the air fryer and bake at 370ºF for 6 minutes, until the vegetables are crisp-tender. Drain and set aside.

Working one at a time, place the potsticker wrappers on a work surface. Top each wrapper with a scant 1 tbsp. of the filling. Fold half of the wrapper over the other half to form a half-circle. Dab with water and press both edges together.

Spread 1 1/4 tsp. of olive oil on the baking pan. Put half of the potstickers, seam-side up, in the pan. Air fry for 5 minutes. Add 1 tbsp. of water and return the pan to the air fryer.

Air fry for 4 minutes more, or until hot. Repeat with the remaining potstickers, the remaining 1 1/4 tsp. of oil, and another tbsp. of water. Serve immediately.

Nutrition: Calories: 87.5, Fat: 2.8g, Protein: 2.5g, Carbs: 13.5g, Fiber: 1g, Sugar: 1g

60. Garlic Roasted Mushrooms

Preparation Time: 3 minutes   **Cooking Time: 22 minutes**
Servings: 4

Ingredients:
- 16 garlic cloves, peeled
- 2 tsp. olive oil, divided
- 16 button mushrooms
- 1/2 tsp. marjoram, dried
- 1/8 tsp. freshly ground black pepper
- 1 tbsp. white wine or low-sodium vegetable broth

Directions: In a baking pan, mix the garlic with 1 tsp. of olive oil. Roast in the air fryer at 350ºF for 12 minutes. Add the mushrooms, marjoram, and pepper; stir to coat.

Drizzle with the remaining 1 tsp. of olive oil and white wine. Return to the air fryer and roast for 10 minutes more, or until the mushrooms and garlic cloves are tender. Serve.

Nutrition: Calories: 127.7, Fat: 3.5g, Protein: 13.5g, Carbs: 16.5g, Fiber: 4g, Sugar: 7.7g

61. Onion Bites

Preparation Time: 10 minutes   **Cooking Time: 10 minutes**
Servings: 20 onion bites

Ingredients:
- 20 white boiler onions
- 1 cup buttermilk
- 2 eggs
- 1 cup flour
- 1 cup whole-wheat bread crumbs
- 1 tbsp. smoked paprika
- 1 tsp. salt
- 1 tsp. ground black pepper
- 1 tsp. garlic, granulated
- 3/4 tsp. chili powder
- Olive oil spray

Directions: Place a parchment liner in the air fryer basket.

Slice off the root end of the onions, taking off as little as possible.

Peel off the papery skin and make cuts halfway through the tops of the onions. Don't cut too far down; you want the onion to hold together still. In a large bowl, beat the buttermilk and eggs together.

Mix the flour, bread crumbs, paprika, salt, pepper, garlic, and chili powder in a medium bowl.

Add the prepared onions to the buttermilk mixture and allow to soak for at least 10 minutes.

Remove the onions from the batter and dredge them with the bread crumb mixture.

Place the prepared onions in the air fryer basket in a single layer. Spray lightly with olive oil and air fry at 360ºF for 8–10 minutes, until golden and crispy. Repeat with any remaining onions and serve.

Nutrition: Calories: 165.5, Fat: 1.8g, Protein: 6.4g, Carbs: 30.5g, Fiber: 4g, Sugar: 6.7g

62. Parmesan Cauliflower

Preparation Time: 12 minutes   **Cooking Time: 20 minutes**
Servings: 20 cauliflower bites

Ingredients:
- 4 cups cauliflower florets
- 1 cup whole-wheat bread crumbs
- 1 tsp. coarse sea salt or kosher salt
- 1/4 cup Parmesan cheese, grated
- 1/4 cup butter
- 1/4 cup mild hot sauce
- Olive oil spray

Directions: Place a parchment liner in the air fryer basket.

Cut the cauliflower florets in half and set them aside.

In a small bowl, mix the bread crumbs, salt, and Parmesan; set aside.

In a small microwave-safe bowl, combine the hot sauce and butter. Heat in the microwave until the butter is melted, about 15 seconds. Whisk.

Holding the stems of the cauliflower florets, dip them in the butter mixture to coat. Shake off any excess mixture. Dredge the dipped florets with the bread crumb mixture, then put them in the air fryer basket. There's no need for a single layer; just toss them all in there.

Spray the cauliflower lightly with olive oil and air fry at 350ºF for 15 minutes, shaking the basket a few times throughout the cooking process. The florets are done when they are lightly browned and crispy. Serve warm.

Nutrition: Calories: 105.5, Fat: 5.7g, Protein: 3.5g, Carbs: 9.5g, Fiber: 1g, Sugar: 1g

63. Parmesan French Fries

Preparation Time: 5 minutes
Servings: 16 fries

Cooking Time: 20 minutes

Ingredients:
- 2 russet potatoes, washed
- 1 tbsp. olive oil
- 1 tbsp. garlic, granulated
- 1/4 cup Parmesan cheese, grated
- 1/4 tsp. salt
- 1/4 tsp. ground black pepper
- 1 tbsp. fresh parsley, finely chopped (optional)

Directions: Cut the potatoes into thin wedges and place them in a bowl.

Drizzle the oil over the russet potatoes, and toss to coat.

Sprinkle with the garlic, Parmesan cheese, salt, and pepper, and toss again.

Place in the air fryer basket and cook at 400ºF for 20 minutes, stirring halfway through to ensure even cooking. Top with the parsley, and serve warm.

Nutrition: Calories: 208.7, Fat: 4.6g, Protein: 6.5g, Carbs: 34.7g, Fiber: 2g, Sugar: 1g

64. Corn Tortilla Chips

Preparation Time: 5 minutes
Servings: 4

Cooking Time: 8 minutes

Ingredients:
- 4 (6-inch) corn tortillas
- 1 tbsp. canola oil
- 1/4 tsp. kosher salt

Directions: Stack the corn tortillas, cut them in half, then slice them into thirds.

Spray the air fryer basket with non-stick cooking spray, brush the tortillas with canola oil and place them in the basket. Air fry at 360ºF for 5 minutes.

Pause the fryer to shake the basket, then air fry for 3 more minutes or until golden brown and crispy.

Remove the chips from the fryer and place them on a plate lined with a paper towel. Sprinkle with the kosher salt on top before serving warm.

Nutrition: Calories: 71.6, Fat: 3.6g, Protein: 1.6g, Carbs: 7.8g, Fiber: 1g, Sugar: 0g

65. Cream Buns with Strawberries

Preparation Time: 10 minutes
Servings: 6

Cooking Time: 12 minutes

Ingredients:
- 240g all-purpose flour
- 50g granulated sugar
- 8g baking powder
- 1g of salt
- 85g chopped cold butter
- 84g chopped fresh strawberries
- 120 ml whipping cream
- 2 large eggs
- 10 ml vanilla extract
- 5 ml of water

Directions: Sift flour, sugar, baking powder and salt in a large bowl. Put the butter with the flour with the use of a blender or your hands until the mixture resembles thick crumbs.

Mix the strawberries in the flour mixture. Set aside for the mixture to stand. Beat the whipping cream, 1 egg and the vanilla extract in a separate bowl.

Put the cream mixture in the flour mixture until they are homogeneous, and then spread the mixture to a thickness of 38 mm.
Use a round cookie cutter to cut the buns. Spread the buns with a combination of egg and water. Set aside
Preheat the air fryer, set it to 375°F.
Place baking paper in the preheated inner basket. Place the buns on top and cook for 12 minutes.

Nutrition: Calories: 149, Fat: 13.4g, Carbs: 2.8g, Protein: 11.2g, Sugar: 7.6g

66. Blueberry Buns

Preparation Time: 10 minutes   **Cooking Time: 12 minutes**
Servings: 6

Ingredients:
- 240g all-purpose flour
- 50g granulated sugar
- 8g baking powder
- 2g of salt
- 85g chopped cold butter
- 85g of fresh blueberries
- 3g grated fresh ginger
- 113 ml whipping cream
- 2 large eggs
- 4 ml vanilla extract
- 5 ml of water

Directions: Put sugar, flour, baking powder and salt in a large bowl.
Put the butter with the flour using a blender or your hands until the mixture resembles thick crumbs.
Mix the blueberries and ginger in the flour mixture and set aside.
Mix the whipping cream, 1 egg and the vanilla extract in a different container.
Put the cream mixture with the flour mixture until combined.
Shape the dough until it reaches a thickness of approximately 38 mm and cut it into eighths.
Spread the buns with a combination of egg and water. Set aside Preheat the air fryer set it to 380°F.
Place baking paper in the preheated inner basket and place the buns on top of the paper. Cook for 12 minutes.

Nutrition: Calories: 104, Fat: 1.63g, Carbs: 19.3g, Protein: 2.4g, Sugar: 2g

67. French Toast in Sticks

Preparation Time: 5 minutes   **Cooking Time: 10 minutes**
Servings: 4

Ingredients:
- 4 slices of white bread, 38 mm thick, preferably hard
- 2 eggs
- 60 ml of milk
- 15 ml maple sauce
- 2 ml vanilla extract
- Nonstick Spray Oil
- 38g of sugar
- 3ground cinnamon
- Maple syrup, to serve
- Sugar to sprinkle

Directions: Cut each slice of bread into thirds making 12 pieces. Place sideways.
Beat the eggs, milk, maple syrup and vanilla.
Preheat the air fryer, to 330°F.
Dip the sliced bread in the egg mixture and place it in the preheated air fryer. Sprinkle French toast generously with oil spray. Cook French toast for 10 minutes at 330°F. Turn the toast halfway through cooking.
Mix the sugar and cinnamon in a bowl. Cover the French toast with the sugar and cinnamon mixture when you have finished cooking.
Serve with Maple syrup and sprinkle with powdered sugar.

Nutrition: Calories 126, Fat 5.2g, Carbs 16.1g, Sugar 3.2g, Protein 3.1g

68. Muffins Sandwich

Preparation Time: 2 minutes   **Cooking Time: 10 minutes**
Servings: 1

Ingredients:
- Nonstick Spray Oil
- 1 slice of white cheddar cheese
- 1 slice of Canadian bacon
- 1 English muffin, divided
- 15 ml hot water
- 1 large egg
- Salt and pepper to taste

Directions: Spray the inside of an 85g mold with oil spray and place it in the air fryer.
Preheat the air fryer, set it to 350°F.
Add the Cheddar cheese and bacon in the preheated air fryer.
Pour the hot water and the egg into the hot pan and season with salt and pepper. Select Bread, set to 10 minutes. Take out the muffins after 7 minutes, leaving the egg for the full time.
Build your sandwich by placing the cooked egg on top of the muffins and serve.

Nutrition: Calories 401, Fat 25.6g, Carbs 26g, Sugar 14.3g, Protein 3.2g

69. Bacon BBQ

Preparation Time: 2 minutes
Servings: 2
Cooking Time: 8 minutes

Ingredients:
- 13g dark brown sugar
- 5g chili powder
- 1g ground cumin
- 1g cayenne pepper
- 4 slices of bacon, cut in half

Directions: Mix seasonings until well combined.
Dip the bacon in the dressing until it is completely covered. Leave aside.
Preheat the air fryer, set it to 350°F.
Place the bacon in the preheated air fryer. Select Bacon and press Start/Pause.

Nutrition: Calories: 123, Fat: 42g, Carbs: 51g, Protein: 46g, Sugar: 10.2g

70. Garlic Kale Chips

Preparation Time: 6–7 minutes
Servings: 2
Cooking Time: 5 minutes

Ingredients:
- 1 tbsp. yeast flakes
- Sea salt to taste
- 4 cups packed kale
- 2 tbsp. olive oil
- 1 tsp. garlic, minced
- ½ cup ranch seasoning pieces

Directions: In a bowl, place the oil, kale, garlic, and ranch seasoning pieces. Add the yeast and mix well. Dump the coated kale into an air fryer basket and cook at 375°F for 5 minutes.
Shake after 3 minutes and serve.

Nutrition: Calories 51, Fat 1.7g, Carbs 9.9g, Protein 46.3g

71. Garlic Salmon Balls

Preparation Time: 7 minutes
Servings: 2
Cooking Time: 10 minutes

Ingredients:
- 6 oz. tinned salmon
- 1 large egg
- 3 tbsp. olive oil
- 5 tbsp. wheat germ
- ½ tsp. garlic powder
- 1 tbsp. dill, fresh, chopped
- 4 tbsp. spring onion, diced
- 4 tbsp. celery, diced

Directions: Preheat your air fryer to 370°F. In a large bowl, mix the salmon, egg, celery, onion, dill, and garlic. Shape the mixture into small balls and roll in the wheat germ. In a small skillet, warm olive oil over medium-low heat. Add the salmon balls and slowly flatten them. Handover them to your air fryer and cook for 10 minutes.

Nutrition: Calories: 218, Fat 7.5g, Carbs 14.2g, Protein 22g

72. Onion Rings

Preparation Time: 7 minutes
Servings: 3
Cooking Time: 10 minutes

Ingredients:
- 1 onion, cut into slices, separate into rings
- 1 cup of milk
- ¾ cup pork rinds
- 1 1/4 cup almond flour
- 1 egg
- 1 tbsp. baking powder
- ½ tsp. salt

Directions: Preheat your air fryer for 10 minutes. Slice onion, then separate into rings. In a bowl, integrate the baking powder, flour, and salt.
Beat in the eggs and milk, then combines with the flour. Dip the onion rings into the batter to coat them.
Spread the pork rinds on a plate and dip the rings into the crumbs. Place the onion rings in your air fryer and cook for 10 minutes at 360ºF.

Nutrition: Calories: 303, Fat: 17.6g, Carbs: 32g, Protein: 37g

73. Eggplant Fries

Preparation Time: 7 minutes   **Cooking Time: 12 minutes**
Servings: 3

Ingredients:
- 2 eggplants
- ¼ cup olive oil
- ¼ cup almond flour
- ½ cup water

Directions: Preheat your air fryer to 390ºF. Cut the eggplants into ½-inch slices. In a mixing bowl, mix the water, flour, olive oil, and eggplants.
Coat the eggplants and add them to the air fryer and cook for 12 minutes. Serve with yogurt or tomato sauce.

Nutrition: Calories: 102, Fat: 7.2g, Carbs: 11.3g, Protein: 1.7g

74. Roasted Bell Peppers

Preparation Time: 7 minutes   **Cooking Time: 5 minutes**
Servings: 3
Ingredients:
- 2 bell peppers, sliced and seeded
- 1 tsp. olive oil
- 1 pinch sea salt
- 1 lemon
- Pepper

Directions: Preheat the air fryer to 390ºF. Scatter the peppers with salt and oil and cook in the air fryer for 5 minutes.
Place peppers in a bowl, and squeeze lemon juice over the top. Season with salt and pepper.

Nutrition: Calories: 29, Fat: 0.24g, Carbs: 6.1g, Protein: 1.8g

75. Garlic Tomatoes

Preparation Time: 7 minutes   **Cooking Time: 14 minutes**
Servings: 4

Ingredients:
- 4 tomatoes
- 3 tbsp. vinegar
- ½ tsp. thyme, dried
- 1 tbsp. olive oil
- Salt and black pepper to taste
- 1 garlic clove, minced

Directions: Preheat the air fryer to 390ºF. Scrape the tomatoes into halves and remove the seeds. Place them in a bowl and toss with garlic, thyme, oil, salt, and pepper.
Place them into the air fryer and cook for 14 minutes. Drizzle with vinegar and serve.

Nutrition: Calories: 27.9, Fat: 2.3g, Carbs: 2g, Protein: 0.3g

76. Cheese and Onion Nuggets

Preparation Time: 7 minutes   **Cooking Time: 12 minutes**
Servings: 4

Ingredients:
- 7 oz. Edam cheese, grated
- 2 spring onions, diced
- 1 egg, beaten
- 1 tbsp. coconut oil
- 1 tbsp. thyme, dried
- Salt and pepper to taste

Directions: Mix the oil, cheese, thyme, onion, salt, and pepper in a bowl. Make 8 balls and place the Edam cheese in the center.
Place in the fridge for an hour. With a pastry brush, brush the beaten egg over the nuggets. Cook for 12 minutes in the air fryer at 350°F.

Nutrition: Calories:226, Fat:17.1g, Carbs:4.3g, Protein:14g

77. Spiced Nuts

Preparation Time: 7 minutes   Cooking Time: 25 minutes
Servings: 3
Ingredients:
- 1 cup almonds
- 1 cup pecan halves
- 1 cup cashews
- 1 egg white, beaten
- ½ tsp. cinnamon, ground
- Pinch cayenne pepper
- ¼ tsp. cloves, ground
- Pinch salt

Directions: Combine the egg white with spices. Preheat your air fryer to 300°F.
Toss the nuts in the spiced mixture. Cook for 25 minutes, stirring throughout cooking time.

Nutrition: Calories: 88.3, Fat: 7.4g, Carbs: 3.7g, Protein: 2.4g

78. Ketogenic French Fries

Preparation Time: 7 minutes   Cooking Time: 20 minutes
Servings: 4

Ingredients:
- 1 large rutabaga, peeled, cut into spears about ¼-inch wide
- Salt and pepper to taste
- ½ tsp. paprika
- 2 tbsp. coconut oil

Directions: Preheat your air fryer to 450°F. Mix the oil, paprika, salt, and pepper.
Pour the oil mixture over the rutabaga. Cook in the air fryer for 20 minutes or until crispy.

Nutrition: Calories: 112, Fat: 7.1g, Carbs: 12.3g, Protein: 1.8g

79. Garlic Green Tomatoes

Preparation Time: 7 minutes   Cooking Time: 12 minutes
Servings: 2

Ingredients:
- 3 green tomatoes, sliced
- ½ cup almond flour
- 2 eggs, beaten
- Salt and pepper to taste
- 1 tsp. garlic, minced

Directions: Season the tomatoes with garlic, salt, and pepper. Preheat your air fryer to 400°F. Dip the tomatoes first in flour then in the egg mixture.
Spray the tomato rounds with oil and place in the air fryer basket. Cook for 9 minutes, then flip over and cook for additional 3 minutes.

Nutrition: Calories: 122.5, Fat: 3.2g, Carbs: 15.7g, Protein: 8.7g

80. Garlic Cauliflower Nuggets

Preparation Time: 7 minutes   Cooking Time: 20 minutes
Servings: 4

Ingredients:
- 1 crown cauliflower, chopped in a food processor
- ½ cup parmesan cheese, grated
- Salt and pepper to taste
- ¼ cup almond flour
- 2 eggs
- 1 tsp. garlic, minced

Directions: Mix all the ingredients. Shape into nuggets and spray with olive oil. Preheat your air fryer to 400°F.

Cook for 10 minutes on each side.

Nutrition: Calories: 17.5, Fat: 0.5g, Carbs: 1.1g, Protein: 2.3g

81. Zucchini Crisps

Preparation Time: 30 minutes   **Cooking Time: 30 minutes**
Servings: 2
Ingredients:
* *2 zucchinis, sliced into a ⅛-inch thick disk*
* *Pinch sea salt*
* *White pepper to taste*
* *1 tbsp. of olive oil for drizzling*

Directions: Preheat the air fryer to 330°F.
Place zucchini in a bowl with salt. Let them drain in a colander for 30 minutes.
Layer zucchini in a overproof dish. Drizzle with oil and season with pepper. Place baking dish in the air fryer basket and cook for 30 minutes. Adjust seasoning and serve.

Nutrition: Calories: 15, Carbs: 3.1g, Fat: 0.1g, Protein: 0.9g, Fiber: 1.3g

82. Skinny Pumpkin Chips

Preparation Time: 20 minutes   **Cooking Time: 13 minutes**
Servings: 2

Ingredients:
* *1 lb. pumpkin, cut into sticks*
* *1 tbsp. coconut oil*
* *½ tsp. rosemary*
* *½ tsp. basil*
* *Salt and ground black pepper to taste*

Directions: Start by preheating the air fryer to 395°F. Brush the pumpkin sticks with coconut oil; add the spices and toss to combine.
Cook for 13 minutes, shaking the basket halfway through the Cooking Time. Serve with mayonnaise. Enjoy!

Nutrition: Calories: 117.5, Fat; 14.1g, Carbs; 1.7g, Protein; 6.8g, Sugar: 6.5g

83. Ripe Plantains

Preparation Time: 10 minutes   **Cooking Time: 10 minutes**
Servings: 2

Ingredients:
* *2 pcs. ripe plantain, peeled and sliced*
* *1 tbsp. coconut butter, unsweetened*

Directions: Preheat the air fryer to 350°F.
Brush a small amount of coconut butter on all sides of plantain disks.
Place one even layer into the air fryer basket, making sure none overlap or touch. Fry plantains for 10 minutes. Remove from the basket. Place on plates. Repeat step for all plantains. While plantains are still warm. Serve.

Nutrition: Calories: 208.7, Carbs: 28.7g, Fat: 7.5g, Protein: 3.5g, Fiber: 3.5g

Poultry

84. Lemon-Garlic Chicken

Preparation Time: 2 hours
Servings: 4
Cooking Time: 35 minutes

Ingredients:
- Lemon juice ¼ cup
- 1 Tbsp. olive oil
- 1 tsp mustard
- Cloves of garlic
- ¼ tsp salt
- ⅛ tsp black pepper
- Chicken thighs
- Lemon wedges

Directions: In a bowl, whisk together the olive oil, lemon juice, mustard Dijon, garlic, salt, and pepper.
Place the chicken thighs in a large ziploc bag. Spill marinade over chicken & seal bag, ensuring all chicken parts are covered. Cool for at least 2 hours.
Preheat a frying pan to 360 F. Remove the chicken with towels from the marinade, & pat dry.
Place pieces of chicken in the air fryer basket, if necessary, cook them in batches.
Fry till chicken is no longer pink on the bone & the juices run smoothly, 22 to 24 min. Upon serving, press a lemon slice across each piece.

Nutrition: Calories: 257.5, Protein: 19.9g, Carbs: 3.1g, Fat: 18.1g

85. Herb-Marinated Chicken Thighs

Preparation Time: 30 minutes
Servings: 4
Cooking Time: 12 minutes

Ingredients:
- Chicken thighs: 8 skin-on, bone-in,
- Lemon juice: 2 Tablespoon
- Onion powder: half teaspoon
- Garlic powder: 2 teaspoon
- Spike Seasoning: 1 teaspoon.
- Olive oil: 1/4 cup
- Dried basil: 1 teaspoon
- Dried oregano: half teaspoon.
- Black Pepper: 1/4 tsp

Directions: In a bowl, add dried oregano, olive oil, lemon juice, dried sage, garlic powder, Spike Seasoning, onion powder, dried basil, black pepper.
In a ziploc bag, add the spice blend and the chicken and mix well. Marinate the chicken in the refrigerator for six hours or more.
Preheat the air fryer to 360F.
Put the chicken in the air fryer basket, cook for 6 minutes, flip the chicken, and cook for 6 minutes more.
Take out from the air fryer and serve with microgreens.

Nutrition: Calories: 99.6, Protein: 4.5g, Carbs: 1g, Fat: 8.7g

86. Popcorn Chicken in Air Fryer

Preparation Time: 10 minutes
Servings: 4
Cooking Time: 10 minutes

Ingredients:
For Marinade:
- 8 cups, chicken tenders, cut into bite-size pieces
- Freshly ground black pepper: 1/2 tsp
- Almond milk: 2 cups
- Salt: 1 tsp
- Paprika: 1/2 tsp

Dry Mix:
- Salt: 3 tsp
- Flour: 3 cups
- Paprika: 2 tsp
- Oil spray
- Freshly ground black pepper: 2 tsp

Directions: In a bowl, add all marinade ingredients and chicken. Mix well, and put it in a ziploc bag and refrigerator for two hours for the minimum, or six hours.
In a large bowl, add all the dry ingredients.
Coat the marinated chicken to the dry mix. Into the marinade again, then for the second time in the dry mixture.
Spray the air fryer basket with olive oil and place the breaded chicken pieces in one single layer. Spray oil over the chicken pieces too. Cook at 370F for 10 minutes, tossing halfway through.

Serve immediately with salad greens or dipping sauce.

Nutrition: Calories: 339.5, Protein: 20.5g, Carbs: 13.4g, Fat: 9.6g

87. <u>Orange Chicken Wings</u>

Preparation Time: 5 minutes   Cooking Time: 35 minutes
Servings: 2

Ingredients:
- *Chicken Wings, Six pieces*
- *One orange zest and juice*
- *Worcestershire Sauce: 1.5 tbsp.*
- *Black pepper to taste*
- *Herbs (sage, rosemary, oregano, parsley, basil, thyme, and mint)*

Directions: Wash and pat dry the chicken wings
In a bowl, add chicken wings, pour zest and orange juice
Add the rest of the ingredients and rub on chicken wings. Let it marinate for at least half an hour.
Let the Air fryer preheat at 356F.
In an aluminum foil, wrap the marinated wings and put them in an air fryer, and cook for 20 minutes at 356F.
Remove aluminum foil and brush the sauce over wings and cook for 15 minutes more. Then again, brush the sauce and cook for another ten minutes.
Take out from the air fryer and serve hot.

Nutrition: Calories: 270.5, Protein: 29.5g, Carbs: 19.6g, Fat: 14.5g

88. <u>Chicken Pie</u>

Preparation Time: 10 minutes   Cooking Time: 30 minutes
Servings: 2

Ingredients:
- *Puff pastry: 2 sheets*
- *Chicken thighs: 2 pieces, cut into cubes*
- *One small onion, chopped*
- *Small potatoes: 2, chopped*
- *Mushrooms: 1/4 cup*
- *Light soya sauce*
- *One carrot, chopped*
- *Black pepper to taste*
- *Worcestershire sauce: to taste*
- *Salt to taste*
- *Italian mixed dried herbs*
- *Garlic powder: a pinch*
- *Plain flour: 2 tbsp.*
- *Milk, as required*
- *Melted butter*

Directions: In a mixing bowl, add light soya sauce and pepper add the chicken cubes, and coat well.
In a pan over medium heat, sauté potatoes, carrot, and onion. Add some water, if required, to cook the vegetables. Add the chicken cubes and mushrooms and cook them too.
Stir in black pepper, salt, Worcestershire sauce, garlic powder, and dried herbs.
When the chicken is cooked through, add some of the flour and mix well.
Add in the milk and let the vegetables simmer until tender.
Place one piece of puff pastry in the baking tray of the air fryer, poke holes with a fork.
Add on top the cooked chicken filling and eggs and puff pastry on top with holes. Cut the excess pastry off. Glaze with melted butter.
Air fry at 180 F for six minutes, or until it becomes golden brown.
Serve right away and enjoy.

Nutrition: Calories: 223.5, Protein: 20.5g, Carbs: 16.4g, Fat: 17.5 g

89. <u>Blackened Chicken Breast</u>

Preparation Time: 10 minutes   Cooking Time: 20 minutes
Servings: 2

Ingredients:
- *Paprika: 2 teaspoons*
- *Ground thyme: 1 teaspoon*
- *Cumin: 1 teaspoon*
- *Cayenne pepper: half tsp.*
- *Onion powder: half tsp.*
- *Black Pepper: half tsp.*
- *Salt: ¼ teaspoon*
- *Vegetable oil: 2 teaspoons*
- *Pieces of chicken breast halves (without bones and skin)*

Directions: In a mixing bowl, add onion powder, salt, cumin, paprika, black pepper, thyme, and cayenne pepper. Mix it well.

Drizzle oil over chicken and rub. Dip each piece of chicken in blackening spice blend on both sides.
Let it rest for five minutes while the air fryer is preheating. Preheat it for five minutes at 360°F.
Put the chicken in the air fryer and let it cook for ten minutes. Flip and then cook for another ten minutes.
After, let it sit for five minutes, then slice and serve with the side of greens.

Nutrition: Calories: 431.4, Protein: 79.8g, Carbs: 2.8g, Fat: 9.1g

90. <u>Air Fried Chicken Fajitas</u>

Preparation Time: 10 minutes   **Cooking Time: 15 minutes**
Servings: 6

Ingredients:
- Chicken breasts: 4 cups, cut into thin strips
- Bell peppers, sliced
- Salt: half tsp.
- Cumin: 1 tsp.
- Garlic powder: 1/4 tsp
- Chili powder: half tsp.
- Lime juice: 1 tbsp.

Directions: In a bowl, add seasonings, chicken and lime juice, and mix well.
Then add sliced peppers and coat well.
Spray the air fryer with olive oil. Put the chicken and peppers in, and cook for 15 minutes at 400 F. Flip halfway through. Serve with wedges of lemons and enjoy.

Nutrition: Calories: 139.5, Proteins: 22.8g, Carbs: 5.8g, Fat: 4.8g

91. <u>Air Fryer Brown Rice Chicken Fried</u>

Preparation Time: 10 minutes   **Cooking Time: 10 minutes**
Servings: 2

Ingredients:
- Olive Oil Cooking Spray
- Chicken Breast: 1 Cup, Diced & Cooked &
- White Onion: 1/4 cup chopped
- Celery: 1/4 Cup chopped
- Cooked brown rice: 4 Cups
- Carrots: 1/4 cup chopped

Directions: Place foil on the air fryer basket, make sure to leave room for air to flow, roll up on the sides.
Spray with olive oil. Mix all ingredients and add them on the top of the foil, in the air fryer basket.
Give an olive oil spray on the mixture. Cook for five minutes at 390°F.
Open the air fryer and give a toss to the mixture. Cook for five more minutes at 390F.

Nutrition: Calories: 349.6, Protein: 22.4g, Carbs: 19.8g, Fat: 5.6g

92. <u>Buttermilk Chicken in Air-Fryer</u>

Preparation Time: 30 minutes   **Cooking Time: 20 minutes**
Servings: 6

Ingredients:
- Chicken thighs: 4 cups skin-on, bone-in

Marinade:
- Buttermilk: 2 cups
- Black pepper: 2 tsp.
- Cayenne pepper: 1 tsp.
- Salt: 2 tsp.

Seasoned Flour:
- Baking powder: 1 tbsp.
- All-purpose flour: 2 cups
- Paprika powder: 1 tbsp.
- Salt: 1 tsp.
- Garlic powder: 1 tbsp.

Directions: Let the air fry heat at 356F. With a paper towel, pat dry the chicken thighs.
In a mixing bowl, add paprika, black pepper, salt mix well, then add chicken pieces. Add buttermilk and coat the chicken well. Let it marinate for at least 6 hours.
In another bowl, add baking powder, salt, flour, pepper, and paprika. Put one by one of the chicken pieces and coat in the seasoning mix.
Spray oil on chicken pieces and place breaded chicken skin side up in air fryer basket in one layer, cook for 8 minutes, then flip the chicken pieces' cook for another ten minutes.

Nutrition: Calories: 209.6, Protein: 22.5g, Carbs: 11.8g, Fat: 17.5 g

93. Chicken Bites in Air Fryer

Preparation Time: 10 minutes   **Cooking Time: 8 minutes**
Servings: 3

Ingredients:
- Chicken breast: 2 cups
- Kosher salt& pepper to taste
- Smashed potatoes: one cup
- Scallions: ¼ cup
- One Egg beat
- Whole wheat breadcrumbs:
- 1 cup

Directions: Boil the chicken until soft. Shred the chicken with the help of a fork. Add the smashed potatoes, scallions to the shredded chicken. Season with kosher salt and pepper.
Coat with egg and then in bread crumbs.
Put in the air fryer, and cook for 8 minutes at 380F.
Serve warm.

Nutrition: Calories: 233.6, Protein: 25.6g, Carbs: 14.7g, Fat: 8.7 g

94. Chicken Cheese Quesadilla in Air Fryer

Preparation Time: 4 minutes   **Cooking Time: 6 minutes**
Servings: 4

Ingredients:
- Precooked chicken: one cup, diced
- Tortillas: 2 pieces
- Low-fat cheese: one cup (shredded)

Directions: Spray oil the air basket and place one tortilla in it. Add cooked chicken and cheese on top.
Add the second tortilla on top. Put a metal rack on top.
Cook for 6 minutes at 370°F, flip it halfway through so cooking evenly.
Slice and serve with dipping sauce.

Nutrition: Calories: 170.8, Protein: 15.4g, Carbs: 7.6g, Fat: 7.5g

95. Chicken Thighs Smothered Style

Preparation Time: 30 minutes   **Cooking Time: 30 minutes**
Servings: 4

Ingredients:
- 8-ounce of chicken thighs
- 1 tsp paprika
- One pinch salt
- Mushrooms: half cup
- Onions, roughly sliced

Directions: Let the air fryer preheat to 400°F.
Season chicken thighs with paprika, salt, and pepper on both sides.
Place the thighs in the air fryer and cook for 20 minutes.
Meanwhile, sauté the mushroom and onion.
Take out the thighs from the air fryer serve with sautéed mushrooms and onions.

Nutrition: Calories: 465.7, Protein: 40.9g, Carbs: 2.1g, Fat: 31.6g

96. Chicken with Mixed Vegetables

Preparation Time: 10 minutes   **Cooking Time: 10 minutes**
Servings: 2

Ingredients:
- 1/2 onion diced
- Chicken breast: 4 cups, cubed pieces
- Half zucchini chopped
- Italian seasoning: 1 tablespoon
- Bell pepper chopped: 1/2 cup
- Clove of garlic pressed
- Broccoli florets: 1/2 cup
- Olive oil: 2 tablespoons
- Half teaspoon of chili powder, garlic powder, pepper, salt

Directions: Let the air fryer heat to 400 F and dice the vegetables.
In a bowl, add the seasoning, oil and add vegetables, chicken and toss well.

Place chicken and vegetables in the air fryer, and cook for ten minutes, toss half way through, cook in batches. Make sure the veggies are charred and the chicken is cooked through.
Serve hot.

Nutrition: Calories: 229.6, Protein: 26.5g, Carbs: 7.6g, Fat: 9.5g

97. Garlic Parmesan Chicken Tenders

Preparation Time: 5 minutes   **Cooking Time: 12 minutes**
Servings: 4

Ingredients:
- One egg
- Eight raw chicken tenders

To coat:
- Panko breadcrumbs: 1 cup
- Half tsp of salt
- Black Pepper: 1/4 teaspoon

- Water: 2 tablespoons
- Olive oil

- Garlic powder: 1 teaspoon
- Onion powder: 1/2 teaspoon
- Parmesan cheese: 1/4 cup

- Any dipping Sauce

Directions: Add all the coating ingredients in a big bowl.
In another bowl, mix water and egg. Dip the chicken in the egg mix, then in the coating mix.
Put the tenders in the air fry basket in a single layer. Spray with the olive oil.
Cook at 400 degrees for 12 minutes. Flip the chicken halfway through.

Nutrition: Calories: 219.6, Protein: 27.6g, Carbs: 12.5g, Fat: 5.6g

98. Brine-Soaked Turkey

Preparation Time: 10 minutes   **Cooking Time: 45 minutes**
Servings: 8

Ingredients
- 7 lbs. turkey breast, bone-in, skin-on

For the brine
- 1/2 cup salt
- 1 lemon
- 1/2 onion

- 3 garlic cloves, smashed
- 5 sprigs fresh thyme
- 3 bay leaves

- Black pepper

For the turkey breast
- 4 tbsp. butter, softened
- 1/2 tsp. black pepper

- 1/2 tsp. garlic powder
- 1/4 tsp. thyme, dried

- 1/4 tsp. oregano, dried

Directions: Mix the turkey brine ingredients in a pot and soak the turkey in the brine overnight. The next day, remove the soaked turkey from the brine.
Whisk the butter, black pepper, garlic powder, oregano, and thyme. Brush the butter mixture over the turkey, then place it in a baking tray.
Press the POWER button of the air fry oven and turn the dial to select the AIR ROAST mode. Press the TIME button and again turn the dial to set the Cooking Time to 45 minutes.
Now push the TEMP button and rotate the dial to set the temperature at 370°F. Once preheated, place the turkey baking tray in the oven and close the lid.
Slice and serve warm.

Nutrition: Calories: 396.5, Carbs: 58.9g, Fat: 15.6g, Protein: 8.5g

99. Turkey Fajitas Platter in Air Fryer

Preparation Time: 5 minutes   **Cooking Time: 20 minutes**
Servings: 2

Ingredients:
- Cooked Turkey Breast: 1/4 cup
- Six Tortilla Wraps
- One Avocado
- One Yellow Pepper

- One Red Pepper
- Half Red Onion
- Soft Cheese: 5 Tbsp.
- Mexican Seasoning: 2 Tbsp.

- Cumin: 1 Tsp
- Kosher salt& Pepper
- Cajun Spice: 3 Tbsp.
- Fresh Coriander

Directions: Chop up the avocado and slice the vegetables.
Dice up turkey breast into small bite-size pieces.
In a bowl, add onions, turkey, soft cheese, and peppers along with seasonings. Mix it well.
Place it in foil and the air fryer. Cook for 20 minutes at 392 °F.
Serve hot.

Nutritional: Calories: 378.7, Protein: 30.6g, Carbs: 63.8g, Fat: 28.7g

100. Turkey Juicy Breast Tenderloin

Preparation Time: 5 minutes　　　　　　　　　　　　　　　　　**Cooking Time: 25 minutes**
Servings: 3

Ingredients:
- *Turkey breast tenderloin: one-piece*
- *Thyme: half tsp.*
- *Sage: half tsp.*
- *Paprika: half tsp.*
- *Pink salt: half tsp.*
- *Freshly ground black pepper: half tsp.*

Directions: Let the air fryer preheat to 350 °F. In a bowl, mix all the spices and herbs, rub it all over the turkey. Spray oil on the air fryer basket. Put the turkey in the air fryer and let it cook at 350 F for 25 minutes, flip halfway through.

Nutritional: Calories: 161.9, Protein: 13.5g, Carbs: 0.8g, Fat: 0.9g

101. Turkey Breast with Mustard Glaze

Preparation Time: 10 minutes　　　　　　　　　　　　　　　　**Cooking Time: 50 minutes**
Servings: 6

Ingredients:
- *Whole turkey breast: 5 pounds*
- *Olive oil: 2 tsp.*
- *Dried sage: half tsp.*
- *Smoked paprika: half tsp.*
- *Dried thyme: one tsp.*
- *Salt: one tsp.*
- *Freshly ground black pepper: half tsp.*
- *Dijon mustard: 2 tbsp*

Directions: Let the air fryer preheat to 350 ° F. Rub the olive oil all over the turkey breast.
In a bowl, mix salt, sage, pepper, thyme, and paprika. Mix well and coat turkey in this spice rub.
Place the turkey in an air fryer, cook for 25 minutes at 350ºF. Flip the turkey over and cook for another 12 minutes. Flip again and cook for another ten minutes. With an instant-read thermometer, the internal temperature should reach 165ºF.
In the meantime, in a saucepan, mix mustard and with one tsp. of butter.
Brush this glaze all over the turkey when cooked. Cook again for five minutes.

Nutritional: Calories: 378.6, Carbs: 20.5g, Protein: 52.7g, Fat: 22.6g

102. Zucchini Turkey Burgers

Preparation Time: 10 minutes　　　　　　　　　　　　　　　　**Cooking Time: 10 minutes**
Servings: 5

Ingredients:
- *Gluten-free breadcrumbs: 1/4 cup (seasoned)*
- *1 tsp of kosher salt and fresh pepper*
- *Grated zucchini: 1 cup*
- *Red onion: 1 tbsp. (grated)*
- *Lean ground turkey: 4 cups*
- *One clove of minced garlic*

Directions: In a bowl, add zucchini (moisture removed with a paper towel), ground turkey, garlic, salt, onion, pepper, breadcrumbs. Mix well. With your hands make five patties. But not too thick.
Let the air fryer preheat to 375 F.
Put in an air fryer in a single layer and cook for 7 minutes or more. Until cooked through and browned.
Place in buns with ketchup and lettuce and enjoy.

Nutrition: Calories: 160.6, Carbs: 4.1g, Protein: 18.6g, Fat: 6.5g

103. No-breaded Turkey Breast

Preparation Time: 5 minutes   **Cooking Time: 40-60 minutes**
Servings: 10

Ingredients:
- *Turkey breast: 4 pounds, ribs removed, bone with skin*
- *Olive oil: 1 tablespoon*
- *Salt: 2 teaspoons*
- *Dry turkey seasoning (without salt): half tsp.*

Directions: Rub half tbsp of olive oil over turkey breast. Sprinkle salt, turkey seasoning on both sides of turkey breast with half tbsp of olive oil.
Let the air fryer preheat at 350 F. put turkey skin side down in air fryer and cook for 20 minutes until the turkey's temperature reaches 160 F for half an hour to 40 minutes.
Let it sit for ten minutes before slicing.

Nutrition: Calories: 225.6, Carbs: 21.5g, Protein: 32.9g, Fat: 9.5g

104. Breaded Chicken Tenderloins

Preparation Time: 10 minutes   **Cooking Time: 12 minutes**
Servings: 4

Ingredients:
- *Eight chicken tenderloins*
- *Olive oil: 2 tablespoons*
- *One egg whisked*
- *1/4 cup breadcrumbs*

Directions: Let the air fryer heat to 356F.
In a big bowl, add breadcrumbs and oil. Mix well until forms a crumbly mixture.
Dip chicken tenderloin in whisked egg and coat in breadcrumbs mixture.
Place the breaded chicken in the air fryer and cook for 12 minutes.

Nutrition: Calories: 205.5, Protein: 20.5g, Carbs: 16.5g, Fat: 9.5g

105. Parmesan Chicken Meatballs

Preparation Time: 10 minutes   **Cooking Time: 12 minutes**
Servings: 20

Ingredients:
- *Pork rinds: half cup, ground*
- *Ground chicken: 4 cups*
- *Parmesan cheese: half cup grated*
- *Kosher salt: 1 tsp.*
- *Garlic powder: 1/2 tsp.*
- *One egg beaten*
- *Paprika: 1/2 tsp.*
- *Pepper: half tsp.*
- *Whole wheat breadcrumbs: half cup ground*

Directions: Let the Air Fryer pre-heat to 400°F.
Add cheese, chicken, egg, pepper, half cup of pork rinds, garlic, salt, and paprika in a big mixing ball. Mix well into a dough, make into 1and half-inch balls.
Coat the meatballs in whole wheat bread crumbs.
Spray the oil in the air fry basket and add meatballs in one even layer.
Let it cook for 12 minutes at 400°F, flipping once halfway through. Serve with salad greens.

Nutrition: Calories: 239.5, Protein: 20.5g, Carbs: 11.5g, Fat: 9.6g

106. Lemon Rosemary Chicken

Preparation Time: 30 minutes   **Cooking Time: 20 minutes**
Servings: 2

Ingredients:
For marinade:
- *Chicken: 2 and ½ cups*
- *Ginger: 1 tsp, minced*
- *Olive oil: 1/2 tbsp.*
- *Soy sauce: 1 tbsp.*

For the sauce:
- *Half lemon*
- *Honey: 3 tbsp.*
- *Oyster sauce: 1 tbsp.*
- *Fresh rosemary: half cup, chopped*

Directions: In a big mixing bowl, add the marinade ingredients with chicken, and mix well.
Keep in the refrigerator for at least half an hour.
Let the oven preheat to 392°F for three minutes.
Place the marinated chicken in the air fryer in a single layer. And cook for 6 minutes at 392F.
Meanwhile, add all the sauces ingredients in a bowl and mix well except for lemon wedges.
Brush the sauce generously over half-baked chicken add lemon juice on top.
Cook for another 13 minutes at 392F. flip the chicken halfway through. Let the chicken evenly brown.

Nutrition: Calories: 307.6, Protein: 25.6g, Carbs: 6.5g, Fat: 11.8g

107. Air Fryer Chicken & Broccoli

Preparation Time: 10 minutes　　　　　　　　　　　　　　**Cooking Time: 25 minutes**
Servings: 4

Ingredients:
- Olive oil: 2 Tablespoons
- Chicken breast: 4 cups, bone and skinless (cut into cubes)
- Half medium onion, roughly sliced
- Low sodium soy sauce: 1 Tbsp.
- Garlic powder: half teaspoon
- Rice vinegar: 2 teaspoons
- Broccoli: 1-2 cups, cut into florets
- Hot sauce: 2 teaspoons
- Fresh minced ginger: 1 Tbsp.
- Sesame seed oil: 1 teaspoon
- Salt & black pepper, to taste

Directions: In a bowl, add chicken breast, onion, and broccoli. Combine them well.
In another bowl, add ginger, oil, sesame oil, rice vinegar, hot sauce, garlic powder, and soy sauce mix it well.
Then add the broccoli, chicken, and onions to marinade.
Coat well the chicken with sauces. And let it rest in the refrigerator for 15 minutes.
Place chicken mix in one even layer in air fryer basket and cook for 16-20 minutes, at 380 F. halfway through, toss the basket and cook the chicken evenly.
Add five minutes more, if required. Add salt and pepper, if needed. Serve hot with lemon wedges.

Nutrition: Calories: 190.6, Protein: 25.6g, Carbs: 3.6g, Fat: 6.4g

108. Air Fried Maple Chicken Thighs

Preparation Time: 10 minutes　　　　　　　　　　　　　　**Cooking Time: 25 minutes**
Servings: 4

Ingredients:
- One egg
- Buttermilk: 1 cup
- Maple syrup: half cup
- Chicken thighs: 4 pieces
- Granulated garlic: 1 tsp.

Dry Mix:
- Granulated garlic: half tsp.
- All-purpose flour: half cup
- Salt: one tbsp.
- Sweet paprika: one tsp.
- Smoked paprika: half tsp.
- Tapioca flour: ¼ cup
- Cayenne pepper: ¼ teaspoon
- Granulated onion: one tsp.
- Black pepper: ¼ teaspoon
- Honey powder: half tsp.

Directions: In a ziploc bag, add egg, one tsp. of granulated garlic, buttermilk, and maple syrup, add in the chicken thighs and let it marinate for one hour or more in the refrigerator.
In a mixing bowl, add sweet paprika, tapioca flour, granulated onion, half tsp. of granulated garlic, flour, cayenne pepper, salt, pepper, honey powder, and smoked paprika mix it well.
Let the air fry preheat to 380 F. Coat the marinated chicken thighs in the dry spice mix, shake the excess off.
Put the chicken skin side down in the air fryer.
Let it cook for 12 minutes. Flip thighs halfway through and cook for 13 minutes more.

Nutrition: Calories: 415, Protein: 23.8g, Carbs: 20.1g, Fat: 12.8g

109. Mushroom Oatmeal

Preparation Time: 10 minutes　　　　　　　　　　　　　　**Cooking Time: 25 minutes**
Servings: 4

Ingredients:

- *One small yellow onion, chopped*
- *1 cup steel-cut oats*
- *1 Garlic cloves, minced*
- *2 Tablespoons butter*
- *½ cup of water*
- *One and a half cup of canned chicken stock*
- *Thyme springs, chopped*
- *2 Tablespoons extra virgin olive oil*
- *½ cup gouda cheese, grated*
- *1 cup mushroom, sliced*
- *Salt and black pepper to taste*

Directions: Heat a pan over medium heat, which suits your air fryer with the butter, add onions and garlic, stir and cook for 4 minutes.

Add oats, sugar, salt, pepper, stock, and thyme, stir, place in the air fryer and cook for 16 minutes at 360 F.

In the meantime, prepare a skillet over medium heat with the olive oil, add mushrooms, cook them for 3 minutes, add oatmeal and cheese, whisk, divide into bowls and serve for breakfast.

Nutrition: Calories: 283.7, Protein: 17.5g, Carbs: 19.6g, Fat: 7.5g

110. Bell Peppers Frittata

Preparation Time: 10 minutes
Servings: 4

Cooking Time: 20 minutes

Ingredients:

- *2 Tablespoons olive oil*
- *2 cups chicken sausage, casings removed and chopped*
- *One sweet onion, chopped*
- *1 red bell pepper, chopped*
- *1 orange bell pepper, chopped*
- *1 green bell pepper, chopped*
- *Salt and black pepper to taste*
- *8 eggs, whisked*
- *½ cup mozzarella cheese, shredded*
- *2 teaspoons oregano, chopped*

Directions: Add 1 spoonful of oil to the air fryer, add bacon, heat to 320 F, and brown for 1 minute.

Remove remaining butter, onion, red bell pepper, orange and white, mix and simmer for another 2 minutes.

Stir and cook for 15 minutes, add oregano, salt, pepper, and eggs.

Add mozzarella, leave frittata aside for a couple of minutes, divide and serve between plates.

Nutrition: Calories: 211.6, Protein: 12.6g, Carbs: 7.5g, Fat: 3.5g

111. Southwest Chicken in Air Fryer

Preparation Time: 20 minutes
Servings: 4

Cooking Time: 25 minutes

Ingredients:

- *Avocado oil: one tbsp.*
- *Four cups of boneless, skinless, chicken breast*
- *Chili powder: half tsp.*
- *Salt to taste*
- *Cumin: half tsp.*
- *Onion powder: 1/4 tsp.*
- *Lime juice: two tbsp.*
- *Garlic powder: 1/4 tsp*

Directions: In a ziploc bag, add chicken, oil, and lime juice.

Add all spices in a bowl and rub all over the chicken in the ziploc bag. Let it marinate in the fridge for ten minutes.

Take chicken out from the ziploc bag and put it in the air fryer.

Cook for 25 minutes at 400 F, flipping chicken halfway through until internal temperature reaches 165 degrees F.

Nutrition: Calories: 164.5, Protein: 24.6g, Carbs: 1g, Fat: 5.4g

112. No-Breading Chicken Breast in Air Fryer

Preparation Time: 10 minutes
Servings: 2

Cooking Time: 10 minutes

Ingredients:

- *Olive oil spray*
- *Chicken breasts: 4 (boneless)*
- *Onion powder: 3/4 teaspoon*
- *Salt: ¼ cup*
- *Smoked paprika: half tsp.*
- *1/8 tsp. of cayenne pepper*
- *Garlic powder: 3/4 teaspoon*
- *Dried parsley: half tsp.*

Directions: In a large bowl, add six cups of warm water, add salt (1/4 cup) and mix to dissolve.

Put chicken breasts in the warm salted water and let it refrigerate for almost 2 hours.

Remove from water and pat dry.

In a bowl, add all the spices with ¾ tsp. of salt. Spray the oil all over the chicken and rub the spice mix all over the chicken.

Let the air fryer heat at 380F.
Put the chicken in the air fryer and cook for ten minutes. Flip halfway through and serve with salad green.

Nutrition: Calories: 207.5, Protein: 39.4g, Carbs: 1g, Fat: 4g

113. Lemon Pepper Chicken Breast

Preparation Time: 3 minutes   **Cooking Time: 15 minutes**
Servings: 2

Ingredients:
- Two Lemons rind, juice, and zest
- One Chicken Breast
- Minced Garlic: 1 Tsp
- Black Peppercorns: 2 tbsp.
- Chicken Seasoning: 1 Tbsp.
- Salt & pepper, to taste

Directions: Let the air fryer preheat to 356°F.
In a large aluminum foil, add all the seasonings along with lemon rind.
Add salt and pepper to chicken and rub the seasonings all over chicken breast. Put the chicken in aluminum foil. And fold it tightly. Flatten the chicken inside foil with a rolling pin.
Put it in the air fryer and cook at 356°F for 15 minutes.

Nutrition: Calories: 139.6, Protein: 13.2g, Carbs: 23.4g, Fat: 1.3g

114. Chicken Coconut Poppers

Preparation Time: 10 minutes   **Cooking Time: 10 minutes**
Servings: 6

Ingredients:
- ½ cup coconut flour
- 1 tsp. chili flakes
- 1 tsp. ground black pepper
- 1 tsp. garlic powder
- 11 oz. chicken breast, boneless, skinless
- 1 tbsp. olive oil

Directions: Cut the chicken breast into medium cubes and put them in a large bowl.
Sprinkle the chicken cubes with chili flakes, ground black pepper, garlic powder, and stir them well using your hands. After this, sprinkle the chicken cubes with almond flour. Shake the bowl with the chicken cubes gently to coat the meat.
Preheat the air fryer to 365°F. Grease the air fryer basket tray with olive oil.
Place the chicken cubes inside. Cook the chicken poppers for 10 minutes.
Turn the chicken poppers over after 5 minutes of cooking.
Allow the cooked chicken poppers to cool before serving.

Nutrition: Calories: 122.6, Fat: 4.1g, Fiber: 3.9g, Carbs: 6.3g, Protein: 13.7g

115. Paprika Whole Chicken

Preparation Time: 15 minutes   **Cooking Time: 75 minutes**
Servings: 12

Ingredients:
- 6-lb. whole chicken
- 1 tsp. kosher salt
- 1 tsp. ground black pepper
- 1 tsp. ground paprika
- 1 tbsp. minced garlic
- 3 tbsp. butter
- 1 tsp. olive oil
- ¼ cup water
- 3 oz. chive stems

Directions: Rub the whole chicken with kosher salt and ground black pepper inside and outside.
Sprinkle it with the ground paprika and minced garlic.
Dice the chives. Put the diced chives inside the whole chicken.
Then add the butter. Rub the chicken with olive oil.
Preheat the air fryer to 360°F and pour water into the air fryer basket.
Place the chicken on the rack inside the air fryer. Cook the chicken for 75 minutes.
When the chicken is cooked it should have slightly crunchy skin. Cut the cooked chicken into the servings.

Nutrition: Calories: 463.2, Fat: 19.6g, Fiber: 0.2g, Carbs: 0.7g, Protein: 66g

116. Pandan Coconut Chicken

Preparation Time: 20 minutes   **Cooking Time: 10 minutes**
Servings: 4

Ingredients:
- 15 oz. chicken
- 1 pandan leaf
- 3 oz. chive stems, diced
- 1 tsp. minced garlic

- 1 tsp. chili flakes
- 1 tsp. stevia
- 1 tsp. ground black pepper
- 1 tsp. turmeric

- 1 tbsp. butter
- ¼ cup coconut milk
- 1 tbsp. chives powder

Directions: Cut the chicken into 4 big cubes.
Put the chicken cubes in a large bowl. Sprinkle the chicken with minced garlic, diced chives, chili flakes, stevia, ground black pepper, chives powder, and turmeric.
Mix the meat up using your hands. Cut the pandan leaf into 4 parts.
Wrap the chicken cubes into the pandan leaf.
Pour the coconut milk into a bowl with the wrapped chicken and leave it for 10 minutes.
Preheat the air fryer to 380°F. Put the pandan chicken in the air fryer basket and cook for 10 minutes.
When the chicken is cooked – transfer to serving plates and let it chill for at least 2-3 minutes.

Nutrition: Calories: 249.5, Fat: 12.2g, Fiber: 0.9g, Carbs: 2.5g, Protein: 30.2g

117. Bacon Chicken Breast

Preparation Time: 15 minutes   **Cooking Time: 16 minutes**
Servings: 4

Ingredients:
- 1-lb. chicken breast, skinless, boneless
- 4 oz. bacon, sliced
- 1 tsp. paprika

- ¼ cup almond milk
- 1 tsp. salt
- ½ tsp. ground black pepper
- 1 tsp. turmeric

- 1 tbsp. fresh lemon juice
- 2 tbsp. butter
- 1 tsp. olive oil

Directions: Beat the chicken breast lightly to flatten.
Then rub the chicken with paprika, salt, ground black pepper, and turmeric.
Sprinkle the chicken with fresh lemon juice. Then place the butter in the center of the chicken breast and roll it.
Wrap the chicken roll in the sliced bacon and sprinkle with almond milk and olive oil.
Preheat the air fryer to 380°F. Put the bacon chicken in the air fryer basket and cook it for 8 minutes.
Turn the chicken breast over and cook it for 8 minutes more.

Nutrition: Calories: 382.5, Fat: 25g, Fiber: 0.7g, Carbs: 2g, Protein: 35.6g

118. Cheddar Chicken Drumsticks

Preparation Time: 18 minutes   **Cooking Time: 13 minutes**
Servings: 4

Ingredients:
- 1-lb. chicken drumstick
- 6 oz. Cheddar cheese, sliced

- 1 tsp. dried rosemary
- 1 tsp. dried oregano

- ½ tsp. salt
- ½ tsp. chili flakes

Directions: Sprinkle the chicken drumsticks with dried rosemary, dried oregano, salt, and chili flakes.
Massage the drumsticks carefully and leave for 5 minutes to marinade.
Preheat the air fryer to 370°F.
Place the marinated chicken drumsticks in the air fryer tray and cook them for 10 minutes.
Turn the chicken drumsticks over and cover them with a layer of sliced cheese.
Cook the chicken for 3 minutes more at the same temperature.
Then transfer the chicken drumsticks onto a large serving plate.
Serve the dish hot – the cheese should be melted.

Nutrition: Calories: 225.4, Fat: 9.2g, Fiber: 0.3g, Carbs: 1g, Protein: 16.8g

119. Coriander Chicken

Preparation Time: 20 minutes   **Cooking Time: 16 minutes**
Servings: 4

Ingredients:
- 3 oz. fresh coriander root
- 1 tsp. olive oil
- 3 tbsp. minced garlic
- ¼ lemon, sliced
- ½ tsp. salt
- 1 tsp. ground black pepper
- ½ tsp. chili flakes
- 1 tbsp. dried parsley
- 1-lb. chicken thighs

Directions: Peel the fresh coriander and grate it.
Then combine the olive oil with the minced garlic, salt, ground black pepper, chili flakes, and dried parsley.
Combine the mixture and sprinkle over the chicken tights. Add the sliced lemon and grated coriander root.
Mix the chicken thighs carefully and leave them to marinate for 10 minutes in the fridge.
Meanwhile, preheat the air fryer to 365°F. Put the chicken in the air fryer basket tray.
Add all the remaining liquid from the chicken and cook for 15 minutes.
Turn the chicken over and cook it for 1 minute more. Serve hot.

Nutrition: Calories: 186.7, Fat: 11g, Fiber: 1g, Carbs: 3.2g, Protein: 20.3g

120. Chicken Goulash

Preparation Time: 10 minutes   **Cooking Time: 17 minutes**
Servings: 6

Ingredients:
- 4 oz. chive stems
- 2 green peppers, chopped
- 1 tsp. olive oil
- 14 oz. ground chicken
- 2 tomatoes
- ½ cup chicken stock
- 2 garlic cloves, sliced
- 1 tsp. salt
- 1 tsp. ground black pepper
- 1 tsp. mustard

Directions: Chop chives roughly. Spray the air fryer basket tray with olive oil.
Preheat the air fryer to 365°F.
Put the chopped chives in the air fryer basket tray. Add the chopped green pepper and cook the vegetables for 5 minutes. Add the ground chicken. Chop the tomatoes into small cubes and add them to the air fryer mixture too.
Cook the mixture for 6 minutes more.
Add the chicken stock, sliced garlic cloves, salt, ground black pepper, and mustard. Mix well to combine.
Cook the goulash for 6 minutes more.

Nutrition: Calories: 160.6, Fat: 5.8g, Fiber: 1.7g, Carbs: 5.8g, Protein: 20.8g

121. Chicken & Turkey Meatloaf

Preparation Time: 15 minutes   **Cooking Time: 25 minutes**
Servings: 12

Ingredients:
- 3 tbsp. butter
- 10 oz. ground turkey
- 7 oz. ground chicken
- 1 tsp. dried dill
- ½ tsp. ground coriander
- 2 tbsp. almond flour
- 1 tbsp. minced garlic
- 3 oz. fresh spinach
- 1 tsp. salt
- 1 egg
- ½ tbsp. paprika
- 1 tsp. sesame oil

Directions: Put the ground turkey and ground chicken in a large bowl.
Sprinkle the meat with dried dill, ground coriander, almond flour, minced garlic, salt, and paprika.
Then chop the fresh spinach and add it to the ground poultry mixture.
Crack the egg into the meat mixture and mix well until you get a smooth texture.
Great the air fryer basket tray with the olive oil.
Preheat the air fryer to 350°F. Roll the ground meat mixture gently to make the flat layer.
Put the butter in the center of the meat layer.
Make the shape of the meatloaf from the ground meat mixture. Use your fingertips for this step.
Place the Prepared meatloaf in the air fryer basket tray. Cook for 25 minutes.
When the meatloaf is cooked allow it to rest before serving.

Nutrition: Calories: 141.3, Fat: 9.2g, Fiber: 0.8g, Carbs: 6.5g, Protein 13.4g

122. Turkey Meatballs with Dried Dill

Preparation Time: 15 minutes
Servings: 9

Cooking Time: 11 minutes

Ingredients:
- 1-lb. ground turkey
- 1 tsp. chili flakes
- ¼ cup chicken stock
- 2 tbsp. dried dill

- 1 egg
- 1 tsp. salt
- 1 tsp. paprika
- 1 tbsp. coconut flour

- 2 tbsp. heavy cream
- 1 tsp. olive oil

Directions: Crack the egg in a bowl and whisk it with a fork. Add the ground turkey and chili flakes.
Sprinkle the mixture with dried dill, salt, paprika, coconut flour, and mix it up.
Make the meatballs from the ground turkey mixture.
Preheat the air fryer to 360°F. Grease the air fryer basket tray with olive oil.
Then put the meatballs inside. Cook the meatballs for 6 minutes (3 minutes on each side).
Sprinkle the meatballs with heavy cream. Cook the meatballs for 5 minutes more.
When the turkey meatballs are cooked – let them rest for 2-3 minutes.

Nutrition: Calories: 123.4, Fat: 7.3g, Fiber: 0.5g, Carbs: 1g, Protein: 15.2g

123. Chicken Fried Spring Rolls

Preparation Time: 20 minutes
Servings: 4

Cooking Time: 4 minutes

Ingredients:

For the spring roll wrappers:
- 1 egg, beaten
- 8 spring roll wrappers

- 1 tsp. cornstarch
- ½ tsp. olive oil

For the filling:
- 1 cup chicken breast, cooked, shredded
- 1 celery stalk, sliced thinly

- 1 carrot, sliced thinly
- 1 tsp. chicken stock powder, low sodium

- ½ tsp. ginger, chopped finely
- ½ cup sliced mushrooms

Directions: Preheat the Air Fryer to 390°F.
Prepare the filling. In a bowl, combine shredded chicken, mushrooms, carrot, and celery. Add in chicken, stock powder, and ginger. Stir well. Meanwhile, mix cornstarch and egg until thick in a bowl. Set aside.
Spoon some filling into a spring roll wrapper. Roll and seal the ends with the egg mixture.
Light brush spring rolls with oil and place them in the cooking basket.
Cook for 4 minutes. Serve.

Nutrition: Calorie: 149.3, Carbs: 17.6g, Fat: 4.6g, Protein: 9.3g, Fiber: 1.5g

124. Whole Chicken with Italian Seasoning

Preparation Time: 10 minutes
Servings: 4

Cooking Time: 35 minutes

Ingredients:
- 1 whole chicken
- 2 tablespoons oil spray
- 1 teaspoon garlic powder

- 1 teaspoon onion powder
- 1 teaspoon paprika
- 1 teaspoon Italian seasoning

- 2 tablespoons Montreal steak seasoning
- 1½ cup chicken broth

Directions: Whisk all seasonings in a bowl and rub over chicken.
Set a metal rack in the air fryer oven and pour in the broth.
Place the chicken on the metal rack, then put the pressure-cooking lid on.
Press the "Pressure Button" and select 25 minutes of Cooking Time, then press "Start."
Once the air fryer oven beeps, make a natural release and remove its lid.
Transfer the pressure-cooked chicken to a plate. Set the air fryer basket in the oven.
Coat the chicken pieces with oil. Spread the chicken in the air fryer basket.
Put the lid on and press the "Air Fryer Button," then set the time to 10 minutes. Remove the lid and serve.

Nutrition: Calories: 162.5, Fat: 10g, Carbs: 1.2g, Fiber: 0.3g, Sugar: 0.6g, Protein: 12.9g

125. Chicken Pot Pie

Preparation Time: 10 minutes   **Cooking Time: 17 minutes**
Servings: 3

Ingredients:
- 2 tbsp. olive oil
- 1 lb. chicken breast cubed
- 1 tbsp. garlic powder
- 1 tbsp. thyme
- 1 tbsp. pepper
- 1 cup chicken broth
- 12 oz. bag frozen mixed vegetables
- 4 large potatoes cubed
- 10 oz. can chicken soup cream
- 1 cup heavy cream

Directions: Hit the "Sauté Button" on the air fryer oven and add chicken and olive oil.
Sauté chicken for 5 minutes, then stir in spices.
Pour in the broth along with the vegetables and cream of chicken soup. Put the pressure-cooking lid and seal it.
Press the "Pressure Button" and select 10 minutes of Cooking Time, then press "Start."
Once the air fryer oven beeps, do a quick release and remove the lid. Remove the lid and stir in cream.
Press "Sauté Button" and cook for 2 minutes.

Nutrition: Calories: 567.6, Fat: 31.3g, Carbs: 50.2g, Fiber: 3.9g, Sugar: 18.1g, Protein: 23.9g

126. Chicken Casserole

Preparation Time: 10 minutes   **Cooking Time: 9 minutes**
Servings: 4

Ingredients:
- 12 oz. bag egg noodles
- ½ large onion
- ½ cup chopped carrots
- ¼ cup frozen peas
- ¼ cup frozen broccoli pieces
- 2 stalks celery chopped
- 5 cups chicken broth
- 1 tsp. garlic powder
- Salt and pepper to taste
- 1 cup cheddar cheese, shredded
- 1 package French's onions
- ¼ cup sour cream
- 1 can chicken cream and mushroom soup

Directions: Add chicken broth, black pepper, salt, garlic powder, vegetables, and egg noodles to the air fryer oven. Put on the pressure-cooking lid and seal it.
Press the "Pressure Button" and select 4 minutes of Cooking Time, then press "Start."
Once the air fryer oven beeps, remove the lid.
Stir in cheese, ⅓ of French's onions, a can of soup, and sour cream.
Mix well and spread the remaining onion on top. Put on the air fryer lid and seal it.
Press the "Air Fryer Button" and select 5 minutes of Cooking Time, then press "Start."
Once the Air Fryer oven beeps, remove its lid. Serve.

Nutrition: Calories: 493.5, Fat: 18.6g, Carbs: 28.6g, Fiber: 2.6g, Sugar: 3.2g, Protein: 49.5g

127. Ranch Chicken Wings

Preparation Time: 10 minutes   **Cooking Time: 35 minutes**
Servings: 3

Ingredients:
- 12 chicken wings
- 1 tbsp. olive oil
- 1 cup chicken broth
- ¼ cup butter
- ½ cup red hot sauce
- ¼ tsp. Worcestershire sauce
- 1 tbsp. white vinegar
- ¼ tsp. cayenne pepper
- ⅛ tsp. garlic powder
- Seasoned salt to taste
- Black pepper
- Ranch dressing for dipping
- Celery to garnish

Directions: Set the air fryer basket in the air fryer oven and pour the broth into it.
Spread the chicken wings in the basket and put on the pressure-cooking lid.
Press the "Pressure Button" and select 10 minutes of Cooking Time, then press "Start."
Meanwhile, for the sauce preparation, add cayenne pepper, butter, Worcestershire sauce, vinegar, garlic powder, and spicy sauce in a small saucepan. Stir and cook for 5 minutes on medium heat.
Once the air fryer oven beeps, make a quick release and remove its lid.
Remove the wings and toss them with oil, salt, and black pepper.
Set the air fryer basket in the oven and arrange the wings in it. Put on the lid and seal it.
Air fry for 20 minutes. Transfer the wings to the sauce and mix well before serving.

Nutrition: Calories: 413.6, Fat: 31.2g, Carbs: 10.6g, Fiber: 0.3g, Sugar: 0.2g, Protein: 20.8g

128. Chicken Mac and Cheese

Preparation Time: 8 minutes   **Cooking Time: 10 minutes**
Servings: 4

Ingredients:
- 2 ½ cups macaroni
- 2 cups chicken stock
- 1 cup cooked chicken, shredded
- 1 ¼ cup heavy cream
- 8 tbsp. butter
- 1 bag Ritz crackers

Directions: Add chicken stock, 4 tbsp. butter, heavy cream, chicken, and macaroni to the air fryer oven.
Put on the pressure-cooking lid and seal it.
Press the "Pressure Button" and select 4 minutes of Cooking Time, then press "Start."
Crush the crackers and mix them with 4 tbsp. of melted butter.
Once the air fryer oven beeps, do a quick release and remove its lid.
Put on the lid and seal it. Air fry for 5 minutes.

Nutrition: Calories: 610.3, Fat: 43.1g, Carbs: 28.8g, Fiber: 1.2g, Sugar: 1.1g, Protein: 25g

129. Broccoli Chicken Casserole

Preparation Time: 8 minutes   **Cooking Time: 25 minutes**
Servings: 4

Ingredients:
- 1 ½ lb. chicken, cubed
- 2 tsp. chopped garlic
- 2 tbsp. butter
- 1 ½ cup chicken broth
- 1 ½ cup long-grain rice
- 1 (10.75 oz.) can chicken soup cream
- 2 cups broccoli florets
- 1 cup crushed Ritz cracker
- 2 tbsp. melted butter
- 2 cups shredded cheddar cheese
- 1 cup water

Directions: Swell 1 cup water into the air fryer and place a basket in it.
Place the broccoli in the basket evenly. Put on the pressure-cooking lid and seal it.
Press the "Pressure Button" and cook for a minute.
Once the air fryer oven beeps, do a quick release and remove its lid.
Remove the broccoli, hit the "Sauté Button," then add 2 tbsp. of butter.
Toss in chicken and stir cook for 5 minutes. Add garlic and sauté for 30 seconds.
Stir in chicken broth, rice, and cream of chicken soup. Put on the pressure-cooking lid and seal it.
Press the "Pressure Button" and select 12 minutes of Cooking Time, then press "Start."
Once the air fryer oven beeps, do a quick release and remove its lid.
Add broccoli and cheese, then mix well. Toss the cracker with 2 tbsp. butter in a bowl and spread over the pot's chicken. Put on the lid and seal it. Air Fry for 4 minutes.

Nutrition: Calories: 608.6, Fat: 24g, Carbs: 45g, Fiber: 1.4g, Sugar: 1.2g, Protein: 49.8g

130. Chicken Tikka Kebab

Preparation Time: 10 minutes   **Cooking Time: 17 minutes**
Servings: 4

Ingredients:
- 1 lb. chicken thighs boneless skinless, cubed
- 1 tbsp. oil

For marinade:
- ½ cup yogurt Greek
- ¾ tbsp. ginger, grated
- ¾ tbsp. garlic, minced
- 1 tbsp. lime juice
- ½ cup red onion, cubed
- ½ cup green bell pepper, cubed
- ½ cup red bell pepper, cubed
- 2 tsp. red chili powder mild
- ½ tsp. ground turmeric
- 1 tsp. garam masala
- 1 tsp. coriander powder
- Lime wedges and Onion rounds to garnish
- ½ tbsp. dried fenugreek leaves
- 1 tsp. salt

Directions: Preparation of the marinade by mixing yogurt with all its ingredients in a bowl.
Fold in chicken, mix well to coat and refrigerate for 8 hours.
Add onions, bell pepper, and oil to the marinade and mix well.
Yarn the peppers, chicken, and onions on the skewers. Set the air fryer basket in the oven.
Put on the lid and seal it. Cook in the Air Fryer for 10 minutes.
Once the air fryer oven beeps, and remove its lid. Flip the skewers and continue to air fry for 7 minutes.

Nutrition: Calories: 240.3, Fat: 14g, Carbs: 8g, Fiber: 1.6g, Sugar: 3.3g, Protein: 22.2g

131. Bacon-Wrapped Chicken

Preparation Time: 10 minutes   **Cooking Time: 24 minutes**
Servings: 4

Ingredients:
- ¼ cup maple syrup
- 1 tsp. ground black pepper
- 1 tsp. Dijon mustard
- ¼ tsp. garlic powder
- ⅛ tsp. kosher salt
- 4 (6 oz.) skinless, boneless chicken breasts
- 8 slices bacon

Directions: Whisk maple syrup with salt, garlic powder, mustard, and black pepper in a small bowl.
Season the chicken with salt and black pepper, and wrap each chicken breast with 2 slices of bacon.
Place the wrapped chicken in the baking pan of Air fryer oven.
Brush the wrapped chicken with maple syrup mixture. Put on the lid and seal it.
Put in the Air Fryer and bake for 20 minutes. Switch the pot to "Broil" mode and cook for 4 minutes more.

Nutrition: Calories: 440.6, Fat: 18g, Carbs: 13.5g, Fiber: 0.1g, Sugar: 11.2g, Protein: 53.9g

132. Creamy Chicken Thighs

Preparation Time: 10 minutes   **Cooking Time: 30 minutes**
Servings: 2

Ingredients:
- 1 tbsp. olive oil
- 6 chicken thighs, bone-in, skin-on
- Salt
- Freshly ground black pepper
- ¾ cup low-sodium chicken broth
- ½ cup heavy cream
- ½ cup sun-dried tomatoes, chopped
- ¼ cup Parmesan, grated
- Freshly torn basil to serve

Directions: Hit the "Sauté Button" on the Air fryer oven and add oil to heat.
Stir in salt, chicken, and black pepper, then sear for 5 minutes per side.
Add broth, cream, parmesan, and tomatoes. Put on the Air Fryer lid and seal it.
Put in the Air Fryer and bake for 20 minutes.
Once the Air Fryer oven beeps, remove its lid. Garnish with basil and serve.

Nutrition: Calories: 453.6, Fat: 37.1g, Carbs: 2.2g, Fiber: 0.7g, Sugar: 0.6g, Protein: 27.5g

133. Teriyaki Hen Drumsticks

Preparation Time: 30 minutes   **Cooking Time: 20 minutes**
Servings: 4

Ingredients:
- 6 poultry drumsticks
- 1 mug teriyaki sauce

Directions: Mix drumsticks with teriyaki sauce in a zip-lock bag. Let the sauce rest for half an hour.
Preheat your air fryer to 360ºF.
Abode the drumsticks in the air fryer basket and cook for 20 minutes. Shake the basket pair times through food preparation. Garnish with sesame seeds and sliced onions

Nutrition: Calories: 162.6, Carbs: 6.5g, Protein: 16.6g, Fat: 6.7g

134. Rolled Turkey Breast

Preparation Time: 5 minutes   **Cooking Time: 10 minutes**
Servings: 4

Ingredients:
- 1 box cherry tomatoes
- ¼ lb. turkey blanket

Directions: Wrap the turkey and blanket in the tomatoes, close with the help of toothpicks.
Take to Air Fryer for 10 minutes at 390°F.
You can increase the filling with ricotta and other preferred light ingredients.

Nutrition: Calories: 171.3, Carbs: 2.8g, Fat: 1.6g, Protein: 34.6g, Sugar: 1g

135. Chicken in Beer

Preparation Time: 5 minutes
Servings: 4

Cooking Time: 45 minutes

Ingredients:
- 2 ¼ lbs. chicken thigh and thigh
- ½ can of beer
- 4 cloves of garlic
- 1 large onion
- Pepper and salt to taste

Directions: Wash the chicken pieces and, if desired, remove the skin to be healthier.
Place on an ovenproof plate.
In the blender, beat the other ingredients: beer, onion, garlic, and add salt and pepper, all together.
Cover the chicken with this mixture; it has to stay like swimming in the beer.
Take to the preheated air fryer at 390°F for 45 minutes.
It will roast when it has a brown cone on top and the beer has dried a bit.

Nutrition: Calories: 673.6, Carbs: 5.1g, Fat: 40g, Protein: 63.2g, Sugar: 1.4g

136. Chicken Fillet

Preparation Time: 5 minutes
Servings: 4

Cooking Time: 20 minutes

Ingredients:
- 4 chicken fillets
- salt to taste
- 1 garlic clove, crushed
- thyme to taste
- black pepper to taste

Directions: Add seasoning to fillets, wrapping well for flavor. Heat up the Air Fryer for 5 minutes at 350°F. Place the fillets in the basket, a program for 20 minutes at 350°F.
With 5 minutes remaining, turn the fillets and raise the temperature to 390°F.

Nutrition: Calories: 89.6, Carbs: 1g, Fat: 1g, Protein: 17.6g, Sugar: 0g

137. Chicken with Lemon and Bahian Seasoning

Preparation Time: 2 hours
Servings: 4

Cooking Time: 20 minutes

Ingredients:
- 5 pieces chicken to a bird;
- 2 garlic cloves, crushed;
- 4 tbsp. lemon juice;
- 1 coffee spoon of Bahian spices;
- salt and black pepper to taste.

Directions: Place the chicken pieces in a covered bowl and add the spices. Add the lemon juice. Cover the bowl and let the chicken marinate for 2 hours.
Place each piece of chicken in the basket of the air fryer, without overlapping the pieces. Set the fryer for 20 minutes at 390ºF. In half the time, brown evenly.

Nutrition: Calories: 315, Carbs: 4.2g, Fat: 14.6g, Protein: 33.5g, Sugar: 0g

138. Basic BBQ Chicken

Preparation Time: 5 minutes
Servings: 4

Cooking Time: 15 minutes

Ingredients:
- 2 tbsp. Worcestershire Sauce
- 1 tbsp. honey
- ¾ cup ketchup
- 2 tsp. chipotle chili powder
- 6 chicken drumsticks

Directions: Heat up the air fryer to 370°F for 5 minutes.
Use a big bowl to mix the Worcestershire sauce, honey, ketchup, and chili powder. Whisk it up well.
Drop in the drumsticks and turn them so they are all coated with the mixture.
Grease the basket of the air fryer with nonstick spray and place 3 chicken drumsticks in.
Cook for 17 minutes for large drumsticks 15 minutes for smaller ones, flipping when it reaches half the time.
Repeat with the other three drumsticks.

Nutrition: Calories: 144.6, Carbs: 4.1g, Fat: 2.1g, Protein: 13.6g

139. No Frills Turkey Breast

Preparation Time: 5 minutes   **Cooking Time: 40 minutes**
Servings: 4

Ingredients:
- 1 bone-in turkey breast (about 8 lbs.)
- 2 tbsp. olive oil
- 2 tbsp. sea salt
- 1 tbsp. black pepper

Directions: Warm up the air fryer to 360°F for about 8 minutes.
Rub the washed turkey breast with olive oil both on the skin and on the inside of the cavity.
Sprinkle on the sea salt and black pepper.
Remove the basket from the air fryer and spray with butter or olive oil flavored nonstick spray.
Put the turkey in with the breast side down. Cook 20 minutes and carefully turn the breast over.
Spray with cooking oil and cook another 20 minutes.
Let the breast rest at least 15 minutes before cutting and serving.

Nutrition: Calories: 374.6, Carbs: 8g, Fat: 6.5g, Protein: 15.6g

140. Faire-Worthy Turkey Legs

Preparation Time: 5 minutes   **Cooking Time: 27 minutes**
Servings: 4

Ingredients:
- I turkey leg
- 1 tsp. olive oil
- 1 tsp. poultry seasoning
- 1 tsp. garlic powder
- salt and black pepper to taste

Directions: Warm up the air fryer to 350°F for about 4 minutes.
Coat the leg with olive oil. Just use your hands and rub them in.
In a small bowl, mix the poultry seasoning, garlic powder, salt, and pepper. Rub it on the turkey leg.
Coat the inside of the air fryer basket with nonstick spray and place the turkey leg in.
Cook for 27 minutes, turning at 14 minutes. Be sure the leg is done by inserting a meat thermometer in the fleshy part of the leg and it should read 165°F.

Nutrition: Calories: 324.8, Carbs: 8g, Fat: 9.6g, Protein: 18.6g

141. Herb Air Fried Chicken Thighs

Preparation Time: 5 minutes   **Cooking Time: 20 minutes**
Servings: 4

Ingredients:
- 2 lbs. deboned chicken thighs
- 1 tsp. rosemary
- 1 tsp. thyme
- 1 tsp. garlic powder
- 1 large lemon

Directions: Trim fat from thighs and salt and pepper on all sides.
In a bowl, combine the thyme, rosemary, and garlic powder. Sprinkle over the chicken thighs and press the mixture in putting them on a baking sheet.
Cut the lemon and squeeze the juice over all the chicken thighs. Cover with plastic wrap and put in the refrigerator for 30 minutes.
Warm up the air fryer to 360°F for 6 minutes and spray with butter-flavored cooking spray.
Place the thighs in the air fryer basket, as many will fit in one layer.
Cook for 15 minutes, turning after 7 minutes.

Nutrition: Calories: 533.6, Fat: 27.1g, Carbs 2.1g, Sugar 0.5g, Protein 66.8g

142. Lemon Pepper Chicken

Preparation Time: 10 minutes
Servings: 4

Cooking Time: 30 minutes

Ingredients:
- 2 lbs. chicken breasts, boneless & skinless
- 1 ½ tsp granulated garlic
- 1 tbsp. lemon-pepper seasoning
- 1 tsp. salt

Directions: Preheat the air fryer to 360°F.
Season chicken breasts with lemon pepper seasoning, granulated garlic, and salt.
Place chicken into the air fryer basket and cook for 30 minutes. Turn chicken halfway through.
Serve and enjoy.

Nutrition: Calories: 284.6, Fat: 10.1g, Carbs: 1.5g, Sugar 0.3g, Protein 43.1g

143. Spicy Jalapeno Hassel back Chicken

Preparation Time: 10 minutes
Servings: 2

Cooking Time: 15 minutes

Ingredients:
- 2 lbs. chicken breasts, boneless and skinless
- ½ tbsp cheddar cheese, shredded
- 1 tbsp. pickled jalapenos, chopped
- 2 oz. cream cheese, softened
- 2 lbs. bacon slices, cooked and crumbled

Directions: Make five to six slits on top of chicken breasts.
In a bowl, mix together ½ cheddar cheese, pickled jalapenos, cream cheese, and bacon.
Stuff cheddar cheese mixture into the slits.
Place chicken into the air fryer basket and cook at 350°F for 14 minutes.
Sprinkle remaining cheese on top of the chicken and air fry for 1 minute more. Serve and enjoy.

Nutrition: Calories: 735.6: Fat 48.6g, Carbs: 3.5g, Sugar 0.2g, Protein 66.2g

144. Tasty Hassel back Chicken

Preparation Time: 10 minutes
Servings: 2

Cooking Time: 18 minutes

Ingredients:
- 2 lbs chicken breasts, boneless and skinless
- ½ cup sauerkraut, squeezed and remove excess liquid
- 2 tbsp. thin Swiss cheese slices, tear into pieces
- 1 lbs thin deli corned beef slices, tear into pieces
- Salt and Pepper as per taste

Directions: Make five slits on top of chicken breasts. Season chicken with pepper and salt.
Stuff each slit with beef, sauerkraut, and cheese.
Spray chicken with cooking spray and place in the air fryer basket.
Cook chicken at 350°F for 18 minutes. Serve and enjoy.

Nutrition: Calories: 723.2, Fat: 39.1g, Carbs: 3.2g, Sugar 2.3g, Protein: 84.2g

Red Meat

145. Lean Lamb and Turkey Meatballs with Yogurt

Preparation Time: 10 minutes   **Cooking Time: 8 minutes**
Servings: 4

Ingredients:
- 1 egg white
- 4 oz. ground lean turkey
- 1 lb. of lean ground lamb

- 1 tsp. both cayenne pepper, ground coriander, red chili pastes, salt, and ground cumin
- 2 garlic cloves, minced

- 1 ½ tbsp. parsley, chopped
- 1 tbsp. mint, chopped
- ¼ cup of olive oil

For the yogurt:
- 2 tbsp. of buttermilk
- 1 garlic clove, minced

- ¼ cup mint, chopped
- ½ cup Greek yogurt, non-fat

- Salt, to taste

Directions: Set the Air Fryer to 390°F.
Blend all the ingredients for the meatballs in a bowl. Roll and mound them into golf-size round pieces. Arrange in the cooking basket. Cook for 8 minutes.
Meantime, combine all the ingredients for the mint yogurt in a bowl. Mix well.
Serve the meatballs with mint yogurt. Top with olives and fresh mint.

Nutrition: Calories: 154 Carbs: 9 g Fat: 2.5 g Protein: 8.6 g Fiber: 2.4 g

146. Greek Lamb Pita Pockets

Preparation Time: 15 minutes   **Cooking Time: 7 minutes**
Servings: 4

Ingredients:

Dressing:
- 1 cup plain Greek yogurt
- 1 tbsp. lemon juice

- 1 tsp. dried dill weed, crushed
- 1 tsp. ground oregano

- ½ tsp. salt

Meatballs:
- ½ lb. (227 g.) ground lamb
- 1 tbsp. diced onion
- 1 tsp. dried parsley

- 1 tsp. dried dill weed, crushed
- ¼ tsp. oregano
- ¼ tsp. coriander

- ¼ tsp. ground cumin
- ¼ tsp. salt
- 4 pita halves

Directions: Stir dressing ingredients together and refrigerate while preparing lamb.
Combine all meatball ingredients in a bowl and stir to distribute seasonings.
Shape the meat mixture into 12 small meatballs, rounded or slightly flattened if you prefer.
Air fry at 390ºF for 7 minutes, until well done. Remove and drain on paper towels.

Nutrition: Calories: 269.5, Fat: 13.6g, Protein: 18.6g, Carbs: 17.5g, Fiber: 2g, Sugar: 1.5g

147. Air Fried Beef Schnitzel

Preparation Time: 10 minutes   **Cooking Time: 15 minutes**
Servings: 1

Ingredients:
- One lean beef schnitzel
- Olive oil: 2 tablespoons

- Breadcrumbs: ¼ cup
- One egg

- One lemon, to serve

Directions: Let the air fryer heat to 356F.
In a big bowl, add oil and breadcrumbs, mix well until forms a crumbly mixture. Soak beef steak in the beaten egg and dip in the breadcrumbs mixture. Place the breaded beef in the air fryer and cook at 356°F for 15 minutes. Remove from the air fryer and serve with green salad and a slice of lemon.

Nutrition: Calories: 339.6, Protein: 19.6g, Carbs: 13.5g, Fat: 9.5g

148. Air Fried Empanadas

Preparation Time: 10 minutes   **Cooking Time: 20 minutes**
Servings: 2

Ingredients:
- Square gyoza wrappers: eight pieces
- Olive oil: 1 tablespoon
- White onion: 1/4 cup, finely diced
- Mushrooms: 1/4 cup, finely diced
- Half cup lean ground beef
- Chopped garlic: 2 teaspoons
- Paprika: 1/4 teaspoon
- Ground cumin: 1/4 teaspoon
- Six green olives, diced
- Ground cinnamon: 1/8 teaspoon
- Diced tomatoes: half cup
- One egg, lightly beaten

Directions: In a skillet, over a medium flame, add oil, onions, and beef and cook for 3 minutes, until beef turns brown. Add mushrooms and cook for six minutes until it starts to brown. Then add paprika, cinnamon, olives, cumin, and garlic and cook for 3 minutes or more.
Add in the chopped tomatoes, and cook for a minute. Turn off the heat; let it cool for five minutes.
Lay gyoza wrappers on a flat surface add one and a half tbsp. of beef filling in each wrapper. Brush edges with water or egg, fold wrappers, pinch edges.
Put four empanadas in an even layer in an air fryer basket, and cook for 7 minutes at 400°F until nicely browned.
Serve with sauce and salad greens.

Nutrition: Calories: 342.5, Protein: 18.5g, Carbs: 12.1g, Fat: 18.6g

149. Air Fried Steak with Asparagus

Preparation Time: 20 minutes   **Cooking Time: 30 minutes**
Servings: 2

Ingredients:
- Olive oil spray
- Flank steak (2 pounds)- cut into 6 pieces
- Kosher salt and black pepper
- Two cloves of minced garlic
- Asparagus: 4 cups
- Tamari sauce: half cup
- Three bell peppers: sliced thinly
- Beef broth: 1/3 cup
- 1 Tbsp. of unsalted butter
- Balsamic vinegar: 1/4 cup

Directions: Sprinkle salt and pepper on steak and rub.
In a ziploc bag, add Tamari sauce and garlic, then add steak, toss well and seal the bag.
Let it marinate for one hour to overnight.
Place asparagus and bell peppers in the center of the steak.
Roll the steak around the vegetables and close it well with toothpicks.
Preheat the air fryer. Spray the steak with olive oil spray. And place steaks in the air fryer.
Cook for 15 minutes at 400°F.
Remove the steak from the air fryer and let it rest for five minute before slicing.
In the meantime, add balsamic vinegar, butter, and broth over medium flame. Mix well and reduce it by half. Add salt and pepper to taste. Pour over steaks right before serving.

Nutrition: Calories: 469.5, Protein: 29.6g, Carbs: 19.5g, Fat: 14.6g

150. Air Fry Rib-Eye Steak

Preparation Time: 5 minutes   **Cooking Time: 14 minutes**
Servings: 2

Ingredients:
- Lean rib eye steaks: 2 medium-sized
- Salt & freshly ground black pepper, to taste

Directions: Let the air fry preheat at 400 F.
Season the meat with salt and pepper and put in the air fryer basket. Cook for 14 minutes and flip after half time. Take out from the air fryer and let it rest for 5 minutes. Serve with microgreen salad.

Nutrition: Calories: 469.3, Protein: 45.6g, Carbs: 22.6g, Fat: 30.3g

151. Beef Steak Kabobs with Vegetables

Preparation Time: 5 minutes   Cooking Time: 10 minutes
Servings: 4

Ingredients:
- Light Soy sauce: 2 tbsp.
- Lean beef chuck ribs: 4 cups, cut into one-inch pieces
- Low-fat sour cream: 1/3 cup
- Half onion
- 8 skewers: 6 inch
- One bell peppers

Directions: In a mixing bowl, add sour cream and soy sauce. Mix well. Add the lean beef chunks, coat well, and let it marinate for half an hour.
Cut onion, bell pepper into one-inch pieces. In water, soak skewers for ten minutes.
Add bell peppers, onions, and beef on skewers.
Let it cook for 10 minutes in a preheated air fryer at 400°F, flip halfway through. Serve with yogurt dipping sauce.

Nutrition: Calories: 267.6, Protein: 19.6g, Carbs: 14.6g, Fat: 9.3g

152. Air Fryer Hamburgers

Preparation Time: 5 minutes   Cooking Time: 13 minutes
Servings: 4

Ingredients:
- Buns:4
- Lean ground beef chuck: 4 cups
- Salt to taste
- Slices of any cheese: 4 slices
- Black Pepper, to taste

Directions: Let the air fryer preheat to 350 F.
In a bowl, add lean ground beef, pepper, and salt. Mix well and form patties.
Put the patties in the air fryer in one layer only, cook for 6 minutes, flip them halfway through. One minute before you take out the patties, add cheese on top. When cheese is melted, take out from the air fryer.
Add ketchup, any dressing, tomatoes, lettuce and patties to your buns. Serve hot.

Nutrition: Calories: 519.6, Protein: 31.3g, Carbs: 21.6g, Fat: 33.8g

153. Air Fryer Meatloaf

Preparation Time: 10 minutes   Cooking Time: 45 minutes
Servings: 8

Ingredients:
- Ground lean beef: 4 cups
- Bread crumbs: 1 cup (soft and fresh)
- Chopped mushrooms: ½ cup
- Cloves of minced garlic
- Shredded carrots: ½ cup
- Beef broth: ¼ cup
- Chopped onions: ½ cup
- Two eggs beaten
- Ketchup: 3 Tbsp.
- Worcestershire sauce: 1 Tbsp.
- Dijon mustard: 1 Tbsp.

For Glaze:
- Ketchup: half cup
- Dijon mustard: 2 tsp

Directions: In a big bowl, add beef broth and breadcrumbs, stir well. And set it aside in a food processor, add garlic, onions, mushrooms, and carrots, and pulse on high until finely chopped.
In a separate bowl, add soaked breadcrumbs, Dijon mustard, Worcestershire sauce, eggs, lean ground beef, ketchup, and salt. With your hands, combine well and make it into a loaf.
Let the air fryer preheat to 390 F.
Put Meatloaf in the Air Fryer and let it cook for 45 minutes.
In the meantime, add Dijon mustard, ketchup, and brown sugar in a bowl and mix. Glaze this mix over Meatloaf when five minutes are left. Rest the Meatloaf for ten minutes before serving.

Nutrition: Calories: 329.6, Proteins: 19.3g, Carbs: 15.4g, Fat: 9.1 g

154. Beef and Ale Casserole

Preparation Time: 10 minutes   Cooking Time: 1 hour
Servings: 4

Ingredients:
- Three tablespoons plain flour
- 1 ½ lbs. of leg of beef or diced braising steak
- Three tablespoons of olive oil
- Two medium onions, cut into big wedges
- 13 oz of carrots, cut into big chunks
- 7 oz parsnip, cut into large chunks
- 2 cups of strong ale
- Three tablespoons fresh thyme
- One bay leaf

Directions: Heat the oven to 340 ° F.

Spread the flour on a dinner plate. Add beef in the flour.

Pour two tsp of oil into a big frying pan. Fry beef on medium heat for 2-3 minutes. Fry until each side is brown all over. Shift the meat onto a plate and set aside.

Continue following the above instructions with the remaining meat. You can add more oil if required.

Put the remaining oil in a frying pan. Heat it moderately and sauté the onions, carrots, and parsnips for five minutes.

Then put the beef and vegetables into an ovenproof casserole dish. Pour in the ale, sprinkle the thyme and bay leaf. Cover with a lid. Cook in the oven for an hour. Wait till it is properly cooked. Serve immediately.

Nutrition: Calories: 603.6, Protein: 59.3 g, Carbs: 33g, Fat: 22.1g

155. Rosemary Lamb Chops

Preparation Time: 30 minutes
Servings: 2-3

Cooking Time: 20 minutes

Ingredients:
- 2 tsp. oil
- ½ tsp. ground rosemary
- ½ tsp. lemon juice
- 1 lb. (454 g.) lamb chops, 1-inch thick
- Salt and pepper to taste
- Cooking spray

Directions: Mix the oil, rosemary, and lemon juice and rub them into all sides of the lamb chops. Season to taste with salt and pepper.

Cover lamb chops and allow them to rest in the fridge for 15 to 20 minutes.

Spray air fryer basket with cooking spray and place lamb chops in it.

Air fry at 360ºF for 20 minutes.

Nutrition: Calories: 236.5, Fat: 12.7g, Protein: 30.6g, Carbs: 0g, Fiber: 0g

156. Meatloaf

Preparation Time: 10 minutes
Servings: 8

Cooking Time: 45 minutes

Ingredients
- 4 cups ground lean beef
- 1 cup breadcrumbs, soft and fresh
- 1/2 cup mushrooms, chopped

For the glaze
- 1/4 cup honey
- 3 garlic cloves, minced
- 1/2 cup carrots, shredded
- 1/4 cup beef broth
- 1/2 cup onions, chopped

- 1/2 cup ketchup
- 2 eggs beaten
- 3 tbsp. ketchup
- 1 tbsp. Worcestershire sauce
- 1 tbsp. Dijon mustard

- 2 tsp. Dijon mustard

Directions: In a big bowl, add the beef broth and breadcrumbs; stir well. Set it aside in a food processor, add garlic, onions, mushrooms, and carrots, and pulse on HIGH until finely chopped.

Add soaked breadcrumbs, Dijon mustard, Worcestershire sauce, eggs, lean ground beef, ketchup, and salt in a separate bowl. With your hands, combine well and make it into a loaf.

Let the air fryer preheat to 390ºF. Put the meatloaf in the oven and let it cook for 45 minutes.

In the meantime, add Dijon mustard, ketchup, and brown sugar to a bowl and mix. Glaze this mix over the meatloaf when 5 minutes are left. Let it cool for 10 minutes before serving.

Nutrition: Calories: 329.6, Protein: 19.3g, Carbs: 16.3g, Fat: 9.5g

157. Empanadas

Preparation Time: 10 minutes
Servings: 2

Cooking Time: 20 minutes

Ingredients:
- 8 square Gyoza wrappers
- 1 tbsp. olive oil
- 1/4 cup white onion, finely diced
- 1/4 cup mushrooms, finely diced
- 1/2 cup lean ground beef
- 2 tsp. garlic, chopped
- 1/4 tsp. paprika
- 1/4 tsp. ground cumin
- 6 green olives, diced
- 1/8 tsp. ground cinnamon
- 1/2 cup tomatoes, diced
- 1 egg, lightly beaten

Directions: Add oil, onions, and beef over a medium flame in a skillet and cook for 3 minutes until the meat turns brown.

Add the mushrooms and cook for 6 minutes until it starts to brown. Then add the paprika, cinnamon, olives, cumin, and garlic and cook for 3 minutes or more.

Add in the chopped tomatoes, and cook for 1 minute; turn off the heat and let it cool for 5 minutes.

Lay the wrappers on a flat surface add 1 1/2 tbsp. of beef filling in each wrapper. Brush edges with water or egg, fold the wrappers, and pinch the edges. Put 4 empanadas in an even layer in an air fryer basket, and cook for 7 minutes at 400°F until nicely browned. Serve with sauce and salad greens.

Nutrition: Calories: 342.5, Fat: 18.5g, Protein: 18.6g, Carbs: 12.1g

158. Mini Meatloaf

Preparation Time: 15 minutes
Servings: 6

Cooking Time: 25 minutes

Ingredients
- 1 lb. 80/20 ground beef
- 1/4 medium yellow onion, peeled and diced
- 1/2 medium green bell pepper, seeded and diced
- 1 large egg
- 3 tbsp. blanched finely ground almond flour
- 1 tbsp. Worcestershire sauce
- 1/2 tsp. garlic powder
- 1 tsp. parsley, dried
- 2 tbsp. tomato paste
- 1/4 cup water
- 1 tbsp. powdered erythritol

Directions: Combine the ground beef, onion, pepper, egg, and almond flour in a large bowl.

Pour in the Worcestershire sauce, garlic powder and parsley to the bowl. Mix until fully combined.

Divide the mixture and place it into 2 (4-inch) loaf baking pans.

In a small bowl, mix water, tomato paste, and erythritol. Spoon half the mixture over each loaf.

Working in batches (if necessary), place loaf pans into the air fryer basket.

Set the temperature to 350°F and cook for 25 minutes.

Serve warm.

Nutrition: Calories: 169.5, Fat: 8.6g, Protein: 15.3g, Carbs: 2.5g, Fiber: 1g, Sugar: 1.8g

159. Taco-Stuffed Peppers

Preparation Time: 10 minutes
Servings: 4

Cooking Time: 25 minutes

Ingredients
- 1 lb. 80/20 ground beef
- 1 tbsp. chili powder
- 2 tsp. cumin
- 1 tsp. garlic powder
- 1 tsp. salt
- 1/4 tsp. ground black pepper
- 1 can (10 oz.) diced tomatoes and green chiles, drained
- 4 medium green bell peppers
- 1 cup shredded Monterey jack cheese, divided

Directions: In a medium skillet over medium heat, brown the ground beef for about 7 minutes. When no pink remains, drain the fat from the skillet.

Return the skillet to the stovetop and add chili powder, cumin, garlic powder, salt, and black pepper. Add drained can have diced tomatoes and chiles to the skillet. Continue cooking for 3–5 minutes.

While the mixture is cooking, cut each bell pepper in half. Remove the seeds and white membrane.

Spoon the cooked mixture evenly into each bell pepper and top with a 1/4 cup of cheese. Place the stuffed peppers into the air fryer basket. Set the temperature to 350°F and cook for 15 minutes.

When done, peppers will be fork-tender, and cheese will be browned and bubbling. Serve warm.

Nutrition: Calories: 345.6, Fat: 18.5g, Protein: 28.3g, Carbs: 110.2g, Fibers: 3.2g, Sugars: 4.5g

160. Lamb Chops with Herb Butter

Preparation Time: 10 minutes

Cooking Time: 5 minutes

Servings: 4

Ingredients:
- *4 lamb chops*
- *1 tsp. rosemary, diced*
- *1 tbsp. butter*
- *Pepper*
- *Salt*

Directions: Season lamb chops with pepper and salt.

Place the dehydrating tray in a multi-level air fryer basket. Insert the basket in the air fryer oven.

Place the lamb chops on dehydrating tray.

Seal pot with the air fryer lid and select "Air Fry" mode, then set the temperature to 400ºF and cook for 5 minutes.

Stir in rosemary and butter and spread overcooked lamb chops. Serve and enjoy.

Nutrition: Calories: 277.5, Fat: 12.2g, Carbs: 0.2g, Sugar: 0g, Protein: 38.5g

161. Hamburgers

Preparation Time: 5 minutes   **Cooking Time: 6 minutes**
Servings: 4

Ingredients:
- *4 buns*
- *4 cups lean ground beef chuck*
- *4 slices any cheese*
- *Black Pepper to taste*
- *2 sliced tomatoes*
- *1 head of lettuce*
- *Ketchup for dressing*
- *Salt to taste*

Directions: Let the air fryer preheat to 350ºF.

In a bowl, add ground beef, salt, and pepper. Mix well and form into patties.

Place them in the air fryer in a single layer, cook for 6 minutes, flip them halfway through. One minute before removing the patties, add the cheese on top. When cheese is melted, remove from the air fryer.

Add ketchup, tomatoes, lettuce, and patties to your buns and serve.

Nutrition: Calories: 519.5, Carbs: 21.2g, Protein: 31.3g, Fat: 33.5g

162. Flavorful Meatballs

Preparation Time: 15 minutes   **Cooking Time: 25 minutes**
Servings: 6

Ingredients:
- *200 g ground beef*
- *200 g ground chicken*
- *100 g ground pork*
- *30 g minced garlic*
- *1 potato*
- *1 egg*
- *1 tsp. basil*
- *1 tsp. cayenne pepper*
- *1 tsp. white pepper*
- *2 tsp. olive oil*

Directions: Combine ground beef, chicken meat, and pork in the mixing bowl and stir it gently.

Sprinkle it with basil, cayenne pepper, and white pepper.

Add minced garlic and egg. Stir the mixture gently. You should get a fluffy mass.

Peel the potato and grate it. Add grated potato to the mixture and stir it again.

Preheat the air fryer oven to 375°F. Take a tray and spray it with olive oil.

Make the balls from the meat mass and put them on the tray. Lay the tray in the oven and cook it for 25 minutes.

Nutrition: Calories: 203.5, Protein: 26.5g, Fat: 7.1g, Carbs: 6.5g

163. Beef with Mushrooms

Preparation Time: 15 minutes   **Cooking Time: 40 minutes**
Servings: 4

Ingredients:
- *300 g beef*
- *150 g mushrooms*
- *1 onion*
- *1 tsp. olive oil*
- *100 g vegetable broth*
- *1 tsp. basil*
- *1 tsp. chili*
- *30 g tomato juice*

Directions: Take the beef and pierce the meat with a knife. Rub it with olive oil, basil, and chili, and lemon juice.

Chop the onion and mushrooms and pour them with vegetable broth. Cook the vegetables for 5 minutes.

Take a big tray and put the meat in it. Add vegetable broth to the tray too. It will make the meat juicy. Preheat the air fryer oven to 375ºF and cook it for 35 minutes.

Nutrition: Calories: 174.5, Protein: 25.6g, Fat: 5.5g, Carbs: 4.1g

164. Lemon Greek Beef and Vegetables

Preparation Time: 10 minutes
Servings: 4

Cooking Time: 14 minutes

Ingredients:
- ½ lb. (227 g.) 96% lean ground beef
- 2 medium tomatoes, chopped
- 1 onion, chopped
- 2 garlic cloves, minced
- 2 cups fresh baby spinach
- 2 tbsp. freshly squeezed lemon juice
- ⅓ cup low-sodium beef broth
- 2 tbsp. crumbled low-sodium feta cheese

Directions: In a baking pan, crumble the beef. Place in the air fryer basket. Air fry at 370ºF for 6 minutes, stirring once during cooking until browned. Drain off any fat or liquid.
Swell the tomatoes, onion, and garlic into the pan. Air fry for 4 minutes more.
Add the spinach, lemon juice, and beef broth.
Air fry for 4 minutes more, or until the spinach is wilted.
Sprinkle with the feta cheese and serve immediately.

Nutrition: Calories: 97.5, Fat: 1g, Protein: 15.5g, Carbs: 4.6g, Fiber: 1g, Sugar: 1.6g

165. Hot Dogs

Preparation Time: 2 minutes
Servings: 4

Cooking Time: 10 minutes

Ingredients:
- 4 beef hot dogs

Directions: Using a knife, score the hot dogs to create several little slits to prevent bursting during cooking.
Lay the hotdogs in the air fryer. Bake for 5 minutes at 375ºF.
When the timer is up, rotate the hotdogs; cook for 3 minutes more.
Remove from fryer and dig in.

Nutrition: Calories: 110.2, Fat: 5.6g, Carbs: 7.5g, Protein: 4.5g

166. Meatballs and Creamy Potatoes

Preparation Time: 45–50 minutes
Servings: 4–6

Cooking Time: 35 minutes

Ingredients:
- 12 oz. lean ground beef
- 1 medium onion, finely chopped
- 1 tbsp. parsley leaves, finely chopped
- ½ tbsp. fresh thyme leaves
- ½ tsp. minced garlic
- 2 tbsp olive oil
- 1 tsp. salt
- 1 tsp. ground black pepper
- 1 enormous egg
- 3 tbsp. bread crumbs
- 1 cup half & half, or ½ cup whole milk and ½ cup cream mixed
- 7 medium russet potatoes
- ½ tsp. ground nutmeg
- ½ cup grated gruyere cheese

Directions: Place the ground beef, onions, parsley, thyme, garlic, olive oil, salt and pepper, egg, and breadcrumbs in a bowl, and mix well. Place in refrigerator until needed.
In another bowl, place half & half and nutmeg, and whisk to combine.
Peel and wash potatoes, and then slice them thinly, ⅛ to 1/5 of an inch, if needed, to use a mandolin.
Warm up the Air Fryer to 390ºF.
Place potato slices in a bowl with half & half and toss to coat well. Layer the potato slices in an Air Fryer baking accessory and pour over the leftover half & half. Bake for 25 minutes at 390ºF.
Meanwhile, take the meat mixture out of the fridge and shape it into inch and half balls.
When potatoes are cooked, place meatballs on top of them in one layer and cover with the grated Gruyere.
Cook for another 10 minutes.

Nutrition: Calories: 231.2, Fat: 8g, Carbs: 5.8g, Protein: 12.8g

167. Meatballs in Tomato Sauce

Preparation Time: 10 minutes
Servings: 3–4

Cooking Time: 12 minutes

Ingredients:
- 1 egg
- ¾ lb. lean ground beef
- 1 onion, chopped
- 3 tbsp. breadcrumbs
- ½ tbsp. fresh thyme leaves, chopped
- ½ cup tomato sauce
- 1 tbsp. parsley, chopped
- Pinch salt
- Pinch pepper, to taste

Directions: Preheat the Air Fryer to 390°F
Place all ingredients in a bowl. Mix until well-combined. Divide mixture into 12 balls. Place them in the cooking basket. Cook meatballs for 8 minutes.
Put the cooked meatballs in an oven dish. Pour the tomato sauce on top. Put the oven dish inside the cooking basket of the Air Fryer. Cook for 5 minutes at 330°F.

Nutrition: Calorie: 128.4, Carbs: 14.7g, Fat: 17.1g, Protein: 18.2g, Fiber: 1.2g

168. Parmesan Beef Slices

Preparation Time: 14 minutes
Servings: 4

Cooking Time: 25 minutes

Ingredients:
- 12 oz. beef brisket
- 1 tsp. kosher salt
- 7 oz. Parmesan, sliced
- 5 oz. chive stems
- 1 tsp. turmeric
- 1 tsp. dried oregano
- 2 tsp. butter

Directions: Slice the beef brisket into 4 slices. Sprinkle every beef slice with turmeric and dried oregano. Grease the air fryer basket tray with butter. Put the beef slices inside. Dice the chives.
Make a layer using the diced chives over the beef slices. Then make a layer using the Parmesan cheese. Preheat the air fryer to 365°F and cook the beef slices for 25 minutes.

Nutrition: Calories: 347.5, Fat: 17.5g, Fiber 0.9g, Carbs: 4.5g, Protein: 42.5

169. Chili Beef Jerky

Preparation Time: 25 minutes
Servings: 6

Cooking Time: 2.5 hours

Ingredients:
- 14 oz. beef flank steak
- 1 tsp. chili pepper
- 3 tbsp. apple cider vinegar
- 1 tsp. ground black pepper
- 1 tsp. onion powder
- 1 tsp. garlic powder
- ¼ tsp. liquid smoke

Directions: Slice the beefsteak into the medium strips and then tenderize each piece.
Take a bowl and combine the apple cider vinegar, ground black pepper, onion powder, garlic powder, and liquid smoke. Whisk with a fork.
Then transfer the beef pieces to the prepared mixture and stir well. Leave the meat to marinate for up to 8 hours.
Put the marinated beef pieces in the air fryer rack. Cook the beef jerky for 2.5 hours at 150°F.

Nutrition: Calories: 128.5, Fat: 3.5g, Fiber: 0.2, Carbs 1.1g, Protein: 20.6g

170. Steak Tips

Preparation Time: 10 minutes
Servings: 3

Cooking Time: 5 minutes

Ingredients:
- 1 lb. steak, cut into cubes
- 1 tsp. olive oil
- 1 tsp. Montreal steak seasoning
- Pepper
- Salt

Directions: In a bowl, add steak cubes and remaining ingredients and toss well.
Select "Air Fry" mode, set time to 5 minutes and temperature 400°F then press START.

The air fryer display will prompt you to ADD FOOD once the temperature is reached then place steak cubes in the air fryer basket.

Nutrition: Calories: 316.5, Fat: 8.5g, Carbs: 0g, Sugar: 0g, Protein: 54.9g

171. Rosemary Beef Tips

Preparation Time: 10 minutes
Servings: 4
Cooking Time: 12 minutes

Ingredients:
- *1 lb. steak, cut into 1-inch cubes*
- *1 tsp. paprika*
- *2 tsp. onion powder*
- *1 tsp. garlic powder*
- *2 tbsp. coconut aminos*
- *2 tsp. rosemary, crushed*
- *Pepper*
- *Salt*

Directions: Add meat and remaining ingredients into the mixing bowl and mix well and let it sit for 5 minutes.
Select Air Fry mode. Set time to 12 minutes and temperature 380°F then press START.
The air fryer display will prompt you to ADD FOOD once the temperature is reached then place steak cubes in the air fryer basket. Stir halfway through.

Nutrition: Calories: 242.4, Fat: 5.1g, Carbs: 3.1g, Sugar: 0.7g, Protein: 41.8g

172. Spinach Beef Heart

Preparation Time: 15 minutes
Servings: 4
Cooking Time: 20 minutes

Ingredients:
- *1-lb. beef heart*
- *5 oz. chive stems*
- *½ cup fresh spinach*
- *1 tsp. salt*
- *1 tsp. ground black pepper*
- *3 cups chicken stock*
- *1 tsp. butter*

Directions: Remove all the fat from the beef heart.
Dice the chives. Chop the fresh spinach. Combine the diced chives, fresh spinach, and butter together. Stir it.
Cut the beef heart and fill it with the spinach-chives mixture.
Preheat the air fryer to 400°F. Pour the chicken stock into the air fryer basket tray.
Sprinkle the prepared stuffed beef heart with salt and ground black pepper. Put the beef heart in the air fryer and cook it for 20 minutes.
Remove the cooked heart from the air fryer and slice it.
Sprinkle the slices with the remaining liquid from the air fryer.

Nutrition: Calories: 215.6, Fat: 6.1g, Fiber 0.8g, Carbs 3.2g, Protein 33.7g

173. Garlic Beef Steak

Preparation Time: 15 minutes
Servings: 4
Cooking Time: 12 minutes

Ingredients:
- *1 tbsp. butter*
- *2 tbsp. fresh orange juice*
- *1 tsp. lime zest*
- *1-lb. beef steak*
- *1 tsp. ground ginger*
- *1 tsp. dried oregano*
- *1 tbsp. cream*
- *½ tsp. minced garlic*

Directions: Combine the fresh orange juice, butter, lime zest, ground ginger, dried oregano, cream, and minced garlic together.
Combine the mixture well. Then tenderize the steak gently.
Brush the beefsteak with the combined spice, mix carefully and leave the steak for 7 minutes to marinade.
Preheat the air fryer to 360°F.
Put the marinated beef steak in the air fryer basket and cook the meat for 12 minutes. The beef should be well done.

Nutrition: Calories: 244.5, Fat: 9.8g, Fiber: 0.3g, Carbs: 1.5g, Protein: 34.9

174. Paprika Beef Tongue

Preparation Time: 10 minutes
Servings: 6

Cooking Time: 20 minutes

Ingredients:
- 1-lb. beef tongue
- 1 tsp. salt
- 1 tsp. ground black pepper
- 1 tsp. paprika
- 1 tbsp. butter
- 4 cup water

Directions: Preheat the air fryer to 365°F.
Put the beef tongue in the air fryer basket tray and add water.
Sprinkle the mixture with salt, ground black pepper, and paprika.
Cook the beef tongue for 15 minutes. Strain the water from the beef tongue.
Cut the beef tongue into strips.
Toss the butter in the air fryer basket tray and add the beef strips.
Cook the strips for 5 minutes at 360°F.

Nutrition: Calories: 233.5, Fat: 18.1g, Fiber: 0.2g, Carbs: 0.4g, Protein: 15.2g

175. Mushroom Cheese Salad

Preparation Time: 10 minutes
Servings: 2

Cooking Time: 15 minutes

Ingredients:
- 10 mushrooms, halved
- 1 tbsp. fresh parsley, chopped
- 1 tbsp. olive oil
- 1 tbsp. mozzarella cheese, grated
- 1 tbsp. cheddar cheese, grated
- 1 tbsp. dried mix herbs
- Pepper

Directions: Add all ingredients into the bowl and toss well.
Transfer bowl mixture into the air fryer baking dish.
Place in the air fryer and cook at 380°F for 15 minutes. Serve and enjoy.

Nutrition: Calories: 89.5, Fat: 6.5g, Carbs: 1.5g, Sugar: 1g, Protein: 5.5g

176. Cayenne Rib Eye Steak

Preparation Time: 10 minutes
Servings: 2

Cooking Time: 13 minutes

Ingredients:
- 1-lb. rib eye steak
- 1 tsp. salt
- 1 tsp. cayenne pepper
- ½ tsp. chili flakes
- 3 tbsp. cream
- 1 tsp. olive oil
- 1 tsp. lemongrass
- 1 tbsp. butter
- 1 tsp. garlic powder

Directions: Preheat the air fryer to 360°F.
Take a shallow bowl and combine the lemongrass, cayenne pepper, chili flakes, salt, and garlic powder together.
Mix the spices. Sprinkle the rib eye steak with the spice mixture.
Melt the butter and combine it with cream and olive oil. Churn the mixture. Pour the churned mixture into the air fryer basket tray. Add the rib eye steak and cook it for 13 minutes.
When the steak is cooked transfer it to a paper towel to soak all the excess fat.

Nutrition: Calories: 707.5, Fat: 58.5g, Fiber: 0.4g, Carbs: 2.1g, Protein: 40.9g

177. Beef-Chicken Meatball Casserole

Preparation Time: 15 minutes
Servings: 7

Cooking Time: 21 minutes

Ingredients:
- 1 eggplant
- 10 oz. ground chicken
- 8 oz. ground beef
- 1 tsp. minced garlic
- 1 tsp. ground white pepper
- 1 tomato
- 1 egg
- 1 tbsp. coconut flour
- 8 oz. Parmesan, shredded
- 2 tbsp. butter
- ⅓ cup cream

Directions: Combine the ground chicken and ground beef in a large bowl. Add the minced garlic and ground white pepper.

Crack the egg into the bowl with the ground meat mixture and stir it carefully until well combined. Then add the coconut flour and mix. Make the small meatballs from the meat.

Preheat the air fryer to 360°F. Sprinkle the basket tray with the butter and pour the cream.

Peel the eggplant and chop it. Put the meatballs over the cream and sprinkle them with the chopped eggplant.

Slice the tomato and place it over the eggplant. Make a layer of shredded cheese over the sliced tomato.

Put the casserole in the air fryer and cook it for 21 minutes.

Let the casserole cool to room temperature before serving.

Nutrition: Calories: 313.2, Fat 16.1g, Fiber 3.4g, Carbs 7.1g, Protein 34.5g

178. Meatballs in Spicy Tomato Sauce

Preparation Time: 5 minutes   **Cooking Time: 15 minutes**
Servings: 4

Ingredients:
- 3 green onions, minced
- 1 garlic clove, minced
- 1 egg yolk
- ¼-cup saltine cracker crumbs
- Pinch salt
- Freshly ground black pepper
- 1 pound 95 percent lean ground beef
- Olive oil for misting
- 1¼ cups pasta sauce
- 2 tablespoons Dijon mustard

Directions: In a large bowl, combine the green onions, garlic, egg yolk, cracker crumbs, salt, and pepper, and mix well.

Add the ground beef and mix thoroughly with the hands until combined. Form into 1½-inch meatballs. Mist the meatballs with olive oil and put into the basket of the air fryer.

Bake for 8 to 11 minutes or until the meatballs are 165°F. Remove the meatballs from the basket and place in a 6-inch metal bowl. Top with the pasta sauce and Dijon mustard and mix gently.

Bake for 4 minutes until the sauce is hot.

Nutrition: Calories: 359.5, Fat: 11.3g, Carbs: 23.5g, Fiber: 3g, Protein: 39.5g

Pork Recipes

179. Paprika Pulled Pork

Preparation Time: 15 minutes
Servings: 4

Cooking Time: 25 minutes

Ingredients:
- 1 tbsp. chili flakes
- 1 tsp. ground black pepper
- ½ tsp. paprika
- 1 tsp. cayenne pepper
- ⅓ cup cream
- 1 tsp. kosher salt
- 1-lb. pork tenderloin
- 1 tsp. ground thyme
- 4 cup chicken stock
- 1 tsp. butter

Directions: Pour the chicken stock into the air fryer basket tray.
Add the pork steak and sprinkle the mixture with chili flakes, paprika, cayenne pepper, ground black pepper, and salt. Preheat the air fryer to 370°F and cook the meat for 20 minutes.
Strain the liquid and shred the meat with 2 forks.
Then add the butter and cream and mix it.
Cook the pulled pork for 4 minutes more at 360°F. When the pulled pork is cooked allow to rest briefly.

Nutrition: Calories: 197.5, Fat: 6.2, Fiber: 0.5g, Carbs: 2.1g, Protein: 31.2

180. Jamaican Pork with Jerk

Preparation Time: 10 minutes
Servings: 4

Cooking Time: 20 minutes

Ingredients:
- Pork, cut into three-inch pieces
- Jerk paste: ¼ cup

Directions: Rub jerk paste all over the pork pieces. Let it marinate for four hours in the refrigerator.
Let the air fryer preheat to 390°F. spray with olive oil.
Before putting in the air fryer, let the meat sit for 20 minutes at room temperature.
Cook for 20 minutes at 390°F in the air fryer, flip halfway through.
Take out from the air fryer and let it rest for ten minutes before slicing. Serve with microgreens.

Nutrition: Calories: 233.5, Protein: 31.5g, Carbs: 11.4g, Fat: 8.5g

181. Pork Tenderloin with Mustard Glazed

Preparation Time: 10 minutes
Servings: 4

Cooking Time: 18 minutes

Ingredients:
- Yellow mustard: ¼ cup
- One pork tenderloin
- Salt: ¼ tsp
- Freshly ground black pepper: ⅛ tsp
- Minced garlic: 1 Tbsp.
- Dried rosemary: 1 tsp
- Italian seasoning: 1 tsp

Directions: Cut the top of pork tenderloin. Add minced garlic in the cuts, and season with salt and pepper.
In a bowl, add mustard, rosemary, and Italian seasoning mix until combined. Rub this mustard mix all over pork. Let it marinate in the refrigerator for two hours.
Put pork tenderloin in the air fryer basket. Cook for 18 minutes at 400°F. with an instant-read thermometer internal temperature of pork should be 145°F.
Take out from the air fryer and serve.

Nutrition: Calories: 389.5, Protein: 59.6g, Carbs: 10.5g, Fat: 10.4g

182. Air Fryer Breaded Pork Chops

Preparation Time: 10 minutes
Servings: 4

Cooking Time: 18 minutes

Ingredients:

- Whole-wheat breadcrumbs: 1 cup
- Salt: ¼ teaspoon
- Pork chops: 2-4 pieces (center cut and boneless)
- Chili powder: half teaspoon
- Parmesan cheese: 1 tablespoon
- Paprika: 1½ teaspoons
- One egg beaten
- Onion powder: half teaspoon
- Granulated garlic: half teaspoon
- Pepper, to taste

Directions: Let the air fryer preheat to 400 F.
Rub salt on each side of pork chops, and let it rest.
Add beaten egg in a big bowl.
Add breadcrumbs, Parmesan cheese, paprika, garlic, pepper, chili powder, and onion powder in a bowl and mix well. Dip pork chop in beaten egg, then in breadcrumb mixture.
Put it in the air fryer and spray with oil. Cook for 12 minutes at 400 F. Flip and cook for another six minutes.

Nutrition: Calories: 424.6, Protein: 31.5g, Carbs: 18.5g, Fat: 19.6g, Fiber: 5g

183. Air Fryer Pork Chop & Broccoli

Preparation Time: 20 minutes
Servings: 2

Cooking Time: 10 minutes

Ingredients:

- Broccoli florets: 2 cups
- Bone-in pork chop: 2 pieces
- Paprika: half tsp.
- Avocado oil: 2 tbsp.
- Garlic powder: half tsp.
- Onion powder: half tsp.
- Two cloves of crushed garlic
- Salt: 1 teaspoon divided

Directions: Let the air fryer preheat to 350F. Spray the basket with cooking oil.
Add one tbsp. Oil, garlic powder, onion powder, half tsp. of salt, and paprika in a bowl and mix well. Rub this spice mix to the pork chop's sides.
Add pork chops to air fryer basket and cook for five minutes.
In the meantime, add one tsp. oil, garlic, half tsp of salt, and broccoli to a bowl and coat well.
Flip the pork chop, add the broccoli, and cook for five more minutes.
Take out from the air fryer and serve.

Nutrition: Calories: 482.5, Protein: 23.5g, Carbs: 11.5g, Fat: 19.5g

184. Cheesy Pork Chops in Air Fryer

Preparation Time: 5 minutes
Servings: 2

Cooking Time: 8 minutes

Ingredients:

- 4 lean pork chops
- Salt: half tsp.
- Garlic powder: half tsp.
- Shredded cheese: 4 tbsp.
- Chopped cilantro

Directions: Let the air fryer preheat to 350F.
Rub the pork chops with garlic, cilantro, and salt. Put in the air fryer and let it cook for four minutes.
Flip them and cook for two minutes more.
Add cheese on top and cook for another two minutes or until the cheese is melted.
Serve with salad greens.

Nutrition: Calories: 466.5, Protein: 61.5g, Fat: 21.5g

185. Pork Head Chops With Vegetables

Preparation Time: 9 minutes
Servings: 4

Cooking Time: 24 minutes

Ingredients:

- 4 pork head chops
- 2 red tomatoes
- 1 large green pepper
- 4 mushrooms
- 1 onion
- 4 slices cheese
- Salt to taste
- Ground pepper to taste
- Extra-virgin olive oil

Directions: Put the chops on a plate and season with salt and pepper.

Put 2 of the chops in the air fryer basket. Add the tomato slices, cheese slices, pepper slices, onion slices, and mushroom slices. Add some threads of oil. Cook at 375°F for 24 minutes.
Check that the meat is well made and remove it.
Repeat the same operation with the other 2 pork chops.

Nutrition: Calories: 105.3, Fat: 3g, Carbs: 0g, Protein: 21.4g

186. Flavored Pork Chops

Preparation Time: 9 minutes   **Cooking Time: 35 minutes**
Servings: 2

Ingredients:
- *3 garlic cloves, ground*
- *2 tbsp. olive oil*
- *1 tbsp. marinade*
- *4 thawed pork chops*

Directions: Mix the cloves of ground garlic, marinade, and oil. Then apply this mixture to the chops.
Put the chops in the air fryer at 360°F for 35 minutes. Serve.

Nutrition: Calories: 117.5, Fat: 3.1g, Carbs: 0g, Protein: 22.5g

187. Pork Trinoza Wrapped in Ham

Preparation Time: 8 minutes   **Cooking Time: 9 minutes**
Servings: 6

Ingredients:
- *6 pieces Serrano ham, thinly sliced*
- *454 g. pork, halved, with butter and crushed*
- *6 g. salt*
- *1 g. black pepper*
- *227 g. fresh spinach leaves, divided*
- *4 slices Mozzarella cheese, divided*
- *18 g. sun-dried tomatoes, divided*
- *10 ml olive oil, divided*

Directions: Place 3 pieces of ham on baking paper, slightly overlapping each other. Place 1 half of the pork in the ham. Repeat with the other half. Season the inside of the pork rolls with salt and pepper.
Place half of the spinach, cheese, and sun-dried tomatoes on top of the pork loin, leaving a 13 mm. border on all sides.
Roll the fillet around the filling and tie it with a kitchen cord to keep it closed.
Repeat the process for the other pork steak and place them in the fridge.
Warm in the air fryer and press START/PAUSE.
Brush the olive oil on each wrapped steak and place them in the preheated air fryer.
Select STEAK. Set the timer to 9 minutes and press START/PAUSE. Let it cool before cutting.

Nutrition: Calories: 281.5, Fat: 23g, Carbs: 0g, Protein: 16.8g

188. Stuffed Cabbage and Pork Loin Rolls

Preparation Time: 5 minutes   **Cooking Time: 20 minutes**
Servings: 4

Ingredients:
- *500 g. white cabbage*
- *1 onion*
- *8 pork tenderloin steaks*
- *2 carrots*
- *4 tbsp. soy sauce*
- *50 g. extra virgin olive oil*
- *Salt to taste*
- *8 sheets rice*

Directions: Put the chopped cabbage in the Thermo mix glass together with the onion and the chopped carrot.
Select 5 seconds on the speed 5. Add the extra virgin olive oil. Select 5 minutes, left turn, and spoon speed.
Cut the tenderloin steaks into thin strips. Add the meat to the thermo mix glass. Select 5 minutes, room temperature, left turn, spoon speed without beaker.
Add the soy sauce. Select 5 minutes, room temperature, left turn, spoon speed. Rectify salt. Let it cold down.
Hydrate the rice slices. Extend and distribute the filling between them.
Make the rolls, folding so that the edges are completely closed. Set the rolls in the air fryer and paint with the oil.
Select 10 minutes for cooking time and set the temperature to 375°F.

Nutrition: Calories: 119.5, Fat: 3.1g, Carbs: 0g, Protein: 21.4g

189. 12-Minute Pork Loin

Preparation Time: 10 minutes   **Cooking Time: 12 minutes**
Servings: 4

Ingredients:
- One tablespoon water
- One tablespoon Worcestershire sauce
- One tablespoon lemon juice
- One tablespoon Dijon-style mustard
- Four boneless pork top loin chops
- Half tablespoon lemon-pepper seasoning
- One tablespoon butter
- One tablespoon snipped fresh chives

Directions: For the sauce, combine water, Worcestershire sauce, lemon juice, and mustard in a small bowl; set aside.
Trim fat from chops. Use the lemon-pepper seasoning to sprinkle both sides of each chop. In a 10-inch pan, melt butter over medium heat. Add chops and cook for 12 minutes. Rotating once halfway through the cooking period. Withdraw from the heat. Place chops to a serving plate; protect and hold warm.
Pour the sauce into the pan; stir and extract any crusty brown pieces from the bottom of the pan. Pour the gravy over the chops. Sprinkle chives.

Nutrition: Calories: 175.4, Protein: 17.4g, Carbs: 1g, Fat: 9.8g

190. Homemade Flamingos

Preparation Time: 8 minutes   **Cooking Time: 8 minutes**
Servings: 4

Ingredients:
- 400 g. pork fillets, very thin sliced
- 2 eggs, boiled and chopped
- 100 g. Serrano ham, chopped
- 1 egg, beaten
- 1 cup breadcrumbs

Directions: Make a roll with the pork fillets. Introduce half-cooked egg and Serrano ham. So that the roll does not lose its shape, fasten with a string or chopsticks.
Pass the rolls through the beaten egg and then through the breadcrumbs until it forms a good layer.
Warm the air fryer for a few minutes at 375°F. Insert the rolls in the basket and set the timer for 8 minutes.

Nutrition: Calories: 481.5, Fat: 23g, Carbs: 0g, Protein: 16.8g

191. Spiced Pork Chops

Preparation Time: 8 minutes   **Cooking Time: 10 minutes**
Servings: 2

Ingredients:
- 2 pork chops, boneless
- 15 ml. vegetable oil
- 25 g. dark brown sugar, packaged
- 6 g. Hungarian paprika
- 2 g. ground mustard
- 2 g. freshly ground black pepper
- 3 g. onion powder
- 3 g. garlic powder
- Salt and pepper to taste

Directions: Warm the air fryer for a few minutes at 375°F.
Cover the pork chops with oil.
Put all the spices and season the pork chops abundantly, almost as if you were making them breaded.
Place the pork chops in the preheated air fryer.
Select STEAK and set the time to 10 minutes. Remove the pork chops when it has finished cooking.
Let it stand and serve.

Nutrition: Calories: 117.5, Fat: 6.2g, Carbs: 0.3g, Protein: 13.5g

192. Pork Rind

Preparation Time: 9 minutes   **Cooking Time: 50 minutes**
Servings: 4

Ingredients:
- 1 kg pork rinds
- Salt to taste
- 1/2 tsp. black pepper

Directions: Preheat the air fryer. Set the time to 5 minutes and the temperature to 380°F.
Cut the bacon into cubes 1 finger wide. Season with salt and a pinch of pepper.
Place in the basket of the air fryer. Set the time to 45 minutes and press the POWER button.
Shake the basket every 10 minutes so that the pork rinds stay golden brown equally.
Once they are ready, drain a little on the paper towel so they stay dry. Transfer to a plate and serve.

Nutrition: Calories: 281.5, Fat: 23g, Carbs: 0.3g, Protein: 16.9g

193. Herbed Pork Ribs

Preparation Time: 6 minutes   **Cooking Time: 20 minutes**
Servings: 4

Ingredients:
- *500 g. pork ribs*
- *1 tbsp. provencal herbs*
- *Salt to taste*
- *Ground pepper to taste*
- *1 tsp. oil*

Directions: Set the ribs in a bowl and add some oil, Provencal herbs, salt, and ground pepper.
Stir well and leave in the fridge for 1 hour.
Put the ribs in the basket of the air fryer and select 380°F for 20 minutes.
From time to time, shake the basket and remove the ribs.

Nutrition: Calories: 295.6, Fat: 3.1g, Carbs: 5.6g, Protein: 29.6g

194. Air Fryer Pork Satay

Preparation Time: 15 minutes   **Cooking Time: 10 minutes**
Servings: 4

Ingredients:
- *1 (1 lb./454 g.) pork tenderloin, cut into 1 1/2-inch cubes*
- *1/4 cup onion, minced*
- *2 garlic cloves, minced*
- *1 jalapeño pepper, minced*
- *2 tbsp. lime juice, freshly squeezed*
- *2 tbsp. coconut milk*
- *2 tbsp. unsalted peanut butter*
- *2 tsp. curry powder*

Directions: In a medium bowl, mix the pork, lime juice, garlic, onion, jalapeño, peanut butter, coconut milk, and curry powder until well combined. Let position for 10 minutes at room temperature.
Remove the pork from the marinade but reserve the marinade.
Thread the pork onto 8 skewers. Air fry at 380°F for 10 minutes, brushing once with the reserved marinade until the pork reaches at least 145°F on a meat thermometer.
Discard any remaining marinade and serve immediately.

Nutrition: Calories: 194.5, Fats: 24.5g, Protein: 7.6g, Carbs: 1g, Fibers: 1g, Sugars: 2.5g

195. Pulled Pork

Preparation Time: 10 minutes   **Cooking Time: 2 1/2 hours**
Servings: 8

Ingredients:
- *2 tbsp. chili powder*
- *1 tsp. garlic powder*
- *1/2 tsp. onion powder*
- *1/2 tsp. ground black pepper*
- *1/2 tsp. cumin*
- *4 lbs. pork shoulder*

Directions: Mix the chili powder, garlic powder, onion powder, pepper, and cumin in a small bowl.
Rub the spice mixture over the pork shoulder, patting it into the skin.
Place the meat into the air fryer basket, set the temperature to 350°F and the timer for 2 1/2 hours.
Pork skin will be crispy and meat easily shredded with 2 forks when done.

Nutrition: Calories: 536.2, Fats: 34.5g, Protein: 43.5g, Carbs: 1g, Fibers: 1g

196. Pork Loin

Preparation Time: 10 minutes   **Cooking Time: 20 minutes**

Servings: 6

Ingredients:
- 1/2 lb. pork tenderloin patted dry
- Non-stick cooking spray
- 2 tbsps. garlic scape pesto
- Salt to taste
- Pepper to taste

Directions: Adjust the temperature of the air fryer to 375°F.
Rub all sides of the tenderloin with the non-stick cooking spray. Add pepper, garlic scape pesto, and salt.
Sprinkle the air fryer basket with cooking spray.
Place the tenderloin on the air fryer and cook at 400°F for 10 minutes.
Flip over to the other side and cook for another 10 minutes.
Remove from the air fryer and serve.

Nutrition: Calories: 378.7, Fat: 1.6g, Protein: 8.5g, Carbs: 0g

197. Pork Ribs

Preparation Time: 5 minutes
Servings: 4

Cooking Time: 20–25 minutes

Ingredients:
- 12 pork ribs, trimmed excess fat
- 2 tbsp. cornstarch
- 2 tbsp. olive oil
- 1 tsp. dry mustard
- ½ tsp. thyme
- ½ tsp. garlic powder
- 1 tsp. dried marjoram
- Pinch salt
- Freshly ground black pepper, to taste

Directions: Place the ribs on a clean work surface.
In a bowl, combine the olive oil, garlic powder, mustard, cornstarch, thyme, marjoram, salt, and pepper. Rub into the ribs.
Place the ribs in the air fryer basket and roast at 400°F for 10 minutes.
Turn the ribs with tongs and roast for 10 minutes.

Nutrition: Calories: 578.4, Fat: 43.5g, Protein: 40.5g, Carbs: 3.7g, Fiber: 0g, Sugar: 0g

198. Lemon Pork Tenderloin

Preparation Time: 5 minutes
Servings: 4

Cooking Time: 10 minutes

Ingredients:
- 1 lb. pork tenderloin, cut into ½-inch slices
- 1 tbsp. olive oil
- 1 tbsp. freshly squeezed lemon juice
- ½ tsp. grated lemon zest
- ½ tsp. dried marjoram
- Pinch salt
- Freshly ground black pepper to taste

Directions: Put the pork tenderloin slices in a medium bowl.
In a bowl, combine the lemon zest, olive oil, marjoram, lemon juice, salt, and pepper. Mix well.
Pour this marinade over the tenderloin slices.
Place the pork in the air fryer basket and roast at 400°F for 10 minutes.

Nutrition: Calories: 207.5, Fat: 7.6g, Protein: 30.5g, Carbs: 1.6g, Fiber: 0g, Sugar: 0.6g

199. Dijon Tenderloin

Preparation Time: 10 minutes
Servings: 4

Cooking Time: 12 minutes

Ingredients:
- 1 lb. pork tenderloin, cut into 1-inch slices
- Pinch salt
- Freshly ground black pepper to taste
- 2 tbsp. Dijon mustard
- 1 garlic clove, minced
- ½ tsp. dried basil
- 1 cup soft bread crumbs
- 2 tbsp. olive oil

Directions: Pound the pork slices and sprinkle with salt and pepper on both sides. Coat the pork with the Dijon mustard and season with basil and garlic.
On a bowl, combine the bread crumbs and olive oil. Mix well. Coat the pork slices with the bread crumb mixture.

Place the pork in the air fryer basket, leaving a little space between each piece. Air fry at 390ºF for 12 minutes or until the pork is crisp and brown.

Nutrition: Calories: 335.6, Fat: 12.6g, Protein: 33.8g, Carbs: 19.8g, Fiber: 2g, Sugar: 1.5g

200. Pork Satay

Preparation Time: 15 minutes   **Cooking Time: 9 minutes**
Servings: 4

Ingredients:
- *1 lb. pork tenderloin, cut into 1½-inch cubes*
- *¼ cup minced onion*
- *2 garlic cloves, minced*
- *1 jalapeño pepper, minced*
- *2 tbsp. freshly squeezed lime juice*
- *2 tbsp. coconut milk*
- *2 tbsp. unsalted peanut butter*
- *2 tsp. curry powder*

Directions: In a small bowl, mix the pork, garlic, lime juice, coconut milk, jalapeño, peanut butter, onion, and curry powder until well combined.
Remove the pork from the marinade but reserve the marinade.
Thread the pork onto 8 skewers. Air fry at 380ºF for 9 minutes, brushing once with the reserved marinade.

Nutrition: Calories: 194.5, Fat: 6.7g, Protein: 25.6g, Carbs: 6.4g, Fiber: 1g, Sugar: 2.6g

201. Pork Burgers with Red Cabbage Slaw

Preparation Time: 20 minutes   **Cooking Time: 8 minutes**
Servings: 4

Ingredients:
- *½ cup Greek yogurt*
- *2 tbsp. low-sodium mustard, divided*
- *1 tbsp. freshly squeezed lemon juice*
- *¼ cup sliced red cabbage*
- *¼ cup grated carrots*
- *1 lb. lean ground pork*
- *½ tsp. paprika*
- *1 cup mixed baby lettuce greens*
- *2 tomatoes, sliced*
- *8 whole-wheat sandwich buns, cut in half*

Directions: In a small bowl, combine 1 tbsp. mustard, yogurt, cabbage, lemon juice, and carrots; mix and refrigerate.
In a medium bowl, combine the pork, paprika, and the remaining 1 tbsp. mustard. Form into 8 small patties.
Put the patties into the air fryer basket. Air fry at 400ºF for 8 minutes.
Assemble the burgers by placing a lettuce leaf on the bottom of a bun. Add a tomato slice, the patties, and the cabbage mixture. Add the top of the bun and serve.

Nutrition: Calories: 472.3, Fat: 14.5g, Protein: 35.8g, Carbs: 30.7g, Fiber: 8g, Sugar: 7.8g

202. Breaded Pork Chops

Preparation Time: 10 minutes   **Cooking Time: 18 minutes**
Servings: 4

Ingredients:
- *1 cup Whole-wheat breadcrumbs*
- *Salt ¼ tsp.*
- *2–4 pcs. pork chops (boneless)*
- *½ tsp. chili powder*
- *1 tbsp. parmesan cheese*
- *1½ tsp. paprika*
- *1 egg beaten*
- *½ tsp. onion powder*
- *½ tsp. grounded garlic*
- *Pepper to taste*

Directions: Let the air fryer preheat to 400ºF.
Rub salt on each side of pork chops, let it rest.
Add beaten egg in a big bowl.
Add chili powder, breadcrumbs, Parmesan cheese, pepper, garlic, paprika, and onion powder in a bowl and mix well. Dip pork chop in egg, then in breadcrumb mixture.
Place it in the air fryer and spray it with oil.
Cook for 12 minutes at 400ºF. Flip it over halfway through. Cook for another 6 minutes.

Nutrition: Calories: 424.5, Fat: 19.6g, Fiber: 5g, Protein: 31.5g, Carbs: 18.7g

203. Pork Taquitos

Preparation Time: 10 minutes   **Cooking Time: 8 minutes**
Servings: 2

Ingredients:
- 3 cups pork tenderloin, cooked and shredded
- Cooking spray
- 2 ½ shredded mozzarella, fat-free
- 10 tortillas
- 1 lime juice

Directions: Let the air fryer preheat to 380ºF.
Season pork to lime juice.
Place a damp towel over the tortilla, microwave for 10 seconds to soften.
Add the cheese and pork filling to the top of the tortilla. Roll up the tortilla tightly.
Place tortillas on a greased foil pan and drizzle with oil. Cook for 8 minutes, flip halfway through.

Nutrition: Calories: 252.5, Fat: 17.8g, Carbs: 9.8g, Protein: 20.6g

204. Flavorful Egg Rolls

Preparation Time: 10 minutes   **Cooking Time: 15 minutes**
Servings: 3

Ingredients:
- ½ bag coleslaw mix
- ½ onion
- ½ tsp. salt
- ½ cup mushrooms
- Lean ground pork: 2 cups
- 1 stalk celery
- 12 Wrappers (egg roll)

Directions: Put a skillet over medium flame, add onion and lean ground pork and cook for 5 minutes.
Add mushrooms, salt, coleslaw mixture, and celery to skillet and cook for 5 minutes.
Roll out egg roll wrapper flat and add filling (⅓ cup), roll it up, seal with water.
Spray with oil the rolls.
Put in the air fryer for 5 minutes at 400ºF, flipping once halfway through. Serve hot.

Nutrition: Calories: 244.5, Fat: 9.6g, Carbs: 8.7g, Protein: 11.6g

205. Pork Dumplings

Preparation Time: 30 minutes   **Cooking Time: 20 minutes**
Servings: 4

Ingredients:
- 18 dumpling wrappers
- 1 tsp. olive oil
- 4 cups chopped bok choy
- 2 tbsp. rice vinegar
- 1 tbsp. diced ginger
- ¼ tsp. crushed red pepper
- 1 tbsp. diced garlic
- ½ cup lean ground pork
- Cooking spray
- 2 tsp. lite soy sauce
- 1 tsp. Toasted sesame oil
- ⅛ cup finely chopped scallions

Directions: Preheat the air fryer oven to 400ºF.
In a pan, add bok choy and cook for 6 minutes. Add ginger and garlic, and cook for 2 minute. Move this mixture on a paper towel, and wipe off the excess oil.
In a bowl, add bok choy mixture, crushed red pepper, and ground pork and mix well.
Spread a dumpling wrapper on a plate and add 1 tbsp. of filling to the center of the wrapper. Seal the edges with water and crimp them.
Drizzle oil on the air fryer basket, add dumplings and cook at 375ºF for 12 minutes.
Meanwhile, make the sauce: in a bowl, add rice vinegar, sesame oil, soy sauce, and scallions. Mix thoroughly.

Nutrition: Calories: 139.5, Fat: 4.5g, Protein: 12.6g, Carbs: 8.7g

206. Pork Chop with Broccoli

Preparation Time: 20 minutes   **Cooking Time: 10 minutes**
Servings: 2

Ingredients:
- 2 cups broccoli florets
- 2 pcs. bone-in pork chop
- ½ tsp. paprika

- 2 tbsp. avocado oil
- ½ tsp. garlic powder
- ½ tsp. onion powder
- 2 cloves crushed garlic
- 1 tsp. salt divided
- Cooking spray

Directions: Let the air fryer preheat to 350ºF. Spray the basket with cooking oil.
Add 1 tbsp. avocado oil, garlic powder, onion powder, ½ tsp. of salt, and paprika in a bowl, mix well. Rub this mixture to the pork chop's sides.
Add pork chops to air fryer basket and cook for 5 minutes.
Meanwhile, add into a bowl the remaining ½ tsp. of salt, 1 tsp. of avocado oil, garlic, and broccoli and coat well.
Flip the pork chop and add the broccoli. Cook for 5 more minutes.

Nutrition: Calories: 482.5, Fat: 19.6g, Carbs: 11.5g, Protein: 23.5g

207. Cheese Pork Chops

Preparation Time: 5 minutes   **Cooking Time: 8 minutes**
Servings: 2

Ingredients:
- 4 lean pork chops
- ½ tsp. salt
- ½ tsp. garlic powder
- 4 tbsp. shredded cheese
- 2 chopped cilantros

Directions: Let the air fryer preheat to 350ºF.
Rub the pork chops with cilantro, garlic, and salt. Put in the air fryer and cook for 4 minutes.
Flip them and cook for 2 more minutes. Add cheese on top and cook for another 2 minutes.

Nutrition: Calories: 466.5, Protein: 61.3g, Fat: 21.6g

208. Diet Boiled Ribs

Preparation Time: 10 minutes   **Cooking Time: 30 minutes**
Servings: 4

Ingredients:
- 400 g pork ribs
- 1 tsp. black pepper
- 1 g bay leaf
- 1 tsp. basil
- 1 white onion
- 1 carrot
- 1 tsp. cumin
- 700 ml of water

Directions: Cut the ribs on the portions and sprinkle them with black pepper.
Take a big saucepan and pour water into it.
Add the ribs and bay leaf.
Peel the onion and carrot and add them to the water with meat.
Sprinkle it with cumin and basil. Cook it on medium heat in the air fryer for 30 minutes.

Nutrition: Calories: 293.5, Proteins: 27.8g, Fats: 17.2g, Carbs: 4.1g

209. Juicy Pork Chops

Preparation Time: 10 minutes   **Cooking Time: 12 minutes**
Servings: 4

Ingredients:
- pork chops
- 1 tsp. olive oil
- 1 tsp. onion powder
- 1 tsp. paprika
- Pepper
- Salt

Directions: Cover pork chops with olive oil and season with paprika, onion powder, pepper, and salt.
Place the dehydrating tray in a multi-level air fryer basket and place the basket in the instant pot.
Place pork chops on dehydrating tray.
Seal pot with air fryer lid and select "Air fry" mode. Set the temperature to 380ºF and timer for 12 minutes. Turn pork chops halfway through.

Nutrition: Calories: 269.6, Fat: 20.8g, Carbs: 0.6g, Sugar: 0.2g, Protein: 18.8g

210. Tender Pork Chops

Preparation Time: 10 minutes   **Cooking Time: 12 minutes**

Servings: 2

Ingredients:
- *2 pork chops*
- *1 tbsp. olive oil*
- *¼ tsp. garlic powder*
- *½ tsp. onion powder*
- *1 tsp. ground mustard*
- *1 ½ tsp. pepper*
- *1 tbsp. paprika*
- *2 tbsp. brown sugar*
- *1 ½ tsp. salt*

Directions: In a minor container, mix garlic powder, onion powder, mustard, paprika, pepper, brown sugar, and salt. Cover pork chops with olive oil and rub with spice mixture.
Place the dehydrating tray in a multi-level air fryer basket and place the basket in the instant pot.
Place pork chops on dehydrating tray.
Seal pot with air fryer lid and select "Air fry" mode, set the temperature to 400ºF and timer for 12 minutes. Turn pork chops halfway through.

Nutrition: Calories: 374.5, Fat: 27.2g, Carbs 12.6g, Sugar: 9.1g, Protein: 19.5g

211. Pork Chops

Preparation Time: 10 minutes   **Cooking Time: 15 minutes**
Servings: 4
Ingredients:
- *pork chops*
- *Pepper*
- *Salt*

Directions: Season pork chops with pepper and salt.
Place the dehydrating tray in a multi-level air fryer basket and place the basket in the instant pot.
Place pork chops on dehydrating tray.
Seal pot with air fryer lid, set the temperature of the Air Fryer to 400ºF and timer for 15 minutes. Turn pork chops halfway through.

Nutrition: Calories: 255.6, Fat: 19.3g, Carbs: 0g, Sugar 0g, Protein: 18.3g

212. Pork Almond Bites

Preparation Time: 10 minutes   **Cooking Time: 14 minutes**
Servings: 6

Ingredients:
- *1-lb. pork tenderloin*
- *2 eggs*
- *1 tsp. butter*
- *¼ cup almond flour*
- *1 tsp. kosher salt*
- *1 tsp. paprika*
- *1 tsp. ground coriander*
- *½ tsp. lemon zest*

Directions: Chop the pork tenderloin into the large cubes.
Sprinkle the pork cubes with ground coriander, paprika, kosher salt, and lemon zest.
Mix the meat gently. Crack the egg into a bowl and whisk it. Coat the meat cubes with the egg mixture and then the almond flour.
Preheat the air fryer to 365°F.
Put the butter in the air fryer basket tray and then place the pork bites inside. Cook for 14 minutes.
Turn the pork bites over after 7 minutes of cooking.
When the pork bites are cooked – serve them hot.

Nutrition: Calories: 141.5, Fat: 5.1g, Fiber: 0.3g, Carbs: 0.5g, Protein: 22.2

213. Air Fryer Pork Ribs

Preparation Time: 30 minutes   **Cooking Time: 30 minutes**
Servings: 5

Ingredients:
- *1 tbsp. apple cider vinegar*
- *1 tsp. cayenne pepper*
- *1 tsp. minced garlic*
- *1 tsp. mustard*
- *1 tsp. chili flakes*
- *16 oz. pork ribs*
- *1 tsp. sesame oil*
- *1 tsp. salt*
- *1 tbsp. paprika*

Directions: Sprinkle the pork ribs with apple cider vinegar, cayenne pepper, mustard, minced garlic, and chili flakes. Add the sesame oil and salt. Add paprika and mix it into the pork ribs.
Leave the ribs in the fridge for 20 minutes.

Preheat the air fryer to 360°F.
Transfer the pork ribs to the air fryer basket and cook for 15 minutes.
Turn the pork ribs over and cook the meat for 15 minutes more.

Nutrition: Calories: 264.7, Fat: 17.1g, Fiber: 0.7g, Carbs: 1.1g, Protein: 24.8

214. Butter Pork Chops

Preparation Time: 10 minutes   **Cooking Time: 11 minutes**
Servings: 3

Ingredients:
- 1 tsp. peppercorns
- 1 tsp. kosher salt
- 1 tsp. minced garlic
- ½ tsp. dried rosemary
- 1 tbsp. butter
- 13 oz. pork chops

Directions: Rub the pork chops with minced garlic, dried rosemary, and kosher salt.
Preheat the air fryer to 365°F. Put the butter and peppercorns in the air fryer basket tray.
Melt the butter and place the pork chops. Cook for 6 minutes.
Turn the pork chops over and cook for 5 minutes more.
When the meat is cooked, dry with a paper towel. Serve immediately.

Nutrition: Calories: 430.5, Fat: 34.1g, Fiber: 0.3g, Carbs: 0.8g, Protein: 28.2g

Fish and Seafood

215. Asian Sesame Cod

Preparation Time: 5 minutes
Servings: 1

Cooking Time: 10 minutes

Ingredients:
- 1 tablespoon reduced-sodium soy sauce
- 2 teaspoons honey
- 1 teaspoon sesame seeds
- 6 ounces (170 g) cod fillet

Directions: In a lesser bowl, syndicate the soy sauce and honey.
Sprig the air fryer basket with nonstick cooking spray, then place the fish in the basket, brush with the soy mixture, and sprinkle with sesame seeds. Roast at 360°F for 10 minutes or until opaque.
Remove the fryer's fish and allow cooling on a wire rack for 5 minutes before serving.

Nutrition: Calories: 140.4, Fat: 1g, Protein: 26.5g, Carbs: 6.5g, Fiber: 1g, Sugar: 6g

216. Sriracha Calamari

Preparation Time: 10 minutes
Servings: 2

Cooking Time: 13 minutes

Ingredients:
- Club soda: 1 cup
- Sriracha: 1-2 Tbsp.
- Calamari tubes: 2 cups
- Flour: 1 cup
- Pinches of salt
- freshly ground black pepper
- red pepper flakes

Directions: Cut the calamari tubes into rings. Submerge them with club soda. Let it rest for ten minutes.
In the meantime, in a bowl, add freshly ground black pepper, flour, red pepper, and kosher salt and mix well.
Drain the calamari and pat dry with a paper towel. Coat well the calamari in the flour mix and set aside.
Spray oil in the air fryer basket and put calamari in one single layer.
Cook at 375 ° F for 11 minutes. Toss the rings twice while cooking. Meanwhile, to make sauce, add red pepper flakes, and sriracha in a bowl, mix well.
Take calamari out from the basket, mix with sauce and cook for another two minutes more. Serve with salad green.

Nutrition: Calories: 251.5, Protein: 41.5g, Carbs: 2.8g, Fat: 38.5g

217. Shrimp Rolls in Air Fryer

Preparation Time: 10 minutes
Servings: 4

Cooking Time: 10 minutes

Ingredients:
- Deveined raw shrimp: half cup chopped (peeled)
- Olive oil: 2 and 1/2 tbsp.
- Matchstick carrots: 1 cup
- Slices of red bell pepper: 1 cup
- Red pepper: 1/4 teaspoon (crushed)
- Slices of snow peas: 3/4 cup
- Shredded cabbage: 2 cups
- Lime juice: 1 tablespoon
- Sweet chili sauce: half cup
- Fish sauce: 2 teaspoons
- Eight spring roll (wrappers)

Directions: In a skillet, add one and a half tbsp. of olive, until smoking lightly. Stir in bell pepper, cabbage, carrots, and cook for two minutes. Turn off the heat, take out in a dish and cool for five minutes.
In a bowl, add shrimp, lime juice, cabbage mixture, crushed red pepper, fish sauce, and snow peas. Mix well
Lay spring roll wrappers on a plate. Add 1/4 cup of filling in the middle of each wrapper. Fold tightly with water.
Brush the olive oil over folded rolls.
Put spring rolls in the air fryer basket and cook for 6 to 7 minutes at 390°F until light brown and crispy.
You may serve with sweet chili sauce.

Nutrition: Calories: 179.5, Protein: 17.5g, Carbs: 8.7g, Fat: 8.5g

218. Scallops with Tomato Sauce

Preparation Time: 5 minutes
Servings: 2

Cooking Time: 10 minutes

Ingredients:
- Sea scallops eight jumbo
- Tomato Paste: 1 tbsp.
- Chopped fresh basil one tablespoon
- 3/4 cup of low-fat Whipping Cream
- Kosher salt half teaspoon
- Ground Freshly black pepper half teaspoon
- Minced garlic 1 teaspoon
- Frozen Spinach, thawed half cup
- Oil Spray

Directions: Take a seven-inch pan (heatproof) and add spinach in a single layer at the bottom
Rub olive oil on both sides of scallops, season with kosher salt and pepper.
On top of the spinach, place the seasoned scallops
Put the pan in the air fryer and cook for ten minutes at 350°F, until scallops are cooked completely, and internal temperature reaches 135°F. Serve immediately.

Nutrition: Calories: 258.5, Protein: 18.5g, Carbs: 5.4g, Fat: 12.5g

219. Roasted Salmon with Fennel Salad

Preparation Time: 15 minutes
Servings: 4

Cooking Time: 10 minutes

Ingredients:
- Skinless and center-cut: 4 salmon fillets
- Lemon juice: 1 teaspoon (fresh)
- Parsley: 2 teaspoons (chopped)
- Salt: 1 teaspoon, divided
- Olive oil: 2 tablespoons
- Chopped thyme: 1 teaspoon
- Fennel heads: 4 cups (thinly sliced)
- One clove of minced garlic
- Fresh dill: 2 tablespoons, chopped
- Greek yogurt: 2/3 cup (reduced-fat)

Directions: In a bowl, add half teaspoon of salt, parsley, and thyme, mix well. Rub oil over salmon, and sprinkle with thyme mixture.
Put salmon fillets in the air fryer basket, cook for ten minutes at 350°F.
In the meantime, mix garlic, fennel, yogurt, half tsp. of salt, dill, lemon juice in a bowl. Serve with fennel salad.

Nutrition: Calories: 363.5, Protein: 38.5g, Carbs: 8.5g, Fat: 29.5g

220. Lime-Garlic Shrimp Kebabs

Preparation Time: 5 minutes
Servings: 2

Cooking Time: 8 minutes

Ingredients:
- One lime
- Raw shrimp: 1 cup
- Salt: 1/8 teaspoon
- 1 clove of garlic
- Freshly ground black pepper

Directions: In water, let wooden skewers soak for 20 minutes.
Let the Air fryer preheat to 350°F.
In a bowl, mix shrimp, minced garlic, lime juice, kosher salt, and pepper.
Add shrimp on skewers. Place skewers in the air fryer, and cook for 8 minutes. Turn halfway over.

Nutrition: Calories: 75.4, Protein: 13.5g, Carbs: 3.5g, Fat: 8.7g

221. Lemon Garlic Shrimp in Air Fryer

Preparation Time: 5 minutes
Servings: 2

Cooking Time: 8 minutes

Ingredients:
- Olive oil: 1 Tbsp.
- Small shrimp: 4 cups, peeled, tails removed
- One lemon juice and zest
- Parsley: 1/4 cup sliced
- Red pepper flakes (crushed): 1 pinch
- Four cloves of grated garlic
- Sea salt: 1/4 teaspoon

Directions: Let the air fryer preheat to 400°F.
Mix olive oil, lemon zest, red pepper flakes, shrimp, kosher salt, and garlic in a bowl and coat the shrimp well.
Place shrimps in the air fryer basket, coat with oil spray.
Cook at 400 F for 8 minutes. Toss the shrimp halfway through Serve with lemon slices and parsley.

Nutrition: Calories: 139.5, Protein: 20.5g, Carbs: 7.5g, Fat: 17.5g

222. Fish Finger Sandwich

Preparation Time: 10 minutes   **Cooking Time: 15 minutes**
Servings: 3

Ingredients:
- *Greek yogurt: 1 tbsp.*
- *Cod fillets: 4, without skin*
- *Flour: 2 tbsp.*
- *Whole-wheat breadcrumbs: 5 tbsp.*
- *Kosher salt and pepper to taste*
- *Capers: 10–12*
- *Frozen peas: 3/4 cup*
- *Lemon juice*

Directions: Let the air fryer preheat.
Sprinkle kosher salt and pepper on the cod fillets, and coat in flour, then in breadcrumbs.
Spray the fryer basket with oil. Put the cod fillets in the basket. Cook for 15 minutes at 400° F.
Meanwhile, cook the peas in boiling water for a few minutes. Take out from the water and blend with Greek yogurt, lemon juice, and capers until well combined.
On a bun, add cooked fish with pea puree. Add lettuce and tomato.

Nutrition: Calories: 239.5, Protein: 20.5g, Carbs: 6.5g, Fat: 11.5g

223. Air Fried Salmon Cakes

Preparation Time: 9 minutes   **Cooking Time: 7 minutes**
Servings: 2

Ingredients:
- *8 oz. fresh salmon fillet*
- *1 egg*
- *⅛ salt*
- *¼ garlic powder*
- *1 Sliced lemon*

Directions: Let the air fryer preheat to 390°F.
In a bowl, chop the salmon, add the egg and spices. Form tiny cakes.
On the bottom of the air fryer bowl, arrange the sliced lemons and place cakes on top. Cook for 7 minutes.

Nutrition: Calories: 193.1, Fat: 8.7g, Carbs: 1g, Proteins: 25.5g

224. Air Fried Shrimp with Sweet Chili Sauce

Preparation Time: 10 minutes   **Cooking Time: 8 minutes**
Servings: 4

Ingredients:
- *Whole wheat bread crumbs: 3/4 cup*
- *Raw shrimp: 4 cups, deveined, peeled*
- *Flour: half cup*
- *Paprika: one tsp*
- *Chicken Seasoning, to taste*
- *2 tbsp. of one egg white*
- *Kosher salt and pepper to taste*

Sauce:
- *Sweet chili sauce: 1/4 cup*
- *Plain Greek yogurt: 1/3 cup*
- *Sriracha: 2 tbsp.*

Directions: Let the Air Fryer preheat to 400 degrees F.
Add the seasonings to shrimp and coat well.
In three separate bowls, add flour, bread crumbs, and egg whites.
First coat the shrimp in flour, dab lightly in egg whites, then in the bread crumbs.
With cooking oil, spray the shrimp. Place the shrimps in the air fryer, cook for four minutes, turn the shrimp over, and cook for another four minutes. Serve with micro green and sauce.

For the sauce: In a small bowl, mix all the ingredients.

Nutrition: Calories: 228.7, Protein: 22.5g, Carbs: 12.4g, Fat: 9.6g

225. Air Fryer Crab Cakes

Preparation Time: 10 minutes
Servings: 6

Cooking Time: 10 minutes

Ingredients:
- Crab meat: 4 cups
- Two eggs
- Whole wheat bread crumbs: ¼ cup
- Mayonnaise: 2 tablespoons
- Worcestershire sauce: 1 teaspoon
- Old Bay seasoning: 1 and ½ teaspoon
- Dijon mustard: 1 teaspoon
- Freshly ground black pepper to taste
- Green onion: ¼ cup, chopped

Directions: In a bowl, add Dijon mustard, Old Bay seasoning, eggs, Worcestershire, and mayonnaise mix it well. Then add in the chopped green onion and mix.
Fold in the crab meat to mayonnaise mix. Then add breadcrumbs, not to over mix.
Chill the mix in the refrigerator for at least 60 minutes. Then shape into patties.
Let the air-fryer preheat to 350°F. Cook for 10 minutes. Flip the patties halfway through.
Serve with lemon wedges.

Nutrition: Calories: 217.8, Protein: 16.9g, Carbs: 5.1g, Fat: 12.5g

226. Air Fryer Sushi Roll

Preparation Time: 1 hour 30 minutes
Servings: 3

Cooking Time: 10 minutes

Ingredients:
For the Kale Salad:
- Rice vinegar: half teaspoon
- Chopped kale: one and a 1/2 cups
- Garlic powder:1/8 teaspoon
- Sesame seeds: 1 tablespoon
- Toasted sesame oil: 3/4 teaspoon
- Ground ginger: 1/4 teaspoon
- Soy sauce: 3/4 teaspoon

For the Sushi Rolls:
- Half avocado - sliced
- Cooked Sushi Rice - cooled
- Whole wheat breadcrumbs: half cup
- Sushi: 3 sheets

Directions:
Kale Salad: In a bowl, add vinegar, garlic powder, kale, soy sauce, sesame oil, and ground ginger. With your hands, mix with sesame seeds and set it aside.
Sushi Rolls: Lay a sheet of sushi on a flat surface. With damp fingertips, add a tablespoon of rice, and spread it on the sheet. Cover the sheet with rice, leaving a half-inch space at one end.
Add kale salad with avocado slices. Roll up the sushi, use water if needed.
Add the breadcrumbs in a bowl. Coat the sushi roll with Sriracha Mayo, then in breadcrumbs.
Add the rolls to the air fryer. Cook for ten minutes at 390 F, shake the basket halfway through.
Take out from the fryer, and let them cool, then cut with a sharp knife. Serve with light soy sauce.

Nutrition: Calories: 368.7, Protein: 26.8g, Carbs: 14.5g, Fat: 13.1g

227. Air Fryer Tasty Egg Rolls

Preparation Time: 10 minutes
Servings: 3

Cooking Time: 15 minutes

Ingredients:
- Coleslaw mix: half bag
- Half onion
- Salt: 1/2 teaspoon
- Half cups of mushrooms
- Lean ground pork: 2 cups
- One stalk of celery
- Wrappers (egg roll)

Directions: Put a skillet over medium flame, add onion and lean ground pork and cook for 5 minutes.
Add mushrooms, coleslaw mixture, salt, and celery to skillet and cook for five minutes.
Roll out the egg roll and add filling (1/3 cup), roll it up, and seal with water. Spray the rolls with oil.
Put in the air fryer for 8 minutes at 400°F, flipping once halfway through. Serve hot.

Nutrition: Calories: 244.5, Protein: 11.4g, Carbs: 8.7g, Fat: 9.8g

228. Air Fryer Tuna Patties

Preparation Time: 15 minutes   Cooking Time: 10 minutes
Servings: 10

Ingredients:
- Whole wheat breadcrumbs: half cup
- Fresh tuna: 4 cups, diced
- Lemon zest
- Lemon juice: 1 Tablespoon
- 1 egg
- Grated parmesan cheese: 3 Tablespoons
- One chopped stalk celery
- Garlic powder: half teaspoon
- Dried herbs: half teaspoon
- Minced onion: 3 Tablespoons
- Salt to taste
- Freshly ground black pepper

Directions: In a bowl, add lemon zest, bread crumbs, salt, pepper, celery, eggs, dried herbs, lemon juice, garlic powder, parmesan cheese, and onion. Mix everything. Then add in tuna gently. Shape into patties. If the mixture is too loose, cool in the refrigerator.
Add air fryer baking paper in the air fryer basket. Spray the baking paper with cooking spray.
Spray the patties with oil.
Cook for ten minutes at 360°F. turn the patties halfway over. Serve with lemon slices.

Nutrition: Calories: 213.5, Protein: 22.5g, Carbs: 5.5g, Fat: 14.5g

229. Catfish with Green Beans, in Southern Style

Preparation Time: 10 minutes   Cooking Time: 20 minutes
Servings: 2

Ingredients:
- Catfish fillets: 2 pieces
- Green beans: half cup, trimmed
- Freshly ground black pepper and salt, to taste divided
- Crushed red pepper: half tsp.
- Flour: 1/4 cup
- One egg, lightly beaten
- Dill pickle relish: 3/4 teaspoon
- Apple cider vinegar: half tsp
- 1/3 cup whole-wheat breadcrumbs
- Mayonnaise: 2 tablespoons
- Dill
- Lemon wedges

Directions: In a bowl, add green beans, spray them with cooking oil. Coat with crushed red pepper, 1/8 teaspoon of kosher salt, and half tsp. of honey and cook in the air fryer at 400°F until soft and browned, for 12 minutes.
Take out from fryer and cover with aluminum foil.
In the meantime, coat catfish in flour. Then dip in egg to coat, then in breadcrumbs. Place fish in an air fryer basket and spray with cooking oil.
Cook for 8 minutes, at 400ºF, until cooked through and golden brown.
Sprinkle with pepper and salt. In the meantime, mix vinegar, dill, relish, mayonnaise, in a bowl. Serve the sauce with fish and green beans.

Nutrition: Calories: 242.5, Protein: 33.5g, Carbs: 17.5g, Fat: 17.5g

230. Air-Fried Crumbed Fish

Preparation Time: 10 minutes   Cooking Time: 12 minutes
Servings: 2

Ingredients
- 4 fish fillets
- 4 tbsp. olive oil
- 1 egg beaten
- 1/4 cup whole-wheat breadcrumbs

Directions: Let the air fryer preheat to 375°F.
In a bowl, mix breadcrumbs with oil. Mix well.
First, coat the fish in the egg mix (egg beaten with water) than in the breadcrumb mix. Coat well.
Place in the air fryer and let it cook for 12 minutes. Serve hot with salad green and lemon.

Nutrition: Calories: 253.8, Fat: 12.2g, Protein: 15.8g, Carbs: 17.2g, Sugars: 0.3g

231. Parmesan Garlic Crusted Salmon

Preparation Time: 5 minutes   Cooking Time: 15 minutes
Servings: 2

Ingredients:

- 1/4 cup whole-wheat breadcrumbs
- 4 cups salmon
- 1 tbsp. butter, melted
- 1/4 tsp. freshly ground black pepper
- 1/4 cup Parmesan cheese, grated
- 2 tsp. garlic, minced
- 1/2 tsp. Italian seasoning

Directions: Let the air fryer preheat to 400°F, spray the oil over the air fryer basket.
Pat the salmon dry.
In a bowl, mix Parmesan cheese, Italian seasoning, and breadcrumbs. In another pan, mix melted butter with garlic and add to the breadcrumbs mix. Mix well.
Add kosher salt and freshly ground black pepper to salmon. On top of every salmon piece, add the crust mix and press gently.
Let the air fryer preheat to 400ºF and add salmon to it. Cook until done to your liking (about 15 minutes).
Serve hot with vegetable side dishes.

Nutrition: Calories: 339.5, Fat: 18.7g, Protein: 31.5g, Carbs: 7.1g, Sugars: 0.2g

232. Air Fryer Salmon With Maple Soy Glaze

Preparation Time: 6 minutes   **Cooking Time: 8 minutes**
Servings: 4

Ingredients:

- 1 tbsp. pure maple syrup
- 3 tbsp. gluten-free soy sauce
- 1 tbsp. sriracha hot sauce
- 2 garlic cloves, minced
- 4 fillets salmon, skinless

Directions: In a Ziploc bag, mix sriracha, maple syrup, garlic, and soy sauce with salmon.
Mix well and let it marinate for at least 30 minutes.
Let the air fryer preheat to 400°F and spray the basket with oil.
Take fish out from the marinade, pat dry. Put the salmon in the air fryer, cook for 8 minutes or longer.
In the meantime, in a saucepan, add the marinade, let it simmer until reduced to half. Add the glaze over the salmon and serve.

Nutrition: Calories: 291.9, Protein: 35.8g, Fat: 10.5g, Carbs: 4.1g, Sugars: 3.1g

233. Air Fried Cajun Salmon

Preparation Time: 10 minutes   **Cooking Time: 7 minutes**
Servings: 1

Ingredients:

- 1 fresh salmon
- 1 tbsp. Cajun seasoning
- 1 lemon juice

Directions: Let the air fryer preheat to 375°F.
Pat dries the salmon fillet. Rub lemon juice and Cajun seasoning over the fish fillet.
Place in the air fryer and cook for 7 minutes.

Nutrition: Calories: 215.4, Fat: 18.7g, Protein: 19.8g, Carbs: 1g, Sugars: 0.4g

234. Air Fryer Shrimp Scampi

Preparation Time: 5 minutes   **Cooking Time: 7 minutes**
Servings: 2

Ingredients:

- 4 cups raw shrimp
- 1 tbsp. lemon juice
- 1/2 tsp. fresh basil, chopped
- 2 tsp. red pepper flakes
- 4 tbsp. butter
- 1/4 cup chives, chopped
- 1 tbsp. chicken stock
- 1 tbsp. garlic, minced

Directions: Let the air fryer preheat with a metal pan to 330°F.
In the hot pan, add the garlic, red pepper flakes, and half of the butter. Let it cook for 2 minutes. Add the butter, shrimp, chicken stock, minced garlic, chives, lemon juice, basil to the pan. Let it cook for 5 minutes. Bathe the shrimp in melted butter.
Take it out from the air fryer and let it rest for 1 minute. Add the fresh basil leaves and chives and serve.

Nutrition: Calories: 286.5, Fat: 5.1g, Protein: 18.5g, Carbs: 6.3g Sugar: 2.2g

235. Sesame Seeds Fish Fillet

Preparation Time: 10 minutes   **Cooking Time: 12-16 minutes**
Servings: 2

Ingredients:
- *1 tbsp. plain flour*
- *1 egg, beaten*
- *5 frozen fish fillets*

For the coating:
- *2 tbsp. oil*
- *1/2 tsp. Rosemary herbs*
- *Kosher salt and pepper to taste*
- *1/2 cup sesame seeds*
- *5–6 biscuits crumbs*

Directions: Sauté the sesame seeds in a pan for 2 minutes, without oil. Brown them and set it aside.
On a plate, mix all coating ingredients.
Place the aluminum foil on the air fryer basket and let it preheat at 400°F.
First, coat the fish in flour. Then in egg, then in the coating mix.
Place in the air fryer. If fillets are frozen, cook for 10 minutes, then turn the fillet and cook for another 4 minutes.
If not frozen, then cook for 8 minutes and 2 minutes.

Nutrition: Calories: 249.8, Fat: 7.8g, Protein: 20.5g, Carbs: 56.8g, Sugar: 4.2g

236. Lemon Pepper Shrimp in Air Fryer

Preparation Time: 6 minutes   **Cooking Time: 8 minutes**
Servings: 2

Ingredients
- *1 1/2 cup peeled raw shrimp, deveined*
- *1/4 tsp. garlic powder*
- *1 lemon, juiced*
- *1 tsp. lemon pepper*
- *1/2 tbsp. olive oil*
- *1/4 tsp. paprika*

Directions: Let the air fryer preheat to 400ºF.
Mix lemon pepper, olive oil, paprika, garlic powder, and lemon juice in a bowl. Mix well. Add the shrimps and coat well. Add the shrimps to the air fryer, cook for 8 minutes and top with lemon slices and serve.

Nutrition: Calories: 236.5, Fat: 5.5g, Protein: 36.5g, Carbs: 2g, Sugars 0.4g

237. Shrimp and Okra

Preparation Time: 15 minutes   **Servings: 4**

Ingredients:
- *1 lb. shrimp; peeled and deveined*
- *1/2 cup chicken stock*
- *1 tbsp. parsley; chopped.*
- *2 tbsp. coconut aminos*
- *A pinch salt and black pepper*
- *1 1/2 cups okra*
- *3 tbsp. balsamic vinegar*

Directions: In a pan that fits your air fryer, mix all the ingredients, toss, introduce in the fryer and cook at 380°F for 10 minutes. Divide into bowls and serve.

Nutrition: Calories: 250.6, Fat: 9.8g, Fiber: 3g, Carbs: 3.8g, Protein: 8.7g

238. Swordfish Steaks and Tomatoes

Preparation Time: 15 minutes   **Servings: 2**

Ingredients:
- *30 oz. canned tomatoes; chopped.*
- *2 tbsp. capers, drained*
- *Pinch salt and black pepper*
- *1 tbsp. red vinegar*
- *2 (1-inch thick) swordfish steaks*
- *2 tbsp. oregano, chopped.*

Directions: In a pan that fits the air fryer, combine all the ingredients, toss, put the pan in the fryer and cook at 390ºF for 10 minutes; flipping the fish halfway. Divide the mix between plates and serve.

Nutrition: Calories: 279.5, Fat: 11.8g, Fiber: 4g, Carbs: 5.6g, Protein: 11.5g

239. Buttery Cod

Preparation Time: 13 minutes   Servings: 2

Ingredients:
- 2 (4 oz.) cod fillets
- 1/2 medium lemon, sliced
- 2 tbsp. salted butter; melted.
- 1 tsp. Old Bay seasoning

Directions: Place cod fillets into a 6-inch round baking dish. Brush each fillet with butter and sprinkle with Old Bay seasoning. Lay 2 lemon slices on each fillet.
Secure the dish with foil and place it into the air fryer basket. Adjust the temperature to 350ºF and set the timer for 8 minutes; flip halfway through the Cooking Time.
When cooked, the internal temperature should be at least 145ºF. Serve warm.

Nutrition: Calories: 178.7, Protein: 14.5g, Fiber: 0g, Fat: 10.7g, Carbs: 0g

240. Lime Baked Salmon

Preparation Time: 22 minutes   Servings: 2

Ingredients:
- 2 (3 oz.) salmon fillets, skin removed
- 1/4 cup jalapeños, sliced and pickled
- 1/2 medium lime, juiced
- 2 tbsp. cilantro, chopped
- 1 tbsp. salted butter; melted.
- 1/2tsp. garlic, finely minced
- 1 tsp. chili powder

Directions: Place the salmon fillets into a 6-inch round baking pan.
Brush each with butter and sprinkle with chili powder and garlic.
Place the jalapeño slices on top and around salmon.
Pour half of the lime juice over the salmon and cover with foil. Place pan into the air fryer basket.
Adjust the temperature to 370ºF and set the timer for 12 minutes.
When fully cooked, salmon should flake easily with a fork and reach an internal temperature of at least 145ºF.
To serve, spritz with the remaining lime juice and garnish with cilantro.

Nutrition: Calories: 166.8, Protein: 18.5g, Fiber: 7g, Fat: 8.7g, Carbs: 5.8g

241. Lime Trout and Shallots

Preparation Time: 17 minutes   Servings: 4

Ingredients:
- 4 trout fillets, boneless
- 3 garlic cloves, minced
- 6 shallots, chopped.
- 1/2 cup butter, melted
- 1/2 cup olive oil
- 1 lime juice
- A pinch salt and black pepper

Directions: In a pan that fits in the air fryer, combines the fish with the shallots and the rest of the ingredients; stir gently. Put the pan in the machine and cook at 390ºF for 12 minutes; flipping the fish halfway.
Cut between plates and serve with a side salad.

Nutrition: Calories: 269.5, Fat: 11.8g, Fiber: 4g, Carbs: 5.5g, Protein: 12.6g

242. Crab Legs

Preparation Time: 20 minutes   Servings: 4

Ingredients:
- 3 lb. crab legs
- 1/4 cup salted butter, melted and divided
- 1/2 medium lemon juice
- 1/4 tsp. garlic powder.

Directions: Take a large bowl, drizzle 2 tbsp. of butter over crab legs. Set the crab legs into the air fryer basket. Adjust the temperature to 400ºF and set the timer for 15 minutes.
In a small bowl, mix the remaining butter, garlic powder, and lemon juice
To serve, crack open the crab legs and detach meat. Dip in the lemon butter.

Nutrition: Calories: 122.8, Protein: 17.5g, Fiber: 0g, Fat: 5.8g, Carbs: 3.8g

243. Cajun Salmon

Preparation Time: 12 minutes   Servings: 2

Ingredients:
- 2 (4 oz.) salmon fillets, skin removed
- 2 tbsp. unsalted butter, melted.
- 1 tsp. paprika
- 1/4 tsp. ground black pepper
- 1/8 tsp. ground cayenne pepper
- 1/2 tsp. garlic powder.

Directions: Brush each fillet with butter.
Combine the remaining ingredients in a small bowl and then rub them onto the fish.
Place the fillets into the air fryer basket.
Bring the temperature to 390ºF and set the timer for 7 minutes. When fully cooked, the internal temperature will be 145ºF. Serve immediately.

Nutrition: Calories: 252.6, Protein: 29.7g, Fiber: 4g, Fat: 15.7g, Carbs: 3.8g

244. Trout and Zucchinis

Preparation Time: 20 minutes   Servings: 4

Ingredients:
- 3 zucchinis, cut in medium chunks
- 4 trout fillets; boneless
- 1/4 cup tomato sauce
- 1 garlic clove; minced
- 1/2 cup cilantro; chopped.
- 1 tbsp. lemon juice
- 2 tbsp. olive oil
- Salt and black pepper to taste.

Directions: In a pan that fits in the air fryer, mix the fish with the other ingredients, toss, introduce it in the fryer, and cook at 380ºF for 15 minutes. Divide everything between plates and serve right away.

Nutrition: Calories: 219.6, Fat: 11.7g, Fiber: 4g, Carbs: 5.8g, Protein: 9.6g

245. Crab Cakes

Preparation Time: 20 minutes   Servings: 4

Ingredients:
- 1/2 medium green bell pepper; seeded and chopped
- 1/4 cup green onion, chopped
- 1 large egg.
- 2 cans (6 oz.) lump crabmeat
- 1/4 cup ground almond flour, blanched finely
- 1/2 tbsp. lemon juice
- 2 tbsp. full-fat mayonnaise
- 1/2 tsp. Old Bay seasoning
- 1/2 tsp. Dijon mustard

Directions: Take a large bowl, mix all the ingredients. Set into 4 balls and flatten into patties.
Place the patties in the basket of the air fryer.
Adjust the temperature to 350ºF and set the timer for 10 minutes.
Flip the patties halfway through the Cooking Time. Serve warm.

Nutrition: Calories: 150.7, Protein: 14.5g, Fiber: 9g, Fat: 9.8g, Carbs: 2.8g

246. Roasted Red Snapper

Preparation Time: 20 minutes   Servings: 4

Ingredients:
- 4 red snapper fillets; boneless
- 2 garlic cloves; minced
- 1 tbsp. hot chili paste
- 2 tbsp. olive oil
- 2 tbsp. coconut aminos
- 2 tbsp. lime juice
- Pinch salt and black pepper

Directions: Take a bowl and mix all the ingredients, except the fish, and whisk well.
Rub the fish with this mix, place it in your air fryer's basket and cook at 380ºF for 15 minutes.
Serve with a side salad.

Nutrition: Calories: 219.8, Fat: 12.8g, Fiber: 4g, Carbs: 5.8g, Protein: 11.2g

247. Shrimp Scampi

Preparation Time: 18 minutes   Servings: 4

Ingredients:
- 1 lb. medium shrimp, peeled and deveined
- 1/2 medium lemon
- 1/4 cup heavy whipping cream.
- 1 tbsp. fresh parsley, chopped
- 4 tbsp. salted butter
- 1/4 tsp. xanthan gum
- 1/4 tsp. red pepper flakes
- 1 tsp. roasted garlic, minced

Directions: In a saucepan over medium heat, dissolve butter. Zest the lemon, and then squeeze the juice into the pan. Add the garlic.

Pour in the cream, xanthan gum, and red pepper flakes. Pour until the mixture begins to thicken, about 2–3 minutes.

Place the shrimp into a 4 cup round baking dish. Pour the cream sauce over the shrimp and cover with foil. Place the dish into the air fryer basket.

Adjust the temperature to 400ºF and set the timer for 8 minutes. Stir twice during cooking.

Garnish with parsley and serve warm.

Nutrition: Calories: 239.8, Protein: 17.4g, Fiber: 4g, Fat: 9.8g, Carbs: 3.8g

248. Tuna Zoodle Casserole

Preparation Time: 30 minutes   **Servings: 4**

Ingredients:
- 1 oz. pork rinds, finely ground
- 2 medium zucchinis, spiralized
- 2 cans (5 oz) albacore tuna
- 1/4 cup white onion, diced
- 1/4 cup white mushrooms, chopped
- 2 stalks celery, finely chopped
- 1/2 cup heavy cream
- 1/2 cup vegetable broth
- 2 tbsp. full-fat mayonnaise
- 2 tbsp. butter, salted
- 1/2 tsp. red pepper flakes
- 1/4 tsp. xanthan gum

Directions: In a saucepan over medium heat, dissolve the butter. Add the onion, mushrooms, and celery, and sauté until fragrant, about 3–5 minutes.

Pour in heavy cream, vegetable broth, mayonnaise, and xanthan gum. Reduce heat and continue cooking an additional 3 minutes until the mixture begins to thicken.

Add the red pepper flakes, zucchini, and tuna.

Turn off the heat and stir until zucchini noodles are coated.

Pour into 4 cups round baking dish. Top with ground pork rinds and cover the top of the dish with foil. Place into the air fryer basket. Adjust the temperature to 370ºF and set the timer to 15 minutes.

When there are 3 minutes left, remove the foil to brown the top of the casserole. Serve warm.

Nutrition: Calories: 338.7, Protein: 17.5g, Fiber: 8g, Fat: 20.7g, Carbs: 1g

249. Sea Bass and Rice

Preparation Time: 10 minutes   **Cooking Time: 20 minutes**
Servings: 4

Ingredients:
- 1 lb. sea bass fillets, boneless, skinless, and cubed
- 1 cup wild rice
- 2 cups chicken stock
- 2 scallions, chopped
- 1 red bell pepper, chopped
- 1 tsp. turmeric powder
- 1 tbsp. chives, chopped
- Salt and black pepper to the taste
- A drizzle olive oil

Directions: Grease the air fryer's pan with the oil, add the fish, rice, stock, and the other ingredients, stir gently, cook at 380ºF for 20 minutes, stirring halfway. Divide between plates and serve.

Nutrition: Calories: 289.5, Fat: 11.8g, Fiber: 2g, Carbs: 15.8g, Protein: 19.2g

250. Sea Bass and Cauliflower

Preparation Time: 5 minutes   **Cooking Time: 20 minutes**
Servings: 4

Ingredients:
- 1 lb. sea bass fillets, boneless and cubed
- 1 cup cauliflower florets
- 2 tbsp. butter, melted
- 1 tsp. garam masala
- 1/2 cup chicken stock
- 1 tbsp. parsley, chopped
- Salt and black pepper to the taste

90

Directions: In your air fryer, combine the fish with the cauliflower and the other ingredients, stir gently, and cook at 380ºF for 20 minutes. Divide everything between plates and serve.

Nutrition: Calories: 271.8, Fat: 3.8g, Fiber: 3g, Carbs: 13.8g, Protein: 4.3g

251. Air Fried Catfish

Preparation Time: 5 minutes
Servings: 4

Cooking Time: 20 minutes

Ingredients:
- 4 catfish fillets
- 1 tbsp. olive oil

- 1/4 cup fish seasoning
- 1 tbsp. fresh parsley, chopped

- Cooking spray

Directions: Preheat the air fryer to 400ºF. Spray the air fryer basket with cooking spray.
Season the fish with seasoning and place it into the air fryer basket.
Drizzle the fillets with oil and cook for 10 minutes.
Turn the fish to another side and cook for 10 more minutes. Garnish with parsley and serve.

Nutrition: Calories: 119.8, Fat: 3.2g, Carbs: 1g, Protein: 21.2g

252. Garlic Parmesan Shrimp

Preparation Time: 5 minutes
Servings: 2

Cooking Time: 10 minutes

Ingredients:
- 1 lb. shrimp, deveined and peeled
- 1/2 cup Parmesan cheese, grated

- 1/4 cup cilantro, diced
- 1 tbsp. olive oil
- 1 tsp. salt
- 1 tsp. fresh cracked pepper

- 1 tbsp. lemon juice
- 6 garlic cloves, diced

Directions: Warm the air fryer to 350ºF and grease the air fryer basket.
Drizzle the shrimp with olive oil and lemon juice; season with garlic, salt, and cracked pepper.
Secure the bowl with plastic wrap and refrigerate for a few hours.
Stir in the Parmesan cheese and cilantro to the bowl and transfer to the air fryer basket.
Cook for 10 minutes and serve immediately.

Nutrition: Calories: 281.8, Fat: 23.1g, Carbs: 0g, Protein: 16.9g

253. Mango Shrimp Skewers

Preparation Time: 5 minutes
Servings: 2

Cooking Time: 10 minutes

Ingredients:
- 2 tbsp. olive oil
- 1/2 tsp. garlic powder

- 1 tsp. dry mango powder
- 2 tbsp. fresh lime juice

- Salt and black pepper to taste

Directions: Mix the garlic powder, mango powder, lime juice, salt, and pepper in a bowl. Add the shrimp and toss to coat. Cover and allow to marinate for minutes.
Warm your air fryer to 390ºF. Spray the air fryer basket with cooking spray. Transfer the marinated shrimp to the cooking basket and drizzle the olive oil. Cook for 5 minutes, slide out the fryer basket, and shake the shrimp; cook for 5 minutes. Leave to cool and serve.

Nutrition: Calories: 219.8, Fat: 12.8g, Fiber: 4g, Carbs: 5.8g, Protein: 11.8g

254. Creamy Shrimp Nachos

Preparation Time: 5 minutes
Servings: 4

Cooking Time: 10 minutes

Ingredients:

- 1 lb. shrimp, cleaned and deveined
- 1 tbsp. olive oil
- 2 tbsp. fresh lemon juice
- 1 tsp. paprika
- 1/4 tsp. cumin powder
- 1/2 tsp. shallot powder
- 1/2 tsp. garlic powder
- Coarse sea salt and black pepper, to flavor
- 1 bag (9 oz.) corn tortilla chips
- 1/4 cup pickled jalapeño, minced
- 1 cup Pepper Jack cheese, grated
- 1/2 cup sour cream

Directions: Set the shrimp with olive oil, lemon juice, paprika, cumin powder, shallot powder, garlic powder, salt, and black pepper. Cook in the preheated air fryer at 390ºF for 5 minutes.

Place the tortilla chips on the aluminum foil-lined cooking basket. Top with the shrimp mixture, jalapeño, and cheese. Cook for another 2 minutes or until cheese has melted.

Serve garnished with sour cream.

Nutrition: Calories: 224.9, Fat: 3.1g, Carbs: 0g, Protein: 21.2g

255. Peppery and Lemony Haddock

Preparation Time: 5 minutes
Servings: 4

Cooking Time: 15 minutes

Ingredients:

- 1 cup breadcrumbs
- 2 tbsp. lemon juice
- 1/2 tsp. black pepper
- 1/4 cup dry air fryer to flakes
- 1 egg, beaten
- 1/4 cup Parmesan cheese
- 3 tbsp. flour
- 1/4 tsp. salt

Directions: Combine the flour, black pepper, and salt in a small bowl. In another bowl, combine lemon, breadcrumbs, Parmesan cheese, and potato flakes.

Dip the fillets in the flour first, then in the egg, and coat them with the lemony crumbs. Arrange on a lined sheet and place it in the air fryer; cook for 15 minutes at 370ºF.

Nutrition: Calories: 150.9, Protein: 14.5g, Fiber: 9g, Fat: 9.8g, Carbs: 2.8g

256. Pistachio Crusted Salmon

Preparation Time: 5 minutes
Servings: 1

Cooking Time: 15 minutes

Ingredients:

- 1 tsp. mustard
- 1 tbsp. pistachios
- Pinch sea salt
- Pinch garlic powder
- Pinch black pepper
- 1 tsp. lemon juice
- 1 tsp. Parmesan cheese, grated
- 1 tsp. olive oil

Directions: Warm the air fryer to 350ºF, and whisk mustard and lemon juice together.

Season the salmon with salt, pepper, and garlic powder.

Brush the olive oil on all sides. Brush the mustard mixture onto salmon.

Chop the pistachios finely and combine them with the Parmesan cheese; sprinkle on top of the salmon. Set the salmon in the air fryer basket with the skin side down; cook for 15 minutes or to your liking.

Nutrition: Calories: 139.8, Fat: 6.8g, Protein: 18.2g, Carbs: 2.9g, Sugars: 1g, Fiber: 1g

257. Fried Crawfish

Preparation Time: 5 minutes
Servings: 4

Cooking Time: 15 minutes

Ingredients:

- 1 lb. crawfish
- 1 tbsp. avocado oil
- 1 tsp. onion powder
- 1 tbsp. rosemary, chopped

Directions: Preheat the air fryer to 340ºF.

Place the crawfish in the air fryer basket and sprinkle with avocado oil and rosemary.

Add the onion powder and stir the crawfish gently; cook for 15 minutes.

Nutrition: Calories: 37.8, Protein: 1.3g, Fiber: 0g, Fat: 3g, Carbs: 1.9g, Sugar: 0g

258. Easy Tuna Wraps

Preparation Time: 10 minutes   **Cooking Time: 6 minutes**
Servings: 4

Ingredients:

- 1 pound (454 g) fresh tuna steak, cut into 1-inch cubes
- 1 tablespoon grated fresh ginger
- 2 garlic cloves, minced
- 1/2 teaspoon toasted sesame oil
- 4 low-sodium whole-wheat tortillas
- 1/4 cup low-fat mayonnaise
- 2 cups shredded romaine lettuce
- 1 red bell pepper, thinly sliced

Directions: In a medium bowl, mix the tuna, ginger, garlic, and sesame oil. Let it stand for 10 minutes, and then transfer to the air fryer basket.
Air fry at 390°F for 6 minutes, or until done to your liking and lightly browned.
Make wraps with the tuna, tortillas, mayonnaise, lettuce, and bell pepper. Serve immediately.

Nutrition: Calories: 288.7, Fat: 6.9g, Protein: 31.3g, Carbs: 25.7g, Fiber: 1g, Sugar 1g

259. Crispy Air Fryer Fish

Preparation Time: 11 minutes   **Cooking Time: 17 minutes**
Servings: 4

Ingredients:

- 2 tsp. old bay
- 4–6, cut in half, whiting fish fillets
- ¼ cup fine cornmeal
- ¼ cup flour
- 1 tsp paprika
- ½ tsp. garlic powder
- 1 ½ tsp. salt
- ½ freshly ground black pepper

Directions: In a Ziploc bag, add all ingredients and coat the fish fillets with it.
Spray oil on the air fryer basket and put the fish in it.
Cook for ten minutes at 400°F. Flip fish and coat with oil spray. Cook for another 7 minutes.
Serve with salad green.

Nutrition: Calories: 253.9, Fat: 12.2g, Carbs: 7.9g, Proteins: 17.8g

260. Mustard-Crusted Sole

Preparation Time: 5 Minutes   **Cooking Time: 8 to 11 Minutes**
Servings: 4

Ingredients:

- 5 teaspoons low-sodium yellow mustard
- 1 tablespoon freshly squeezed lemon juice
- 4 (31/2-ounce / 99-g) sole fillets
- 1/2 teaspoon dried thyme
- 1/2 teaspoon dried marjoram
- 1/8 Teaspoon freshly ground black pepper
- 1 slice low-sodium whole-wheat bread, crumbled
- 2 teaspoons olive oil

Directions: In a minor bowl, blend the mustard and lemon juice. Spread this evenly over the fillets. Place them in the air fryer basket.
In another small bowl, mix the thyme, marjoram, pepper, bread crumbs, and olive oil. Mix until combined.
Gently but firmly press the spice mixture onto each fish fillets top.
Bake at 320°F for 8 to 11 minutes, or until the fish grasps an inner temperature of at least 145°F on a meat thermometer and the topping is browned and crisp. Serve immediately.

Nutrition: Calories: 142.9, Fat: 3.8g, Protein: 20.3g, Carbs: 4.7g, Fiber: 1g, Sugar 1g

261. Air Fried Lemon Cod

Preparation Time: 5 minutes   **Cooking Time: 10 minutes**
Servings: 1

Ingredients:

- 1 cod fillet
- 1 tbsp. chopped dried parsley
- Kosher salt and pepper to taste
- 1 tbsp. garlic powder
- 1 lemon

Directions: In a bowl, mix all ingredients and coat the fish fillet with spices.

Lay the sliced lemon at the bottom of the air fryer basket.
Put spiced fish on top. Cover the fish with lemon slices.
Cook for 10 minutes at 375°F.

Nutrition: Calories: 100.8, Fat: 1g, Carbs: 9.7g, Proteins: 16.5g

262. Salmon Fillets

Preparation Time: 5 minutes   **Cooking Time: 15 minutes**
Servings: 2

Ingredients:
- ¼ cup low-fat Greek yogurt
- 2 salmon fillets
- 1 tbsp. fresh dill (chopped)
- 1 lemon juice
- ½ garlic powder
- Kosher salt and pepper

Directions: Cut lemon into slices and lay it at the bottom of the air fryer basket.
Season the salmon with salt and pepper. Put salmon on top of lemons.
Cook at 330°F for 15 minutes.
Meanwhile, mix lemon juice, garlic powder, salt, and pepper with yogurt and dill. Serve the fish with sauce.

Nutrition: Calories: 193.8, Fat: 6.8g, Carbs: 5.7g, Proteins: 25.2g

263. Salmon with Fennel and Carrot

Preparation Time: 15 minutes   **Cooking Time: 14 minutes**
Servings: 2

Ingredients:
- 1 fennel bulb, thinly sliced
- 1 large carrot, peeled and sliced
- 1 small onion, thinly sliced
- 1/4 cup low-fat sour cream
- 1/4 teaspoon coarsely ground pepper
- 2 (5-ounce / 142-g) salmon fillets

Directions: Combine the fennel, carrot, and onion in a bowl and toss.
Put the vegetable mixture into a baking pan. Prepare in the air fryer at 400ºF for 4 minutes.
Remove the pan from the air fryer. Stir in the sour cream and sprinkle the vegetables with the pepper.
Top with the salmon fillets.
Return the pan to the air fryer. Roast for another 10 minutes or until the salmon just barely flakes when tested with a fork.

Nutrition: Calories: 253.8, Fat: 8.7g, Protein: 31.2g, Carbs: 11.8g, Fiber: 3g, Sugar 4.8g

264. Air Fried Fish and Chips

Preparation Time: 11 minutes   **Cooking Time: 35 minutes**
Servings: 4

Ingredients:
- 4 cups any fish fillet
- ¼ cup flour
- 1 cup whole-wheat breadcrumbs
- 1 egg
- 2 tbsp. oil
- 2 potatoes
- 1 tsp. salt

Directions: Cut the potatoes in fries. Then coat with oil and salt.
Cook for 20 minutes at 400°F in the Air Fryer, toss the fries halfway through.
Meanwhile, coat fish in flour, then in the whisked egg, and finally in breadcrumbs mix.
Place the fillet in the air fryer and cook at 330°F for 15 minutes.
Flip it halfway through, if needed. Serve with tartar sauce and salad green.

Nutrition: Calories: 408.7, Fat: 10.7g, Carbs: 43.5g, Proteins: 30.4g

265. Grilled Salmon with Lemon

Preparation Time: 9 minutes   **Cooking Time: 8 minutes**
Servings: 4

Ingredients:
- 2 tbsp. olive oil
- 2 salmon fillets
- ⅓ cup lemon juice
- ⅓ cup water
- ⅓ cup gluten-free light soy sauce
- ⅓ cup honey
- Scallion slices to garnish
- Freshly ground black pepper, garlic powder, kosher salt to taste

Directions: Season salmon with pepper and salt.
In a bowl, mix honey, soy sauce, lemon juice, water, oil. Add salmon to this marinade and let it rest for at least 2 hours. Let the air fryer preheat at 375°F.
Place fish in the air fryer and cook for 8 minutes. Move to a dish and top with scallion slices.

Nutrition: Calories: 210.5, Fat: 8.7g, Carbs: 4.3g, Proteins: 15.3g

266. Ranch Tilapia fillets

Preparation Time: 7 minutes
Servings: 2 fillets

Cooking Time: 17 minutes

Ingredients:
- 2 tablespoons flour
- 1 egg, lightly beaten
- 1 cup crushed cornflakes
- 2 tablespoons ranch seasoning
- 2 tilapia fillets
- Olive oil spray

Directions: Place a parchment liner in the air fryer basket.
Scoop the flour out onto a plate; set aside.
Put the beaten egg in a medium shallow bowl.
Abode the cornflakes in a zip-top bag and crush with a rolling pin or another small, blunt object.
On another plate, mix to combine the crushed cereal and ranch seasoning.
Dredge the tilapia fillets in the flour, then dip in the egg, and then press into the cornflake mixture.
Place the prepared fillets on the liner in the air fryer in a single layer.
Spray with olive oil, and air fry at 400°F for 8 minutes. Carefully flip the fillets and spray with more oil.
Air fry for an additional 9 minutes, until golden and crispy, and serve.

Nutrition: Calories: 394.3, Fat: 6.7g, Protein: 34.5g, Carbs: 48.7g, Fiber: 3g, Sugar 4g

267. Air-Fried Fish Nuggets

Preparation Time: 15 minutes
Servings: 4

Cooking Time: 12 minutes

Ingredients:
- 2 cups (skinless) fish fillets in cubes
- 1 egg beaten
- 5 tbsp. flour
- 5 tbsp. water
- Kosher salt and pepper to taste
- ½ cup breadcrumbs mix
- ¼ cup whole-wheat breadcrumbs
- Oil for spraying

Directions: Season the fish cubes with kosher salt and pepper.
In a bowl, add flour and gradually add water, mixing as you add. Then mix in the egg. And keep mixing but do not over mix. Coat the cubes in batter, then in the breadcrumb mix. Coat well.
Place the cubes in a baking tray and spray with oil. Let the air fryer preheat to 400°F.
Place cubes in the air fryer and cook for 12 minutes or until well cooked and golden brown.
Serve with salad greens.

Nutrition: Calories: 183.4, Fat: 2.7g, Carbs: 9.6g, Proteins: 19.3g

268. Garlic Rosemary Grilled Prawns

Preparation Time: 5 minutes
Servings: 2

Cooking Time: 11 minutes

Ingredients:
- ½ tbsp. melted butter
- 8 green capsicum slices
- 8 prawns
- ⅛ cup rosemary leaves
- Kosher salt and freshly ground black pepper
- 3-4 cloves minced garlic

Directions: In a bowl, mix all the ingredients and marinate the prawns in it for at least 60 minutes or more.

Add 2 prawns and 2 slices of capsicum on each skewer.
Let the air fryer preheat to 380°F.
Cook for 5 to 6 minutes. Then change the temperature to 400°F and cook for another 5 minutes.
Serve with lemon wedges.

Nutrition: Calories: 193.4, Fat: 9.7g, Carbs: 11.7g, Proteins: 26.4g

269. Chilean Sea Bass with Green Olive Relish

Preparation Time: 10 minutes
Servings: 4

Cooking Time: 10 minutes

Ingredients:
- Olive oil spray
- 2 (6-ounce / 170-g) Chilean sea bass fillets or other firm-fleshed white fish
- 3 tablespoons extra-virgin olive oil
- 1/2 teaspoon ground cumin
- 1/2 teaspoon kosher salt
- 1/2 teaspoon black pepper
- 1/3 cup pitted green olives, diced
- 1/4 cup finely diced onion
- 1 teaspoon chopped capers

Directions: Spray the air fryer basket with the olive oil spray. Drizzle the fillets with the olive oil and sprinkle with the cumin, salt, and pepper.
Abode the fish in the air fryer basket. Bake at 325ºF for 10 minutes, or until the fish flakes easily with a fork.
For the meantime, in a lesser bowl, stir together the olives, onion, and capers.
Serve the fish topped with the relish.

Nutrition: Calories: 365.8, Fat: 25.3g, Protein: 31.2g, Carbs: 1.7g, Fiber: 1g, Sugar: 0g

270. Sweet & Sour Tuna

Preparation Time: 10 minutes
Servings: 4

Cooking Time: 9 minutes

Ingredients:
- 2lb. (6- oz.) tuna steaks, pat dried
- ½ cup low-sodium chicken broth
- 2 tbsp. Yacon syrup
- 2 tbsp. balsamic vinegar
- 2 tbsp. kaffir lime leaves, minced
- 1 (½-inch) piece fresh ginger, minced
- Ground black pepper, as required

Directions: In the pot of Instant pot, place all the ingredients and mix well.
Add the tuna steaks and mix with broth mixture. Secure the lid and place the pressure valve in the "Seal" position. Press "Manual" and cook under "High Pressure" for about 6 minutes.
Press "Cancel" and carefully allow a "Quick" release.
Open the lid and with a slotted spoon, transfer the tuna steaks onto a plate.
Press "Sauté" and cook for about 2-3 minutes or until sauce becomes slightly thick.
Press "Cancel" and pour the sauce over tuna steaks. Serve immediately.

Nutrition: Calories: 328.7, Fats: 10.1g, Carbs: 3g, Sugar: 1.5g, Proteins: 5.5g

271. Parmesan Broccoli and Asparagus

Preparation Time: 20 minutes
Servings: 4

Cooking Time: 15 minutes

Ingredients:
- ½ lb. asparagus, trimmed
- 1 broccoli head, florets separated
- Juice of 1 lime
- 1 tbsp. parmesan, grated
- 2 tbsp. olive oil
- Salt and black pepper to taste.

Directions: Take a bowl and mix the asparagus with the broccoli and all the other ingredients except the parmesan, toss, transfer to your air fryer's basket and cook at 400°F for 15 minutes.
Divide between plates, sprinkle the parmesan on top, and serve.

Nutrition: Calories: 171.8, Fat: 4.7g, Fiber: 2g, Carbs: 3.8g, Protein: 9.1g

272. Asparagus With Garlic

Preparation Time: 5 minutes   **Cooking Time: 5 minutes**
Servings: 4

Ingredients:
- 1-lb. asparagus, rinsed, ends snapped off where they naturally break (see Tip)
- 2 tsp. olive oil
- 2 garlic cloves, minced
- 2 tbsp. balsamic vinegar
- ½ tsp. dried thyme

Directions: In a huge bowl, mix the asparagus with olive oil. -Transfer to the air fryer basket.
Sprinkle with garlic. Roast for 4 to 5 minutes for crisp-tender, or more if you prefer.
Drizzle with the balsamic vinegar and sprinkle with the thyme leaves. Serve immediately.

Nutrition: Calories: 40.7, Fat: 1g, Protein: 3.3g, Carbs: 5.6g

273. Crunchy Cauliflower

Preparation Time: 20 minutes   **Cooking Time: 15 minutes**
Servings: 5

Ingredients:
- 2 oz. cauliflower
- 1 tbsp. potato starch
- 1 tsp. olive oil
- Salt & pepper to taste

Directions: Set the air fryer toaster oven to 400°F and preheat it for 3 minutes. Slice cauliflower into equal pieces and if you are using potato starch then toss with the florets into the bowl.
Add some olive oil and mix to coat.
Use olive oil cooking spray for spraying the inside of the air fryer toaster oven basket then add cauliflower.
Cook for eight minutes then shake the basket and cook for another 5 minutes depending on your desired level of crispiness. Sprinkle roasted cauliflower with fresh parsley, kosher salt, and seasonings or sauce of your choice.

Nutrition: Calories: 35.7, Fat: 1g, Protein: 1.3g, Carbs: 4.5g, Fiber: 2g

274. Butter Endives Recipe

Preparation Time: 15 minutes   **Cooking Time: 10 minutes**
Servings: 4

Ingredients:
- 4 endives, trimmed and halved
- Salt and black pepper to taste
- 1 tbsp. lime juice
- 1 tbsp. butter, melted

Directions: Place the endives in your air fryer, then add the salt and pepper to taste, lemon juice, and butter.
Cook at a temperature of 360°F for 10 minutes. Cut into different plates and serve right away.

Nutrition: Calories: 99.6, Fat: 2.6g, Fiber: 4g, Carbs: 7.8g, Protein: 4.5g

275. Garlic-Roasted Bell Peppers

Preparation Time: 5 minutes   **Cooking Time: 20 minutes**
Servings: 4

Ingredients:
- 2 bell peppers, any colors, stemmed, seeded, membranes removed, and cut into fourths
- 1 tsp. olive oil
- 2 garlic cloves, minced
- ½ tsp. dried thyme

Directions: Put the peppers in the basket of the air fryer and drizzle with olive oil. Toss gently. Roast for 15 minutes.
Sprinkle with thyme and garlic. Roast for 3 to 5 minutes more, or until tender. Serve immediately.

Nutrition: Calories: 35.6, Fat: 0.9g, Protein: 1.5g, Carbs: 4.8g, Fiber: 2g

276. Sweet Beets Salad

Preparation Time: 20 Minutes
Servings: 4

Cooking Time: 10 minutes

Ingredients:
- 1 ½-lb. beets; peeled and quartered
- 2 tbsps. brown sugar
- 2 scallions; chopped
- 2 tbsp. cider vinegar
- ½ cup orange juice
- 2 cups Arugula
- 2 tbsps. mustard
- A drizzle olive oil
- 2 tbsps. orange zest; grated

Directions: Season the beets with orange juice and oil in a bowl.
Spread the beets in the air fryer basket and seal the fryer. Cook for 10 minutes at 350°F on Air fryer mode.
Place these cooked beets in a bowl then toss in arugula, orange zest, and scallions.
Whisk vinegar, mustard, and sugar in a different bowl. Add this mixture to the beets and mix well.

Nutrition: Calories: 150.8, Fat: 1.7g, Fiber: 4g, Carbs: 13.8g, Protein: 4.2g

277. Veg Buffalo Cauliflower

Preparation Time: 20 minutes
Servings: 3

Cooking Time: 25 minutes

Ingredients:
- 1 medium head cauliflower
- 1 tsp. avocado oil
- 2 tbsp. red hot sauce
- 1 tbsp. nutritional yeast
- 1 ½ tsp. maple syrup
- ¼ tsp. sea salt
- 1 tbsp. cornstarch or arrowroot starch

Directions: Set your air fryer toaster oven to 360°F.
Place all the ingredients into a bowl except cauliflower. Mix them to combine. Put the cauliflower and mix to coat equally. Put half of cauliflower into an air fryer and cook for 15 minutes but keep shaking them until your get desired consistency.
Do the same for the cauliflower which is left but lower the cooking time to 10 minutes.
Keep the cauliflower tightly sealed in the refrigerator for 3-4 days. For heating again add back to the air fryer for 1-2 minutes until crispness.

Nutrition: Calories: 247.8, Fat: 19.8g, Protein: 4.2g, Carbs: 12.7g, Fiber: 2g

278. Dill Mashed Potato

Preparation Time: 10 minutes
Servings: 2

Cooking Time: 15 minutes

Ingredients:
- 2 potatoes
- 1 tbsp. fresh dill, chopped
- 1 tsp. butter
- ½ tsp. salt
- ¼ cup half and half

Directions: Preheat the air fryer to 390°F.
Rinse the potatoes thoroughly and place them in the air fryer. Cook for 15 minutes.
Peel the potatoes and mash them with the help of the fork.
Then add chopped fresh dill and salt. Stir it gently and add butter and half and half.
Take the hand blender and blend the mixture well.

Nutrition: Calories: 210.7, Fat: 5.2g, Fiber: 5.5g, Carbs: 36g, Protein: 5.6g

279. Brussels Sprouts & Potatoes Dish

Preparation Time: 10−20 minutes
Servings: 4

Cooking Time: 5 minutes

Ingredients:
- 1 ½ lb. brussels sprouts, washed and trimmed
- 1 ½ tbsp. breadcrumbs
- ½ cup beef stock
- 1 cup new potatoes, chopped
- 1 ½ tbsp. butter
- Salt and black pepper to taste

Directions: Put sprouts and potatoes in your air fryer oven.

Add stock, salt, and pepper, close the lid and cook at high for 5 minutes.
Quickly release the pressure, open the lid; set on "Sauté" mode; add butter and breadcrumbs, toss to coat well, divide among plates and serve.

Nutrition: Calories: 149.3, Fat: 7.8g, Protein: 1.3g, Sugar: 1.8g

280. Roasted Potatoes

Preparation Time: 10–20 minutes   **Cooking Time: 17 minutes**
Servings: 4

Ingredients:
- 2 lb. baby potatoes
- 5 tbsp. vegetable oil
- ½ cup stock
- 1 rosemary spring
- 5 garlic cloves
- Salt and black pepper to taste

Directions: Set your air fryer oven on "Sauté" mode; add oil and heat it.
Add potatoes, rosemary and garlic, stir and brown them for 10 minutes.
Prick each potato with a knife, add the stock, salt, and pepper to the pot, seal the air fryer oven lid and cook at high for 7 minutes.
Quickly release the pressure, open the air fryer oven lid, divide potatoes among plates and serve.

Nutrition: Calories: 249.5, Fat: 14.5g, Protein: 2.2g, Sugar: 0.9g

281. Ginger and Green Onion Fish

Preparation Time: 15 minutes   **Cooking Time: 15 minutes**
Servings: 2

Ingredients:
Bean Sauce:
- 2 tablespoons low-sodium soy sauce
- 1 tablespoon rice wine
- 1 tablespoon doubanjiang (Chinese black bean paste)
- 1 teaspoon minced fresh ginger
- 1 clove garlic, minced

Vegetables and Fish:
- 1 tablespoon peanut oil
- 1/4 cup julienned green onions
- 1/4 cup chopped fresh cilantro
- 2 tablespoons julienned fresh ginger
- 2 (6-ounce / 170-g) white fish fillets, such as tilapia

Directions:
For the sauce: In a small bowl, combine all the ingredients and stir until well combined; set aside.
For the vegetables and fish: In a medium bowl, combine the peanut oil, green onions, cilantro, and ginger. Toss to combine.
Cut two squares of parchment large enough to hold one fillet and half of the vegetables. Place one fillet on each parchment square, top with the vegetables, and pour over the sauce. Bend over the parchment paper and tuck the sides in small, tight folds to hold the fish, vegetables, and sauce securely inside the packet.
Abode the packets in a single layer in the air fryer basket—roast at 350°F for 15 minutes.
Transfer each packet to a dinner plate. Cut open with scissors just before serving.

Nutrition: Calories: 236.8, Fat: 8.9g, Protein: 36.3g, Carbs: 3.2g, Fiber: 0g, Sugar: 0g

282. Lemon Scallops with Asparagus

Preparation Time: 10 minutes   **Cooking Time: 9 minutes**
Servings: 4

Ingredients:
- 1/2 pound (227 g) asparagus, ends trimmed and cut into 2-inch pieces
- 1 cup sugar snap peas
- 1 pound (454 g) sea scallops
- 1 tablespoon lemon juice
- 2 teaspoons olive oil
- 1/2 teaspoon dried thyme
- Pinch salt
- Freshly ground black pepper, to taste

Directions: Abode the asparagus and sugar snap peas in the air fryer basket. Air fry at 400°F for 2 minutes or until the vegetables are just getting tender.
Meanwhile, pull out the small muscle attached to the side of the scallops and discard it.

In a bowl, toss the scallops with thyme, olive oil, lemon juice, salt, and pepper. Place into the air fryer basket on top of the vegetables.
Air fry for 7 minutes, tossing the basket once during the Cooking Time, and the vegetables are tender. Serve immediately.

Nutrition: Calories: 162.3, Fat: 3.8g, Protein: 22.2g, Carbs: 9.7g, Fiber: 3g, Sugar: 2.5g

283. Lemon Snapper with Fruit

Preparation Time: 15 minutes
Servings: 4

Cooking Time: 12 minutes

Ingredients:
- 4 (4-ounce / 113-g) red snapper fillets
- 2 teaspoons olive oil
- 3 nectarines, halved and pitted
- 3 plums, halved and pitted
- 1 cup red grapes
- 1 tablespoon freshly squeezed lemon juice
- 1/2 teaspoon dried thyme

Directions: Put the red snapper in the air fryer basket and drizzle with the olive oil. Air fry at 390ºF for 4 minutes. Remove the basket and add the nectarines and plums. Scatter the grapes overall.
Drizzle with the lemon juice and sprinkle with the thyme.
Reappearance the basket to the air fryer and air fry for 8 minutes more, or till the fish flakes when tested with a fork and the fruit is tender. Serve immediately.

Nutrition: Calories: 245.8, Fat: 3.6g, Protein: 25.4g, Carbs: 17.8g, Fiber: 3g, Sugar 9.7g

284. Asian-Inspired Swordfish Steaks

Preparation Time: 10 minutes
Servings: 4

Cooking Time: 18 minutes

Ingredients:
- 4 (4-ounce / 113-g) swordfish steaks
- 1/2 teaspoon toasted sesame oil
- 1 jalapeño pepper, finely minced
- 2 garlic cloves, grated
- 1 tablespoon grated fresh ginger
- 1/2 teaspoon Chinese five-spice powder
- 1/8 Teaspoon freshly ground black pepper
- 2 tablespoons freshly squeezed lemon juice

Directions: Place the swordfish steaks on a work surface and drizzle with the sesame oil.
In a small bowl, mix the ginger, jalapeño, pepper, garlic, five-spice powder, and lemon juice. Rub this mixture into the fish and let it stand for 10 minutes. Put in the air fryer basket.
Roast at 380ºF for 8 minutes, or until the swordfish reaches an inner temperature of at least 140ºF on a meat thermometer.

Nutrition: Calories: 187.8, Fat: 5.9g, Protein: 29.5g, Carbs: 1.7g, Fiber: 0g, Sugar 0.9g

285. Fish Tacos

Preparation Time: 15 minutes
Servings: 4

Cooking Time: 10 minutes

Ingredients:
- 1 pound (454 g) white fish fillets, such as snapper
- 1 tablespoon olive oil
- 3 tablespoons freshly squeezed lemon juice, divided
- 11/2 cups chopped red cabbage
- 1/2 cup of salsa
- 1/3 cup sour cream
- 6 whole-wheat tortillas
- 2 avocados, peeled and chopped

Directions: Skirmish the fish with olive oil and sprinkle with 1 tablespoon of the lemon juice. Set in the air fryer basket and air fry at 400°F meant for 10 minutes.
Meanwhile, combine cabbage, remaining 2 tablespoons lemon juice, salsa, and sour cream in a medium bowl.
As momentarily as the fish is cooked, remove from the air fryer basket and break into large pieces.
Let everyone assemble their taco combining the fish, tortillas, cabbage mixture, and avocados.

Nutrition: Calories: 546.8, Fat: 26.8g, Protein: 33.3g, Carbs: 42.7g, Fiber: 12g, Sugar: 3.7g

286. Spicy Cajun Shrimp

Preparation Time: 7 minutes
Servings: 2 cups

Cooking Time: 12 minutes

Ingredients:
- *1/2 pound (227 g) shrimp, peeled and deveined*
- *1 tablespoon olive oil*
- *1 teaspoon ground cayenne pepper*
- *1/2 teaspoon Old Bay seasoning*
- *1/2 teaspoon paprika*
- *1/8 Teaspoon salt*
- *Juice of half a lemon*

Directions: In a huge bowl, syndicate the shrimp, olive oil, cayenne pepper, Old Bay Seasoning, paprika, and salt; toss to combine.
Transfer to the air fryer basket and roast at 390°F for 12 minutes, until browned.
Whisk a bit of lemon juice over the shrimp before serving.

Nutrition: Calories: 158.7, Fat: 6.9g, Protein: 23.3g, Carbs: 0.9g, Fiber: 0g, Sugar: 0g

287. Garlic Parmesan Roasted Shrimp

Preparation Time: 7 minutes
Servings: 4 cups

Cooking Time: 13 minutes

Ingredients:
- *1 pound (454 g) jumbo shrimp, peeled and deveined*
- *1/3 cup Parmesan cheese*
- *1 tablespoon olive oil*
- *1 teaspoon onion powder*
- *2 teaspoons minced garlic*
- *1/2 teaspoon ground black pepper*
- *1/4 teaspoon dried basil*

Directions: In a large bowl, toss to combine the shrimp, Parmesan cheese, olive oil, onion powder, garlic, pepper, and basil.
Transfer to the air fryer basket and roast at 350°F for 13 minutes, until the shrimp are browned, and serve.

Nutrition: Calories: 161.8, Fat: 5.8g, Protein: 25.3g, Carbs: 1.6g, Fiber: 0g, Sugar: 0g

288. Almond Crusted Cod with Chips

Preparation Time: 10 minutes
Servings: 4

Cooking Time: 25 minutes

Ingredients:
- *2 russet potatoes, peeled, thinly sliced, rinsed, and patted dry*
- *1 egg white*
- *1 tablespoon freshly squeezed lemon juice*
- *1/3 cup ground almonds*
- *2 slices low-sodium whole-wheat bread, finely crumbled*
- *1/2 teaspoon dried basil*
- *4 (4-ounce / 113-g) cod fillets*

Directions: Preheat the oven to warm.
Put the potato slices in the air fryer basket and air fry at 390°F aimed at 13 minutes. With tongs, turn the fries twice during cooking.
For the meantime, in a deep bowl, beat the egg white and lemon juice until frothy.
On a plate, mix the almonds, bread crumbs, and basil.
Single at a time, dip the fillets into the egg white mixture and then into the almond-bread crumb mixture to coat.
Place the coated fillets on a wire rack to dry while the fries cook.
When the potatoes are done, transfer them to a baking sheet and keep warm in the oven on low heat.
Air fry the fish in the air fryer basket for 12 minutes, or until the fish grasps an internal temperature of at least 140°F on a meat thermometer and the coating is browned and crisp. Serve immediately with the potatoes.

Nutrition: Calories: 247.8, Fat: 4.7g, Protein: 27.5g, Carbs: 24.2g, Fiber: 3g, Sugar 2.6g

289. Quick Shrimp Scampi

Preparation Time: 10 minutes
Servings: 2

Cooking Time: 7 minutes

Ingredients:

- 30 (1 pound / 454 g) uncooked large shrimp, peeled, deveined, and tails removed
- 2 teaspoons olive oil
- 1 garlic clove, thinly sliced
- Juice and zest of 1/2 lemon
- 1/8 Teaspoon kosher salt
- Pinch of red pepper flakes
- 1 tablespoon chopped fresh parsley

Directions: Sprig a baking pan with nonstick cooking spray, then combine the shrimp, olive oil, sliced garlic, lemon juice and zest, kosher salt, and red pepper flakes in the pan, tossing to coat. Place in the air fryer basket. Roast at 360°F for 7 minutes or until firm and bright pink.
Remove the fryer's shrimp, place on a serving plate, and sprinkle the parsley on top. Serve warm.

Nutrition: Calories: 320.6, Fat: 12.9g, Protein: 46.3g, Carbs: 4.6g, Fiber: 0g, Sugar: 1g

290. Cream Cheese Stuffed Jalapeños

Preparation Time: 12 minutes
Servings: 10 poppers

Cooking Time: 6-8 minutes

Ingredients:
- 8 ounces (227 g) of cream cheese, at room temperature
- 1 cup of whole-wheat bread crumbs, divided
- 2 tablespoons of fresh parsley, minced
- 1 teaspoon of chili powder
- 10 jalapeño peppers, halved and seeded

Directions: In a small bowl, merge the cream cheese, 1/2 cup of bread crumbs, the parsley, and the chili powder. Whisk to combine. Stuff the cheese mixture into the jalapeños.
Sprinkle the tops of the stuffed jalapeños with the remaining 1/2 cup of bread crumbs.
Set in the Air Fryer basket and air fry at 360°F for 6 to 8 minutes. Serve warm.

Nutrition: Calories: 243.8, Fat: 15.8g, Protein: 6.2g, Carbs: 18.7g, Fiber: 2g, Sugar: 3.6g

291. Panko Coconut Shrimp

Preparation Time: 12 minutes
Servings: 4

Cooking Time: 8 minutes

Ingredients:
- 2 egg whites
- 1 tablespoon water
- ½ cup whole-wheat panko bread crumbs
- ¼ cup unsweetened coconut flakes
- ½ teaspoon turmeric
- ½ teaspoon ground coriander
- ½ teaspoon ground cumin
- 1/8 teaspoon salt
- 1 pound (454 g) large raw shrimp, peeled, deveined, and patted dry
- Nonstick cooking spray

Directions: Preheat the air fry to 400°F.
In a shallow dish, beat the egg whites and water until slightly foamy. Set aside.
In a separate shallow dish, mix the bread crumbs, coconut flakes, turmeric, coriander, cumin, and salt, and stir until well combined.
Dredge the shrimp in the egg mixture, shaking off any excess, then coat them in the crumb-coconut mixture.
Spritz the air fryer basket with nonstick cooking spray and arrange the coated shrimp in the basket.
Air fry for 8 minutes, flipping the shrimp once during cooking, or until the shrimp are golden brown and cooked through.

Nutrition: Calories: 180.2g, Fat: 4g, Protein: 28g, Carbs: 8.5g, Fiber: 2.3g, Sugar: 0.8g

292. Almond Salmon Pie

Preparation Time: 20 minutes
Servings: 8

Cooking Time: 30 minutes

Ingredients:
- ½ cup cream
- 1 ½ cup almond flour
- ½ tsp. baking soda
- 1 tbsp. apple cider vinegar
- 1-lb. salmon
- 1 tbsp. chives
- 1 tsp. dried oregano
- 1 tsp. dried dill
- 1 tsp. butter
- 1 egg
- 1 tsp. dried parsley
- 1 tsp. ground paprika

Directions: Crack the egg in a bowl and whisk it.
Add the cream and keep whisking it for 2 minutes more.

After this, add baking soda and apple cider vinegar. Add almond flour and knead until you have a smooth and non-sticky dough.
Chop the salmon into tiny pieces. Sprinkle the chopped salmon with the dried dill, dried oregano, diced chives, dried parsley, and ground paprika. Mix well and cut the dough into 2 parts.
Cover the air fryer basket tray with parchment.
Put the first part of the dough in the air fryer basket tray and make the crust from it using your fingertips. Then place the salmon filling.
Roll the second part of the dough with a rolling pin and cover the salmon filling. Secure the pie edges.
Preheat the air fryer to 360°F. Put the air fryer basket tray in the air fryer and cook for 15 minutes.
Then reduce to 355°F and cook the pie for 15 minutes more.
When the pie is cooked – remove it from the air fryer basket and allow it to cool.

Nutrition: Calories: 133.8, Fat: 8.6g, Fiber 1.1g, Carbs 3.1g, Protein 13.8g

293. Tasty Tuna Steaks

Preparation Time: 10 minutes
Servings: 2

Cooking Time: 4 minutes

Ingredients:
- 12 tuna steaks, skinless and boneless
- ½ tsp. rice vinegar
- 1 tsp. sesame oil
- 1 tsp. ginger, grated
- 4 tbsp. soy sauce

Directions: Add tuna steaks and remaining ingredients in the zip-lock bag. Seal bag and place in the refrigerator for 30 minutes. Select Air Fry mode.
Set time to 4 minutes and temperature 380°F then press START.
The air fryer display will prompt you to ADD FOOD once the temperature is reached then place marinated tuna steaks in the air fryer basket. Serve and enjoy.

Nutrition: Calories: 979.3, Fat: 34g, Carbs: 3.6g, Sugar 0.5g, Protein: 155g

294. Baked Tilapia

Preparation Time: 10 minutes
Servings: 6

Cooking Time: 15 minutes

Ingredients:
- 6 tilapia fillets
- ½ cup Asiago cheese, grated
- ¼ tsp. basil
- ¼ tsp. thyme
- ¼ tsp. onion powder
- 1 tsp. garlic, minced
- ½ cup mayonnaise
- ⅛ tsp. pepper
- ¼ tsp. salt

Directions: In a small bowl, mix together the grated cheese, basil, thyme, onion powder, garlic, mayonnaise, pepper, and salt.
Place the cooking tray in the air fryer basket. Line air fryer basket with parchment paper.
Select Bake mode. Set time to 15 minutes and temperature 350°F then press START.
The air fryer display will prompt you to ADD FOOD once the temperature is reached then place fish fillets in the air fryer basket and spread cheese mixture on top of each fish fillet. Serve and enjoy.

Nutrition: Calories: 286.8, Fat: 13.3g, Carbs: 4.8g, Sugar: 1.1g, Protein: 37.1g

295. Baked Parmesan Tilapia

Preparation Time: 10 minutes
Servings: 4

Cooking Time: 10 minutes

Ingredients:
- 2 lbs. tilapia
- ¼ tsp. paprika
- ¼ tsp. dried basil
- 2 garlic cloves, minced
- 1 tsp. dried parsley
- 1 tbsp. butter, softened
- 2 tbsp. fresh lemon juice
- ¼ cup mayonnaise
- ½ cup parmesan cheese, grated
- ½ tsp. salt

Directions: In a small bowl, mix together butter, parmesan cheese, lemon juice, mayonnaise, parsley, basil, paprika, garlic, and salt.
Place the cooking tray in the air fryer basket. Line air fryer basket with parchment paper.

Select Bake mode. Set time to 10 minutes and temperature 400°F then press START.
The air fryer display will prompt you to ADD FOOD once the temperature is reached then place fish fillets in the air fryer basket and spread the parmesan mixture on top of each fish fillet. Serve and enjoy.

Nutrition: Calories: 367.8, Fat: 16g, Carbs: 5.1g, Sugar: 1g, Protein: 52.4g

296. Pecan Crusted Fish Fillets

Preparation Time: 10 minutes   **Cooking Time: 17 minutes**
Servings: 2

Ingredients:
- 2 halibut fillets
- ½ lemon juice
- 1 tsp. garlic, minced
- ¼ cup parmesan cheese, grated
- ¼ cup pecans
- 2 tbsp. butter
- Pepper
- Salt

Directions: Add pecans, lemon juice, garlic, parmesan cheese, and butter into the food processor and process until completely blended.
Place the cooking tray in the air fryer basket. Line air fryer basket with parchment paper.
Select Bake mode. Set time to 5 minutes and temperature 400°F then press START.
The air fryer display will prompt you to ADD FOOD once the temperature is reached then season fish fillets with pepper and salt and place them in the air fryer basket.
Spread pecan mixture on top of fish fillets and bake for 12 minutes more. Serve and enjoy.

Nutrition: Calories: 605.7, Fat: 33.4g, Carbs: 3.2g, Sugar: 0.5g, Protein 71.9g

297. Bagel Crust Fish Fillets

Preparation Time: 10 minutes   **Cooking Time: 10 minutes**
Servings: 4

Ingredients:
- 4 white fish fillets
- 1 tbsp. mayonnaise
- 1 tsp. lemon-pepper seasoning
- 2 tbsp. almond flour
- ¼ cup bagel seasoning

Directions: In a small bowl, mix together bagel seasoning, almond flour, and lemon pepper seasoning.
Brush mayonnaise over fish fillets. Sprinkle seasoning mixture over fish fillets.
Place the cooking tray in the air fryer basket. Line air fryer basket with parchment paper.
Select Bake mode. Set time to 10 minutes and temperature 400°F then press START.
The air fryer display will prompt you to ADD FOOD once the temperature is reached then place fish fillets in the air fryer basket. Serve and enjoy.

Nutrition: Calories: 374.8, Fat: 1.8g, Carbs: 6.6g, Sugar: 1g, Protein: 41.7g

298. Air Fryer Scallops

Preparation Time: 10 minutes   **Cooking Time: 4 minutes**
Servings: 2

Ingredients:
- 8 scallops
- 1 tbsp. olive oil
- Pepper
- Salt

Directions: Brush scallops with olive oil and season with pepper and salt.
Place the cooking tray in the air fryer basket.
Select Air Fry mode. Set time to 2 minutes and temperature 390°F then press START.
The air fryer display will prompt you to ADD FOOD once the temperature is reached then add scallops in the air fryer basket. Turn scallops and air fry for 2 minutes more. Serve and enjoy.

Nutrition: Calories: 165.4, Fat: 7.2g, Carbs: 2.2g, Sugar: 0g, Protein: 20.2g

299. Pesto Scallops

Preparation Time: 10 minutes
Servings: 4

Cooking Time: 8 minutes

Ingredients:

- 1 lb. sea scallops
- 2 tsp. garlic, minced
- 3 tbsp. heavy cream

- ¼ cup basil pesto
- 1 tbsp. olive oil
- ½ tsp. pepper

- 1 tsp. salt

Directions: In a small pan, mix together garlic, oil, pepper, cream, pesto, and salt, and simmer for 2-3 minutes.
Select Air Fry mode. Set time to 5 minutes and temperature 320°F then press START.
The air fryer display will prompt you to ADD FOOD once the temperature is reached then add scallops in the air fryer basket. Turn scallops and after 3 minutes.
Transfer scallops into the mixing bowl. Pour pesto sauce over scallops and serve.

Nutrition: Calories: 171.5, Fat: 8.1g, Carbs: 3.4g, Sugar: 0g, Protein: 19.9g

300. Baked Salmon Patties

Preparation Time: 10 minutes
Servings: 4

Cooking Time: 20 minutes

Ingredients:

- 2 eggs, lightly beaten
- 12 oz. can salmon, skinless, boneless, and drained
- ½ cup almond flour

- ½ tsp. pepper
- 1 tbsp. Dijon mustard
- 1 tsp. garlic powder
- 2 tbsp. fresh parsley, chopped

- ½ cup celery, diced
- ½ cup bell pepper, diced
- ½ cup onion, diced

Directions: Add salmon and remaining ingredients into the mixing bowl and mix until well combined.
Make 8 equal shapes of patties from the mixture.
Place the cooking tray in the air fryer basket. Line air fryer basket with parchment paper.
Select Bake mode. Set time to 20 minutes and temperature 400°F then press START.
The air fryer display will prompt you to ADD FOOD once the temperature is reached then place patties in the air fryer basket. Turn patties halfway through. Serve and enjoy.

Nutrition: Calories: 181.7, Fat: 6.1g, Carbs: 4.3g, Sugar 2g, Protein 23.2g

301. Cheesy Salmon Fillets

Preparation Time: 5 minutes
Servings: 2-3

Cooking Time: 20 minutes

Ingredients:

- 2 pieces, 4 oz. each salmon fillets, choose even cuts
- ½ cup sour cream, reduced fat

Garnish:
- Spanish paprika

- ¼ cup cottage cheese, reduced fat

- ½ piece lemon, cut into wedges

- ¼ cup Parmigiano-Reggiano cheese, freshly grated

Directions: Preheat Air Fryer to 330 degrees F.
To make the salmon fillets, mix sour cream, cottage cheese, and Parmigiano-Reggiano cheese in a bowl.
Layer salmon fillets in the Air fryer basket. Fry for 20 minutes or until cheese turns golden brown.
To assemble, place a salmon fillet and sprinkle paprika. Garnish with lemon wedges and squeeze lemon juice on top. Serve.

Nutrition: Calorie: 273.8, Carbs: 1g, Fat: 18.7g, Protein: 24.8g, Fiber: 0.5g

302. Moist & Juicy Baked Cod

Preparation Time: 10 minutes
Servings: 2

Cooking Time: 10 minutes

Ingredients:

- 1 lb. cod fillets

- 1 ½ tbsp. olive oil

- 3 dashes cayenne pepper

- *1 tbsp. lemon juice*
- *¼ tsp. salt*

Directions: In a small bowl, mix together olive oil, cayenne pepper, lemon juice, and salt.
Brush fish fillets with oil mixture.
Place the cooking tray in the air fryer basket. Line air fryer basket with parchment paper.
Select Bake mode. Set time to 10 minutes and temperature 400°F then press START.
The air fryer display will prompt you to ADD FOOD once the temperature is reached then place fish fillets in the air fryer basket. Serve and enjoy.

Nutrition: Calories: 274.8, Fat: 12.1g, Carbs: 0.4g, Sugar 0.2g, Protein 40.9g

Vegetables and Salads

303. Cheese Stuffed Mushrooms

Preparation Time: 15 minutes
Servings: 3

Cooking Time: 7 minutes

Ingredients
- 9 large button mushrooms, stems removed
- 1 tbsp. olive oil
- Salt and ground black pepper, to taste
- 1/2 tsp. rosemary, dried
- 6 tbsp. Swiss cheese, shredded
- 6 tbsp. Romano cheese, shredded
- 6 tbsp. cream cheese
- 1 tsp. soy sauce
- 1 tsp. garlic, minced
- 3 tbsp. green onion, minced

Directions: Brush the mushroom caps with olive oil; sprinkle with salt, pepper, and rosemary.
In a mixing bowl, thoroughly combine the remaining ingredients, mix them well, and divide the filling mixture among the mushroom caps. Cook in the preheated air fryer at 390°F for 7 minutes.
Let the mushrooms cool slightly before serving.

Nutrition: Calories: 344.5, Fat: 27.5g, Carbs: 10.6g, Protein: 14.8g, Sugars: 7.5g

304. Air Fryer Vegetables & Italian Sausage

Preparation Time: 5 minutes
Servings: 4

Cooking Time: 11 minutes

Ingredients:
- One bell pepper
- Italian Sausage: 4 pieces spicy or sweet
- One small onion
- 1/4 cup of mushrooms

Directions: Let the air fryer pre-heat to 400°F for three minutes.
Put Italian sausage in a single layer in the air fryer basket and let it cook for six minutes.
Slice the vegetables while the sausages are cooking.
After six minutes, reduce the temperature to 360°F. flip the sausage halfway through. Add the mushrooms, onions, and peppers in the basket around the sausage.
Cook at 360°F for 8 minutes. After a 4-minute mix around the sausage and vegetables.
Take vegetables and sausage out and serve hot with brown rice.

Nutrition: Calories: 290.5, Protein: 16.5g, Carbs: 9.8g, Fat: 20.5g

305. Sweet Potato Fritters

Preparation Time: 6–7 minutes
Servings: 4

Cooking Time: 4 minutes

Ingredients:
- 1 can sweet potato puree, 15 oz.
- ½ tsp. minced garlic
- ½ cup frozen spinach, thawed, finely chopped, and drained well
- 1 large leek, minced
- 1 serving flax egg
- ¼ cup almond flour
- ¼ tsp. sweet paprika flakes
- 1 tsp. kosher salt
- ½ tsp. ground white pepper

Directions: Heat the Air Fryer to 330°F.
Place all ingredients in a bowl and mix all well. Divide into 16 balls and flatten each to the only an-inch-thick patty.
Place patties in the Air Fryer basket and cook for two minutes at 330°F. Flip and cook for 2 more minutes.
If needed, cook in batches.

Nutrition: Calories: 231.5, Fat: 7.5g, Carbs: 5.8g, Protein: 12.8g

306. Cabbage Wedges

Preparation Time: 10 minutes

Cooking Time: 24 minutes

Servings: 6

Ingredients:
- 1 small head of green cabbage
- 6 strips of bacon, thick-cut, pastured
- 1 teaspoon of onion powder
- ½ teaspoon of ground black pepper
- 1 teaspoon of garlic powder
- ¾ teaspoon of salt
- 1/4 teaspoon of red chili flakes
- 1/2 teaspoon of fennel seeds
- 3 tablespoons of olive oil

Directions: Switch on the Air Fryer, insert fryer basket, grease it with olive oil, then shut with its lid, set the fryer to 350°F, and preheat for 5 minutes.

Open the fryer, add bacon strips in it, close with its lid and cook for 10 minutes until nicely golden and crispy, turning the bacon halfway through the frying.

Meanwhile, prepare the cabbage, remove the cabbage's outer leaves, and then cut it into eight wedges, keeping the core intact.

Prepare the spice mix and for this, place onion powder in a bowl, add black pepper, garlic powder, salt, red chili, and fennel and stir until mixed. Drizzle cabbage wedges with oil and then sprinkle with spice mix until well coated.

When the Air Fryer beeps, open its lid, transfer bacon strips to a cutting board and let it rest.

Add seasoned cabbage wedges into the fryer basket, close with its lid, then cook for 8 minutes at 400°F, flip the cabbage, spray with oil and continue air frying for 6 minutes until nicely golden and cooked.

When done, transfer cabbage wedges to a plate. Chop the bacon, sprinkle it over cabbage and serve.

Nutrition: Calories: 122.5, Carbs: 1.6g, Fat: 10.5g, Protein: 4.6g, Fiber: 0g, Sugar: 1g

307. Buffalo Cauliflower Wings

Preparation Time: 5 minutes
Servings: 6

Cooking Time: 15 minutes

Ingredients:
- 1 tablespoon of almond flour
- 1 medium head of cauliflower
- 1 ½ teaspoon of salt
- 4 tablespoons of hot sauce
- 1 tablespoon of olive oil

Directions: Switch on the Air Fryer, insert fryer basket, grease it with olive oil, then shut with its lid, set the fryer to 400°F, and preheat for 5 minutes.

Meanwhile, cut cauliflower into bite-size florets and set aside.

Place flour in a large bowl, whisk in salt, oil, and hot sauce until combined, add cauliflower florets and toss until combined.

Open the fryer, add cauliflower florets in it in a single layer, close with its lid and cook for 15 minutes until nicely golden and crispy, shaking halfway through the frying.

When the Air Fryer beeps, open its lid, transfer cauliflower florets onto a serving plate and keep warm.

Cook the remaining cauliflower florets the same way and serve.

Nutrition: Calories: 47.5, Carbs: 0.6g, Fat: 3.5g, Protein: 1.6g, Fiber: 0.5g

308. Okra

Preparation Time: 10 minutes
Servings: 4

Cooking Time: 10 minutes

Ingredients:
- 1 cup of almond flour
- 8 ounces of fresh okra
- 1/2 teaspoon of sea salt
- 1 cup of milk, reduced-fat
- 1 egg, pastured

Directions: Snap the egg in a basin, pour in the milk, and whisk until blended.

Cut the stem from each okra, then cut it into ½-inch pieces, add them into the egg and stir until well coated.

Mix flour and salt and add it into a large plastic bag.

Working on one okra piece at a time, drain the okra well by letting excess egg drip off, add it to the flour mixture, then seal the bag and shake well until okra is well coated.

Place the coated okra on a grease Air Fryer basket, coat the remaining okra pieces the same way and place them into the basket.

Switch on the Air Fryer, insert fryer basket, spray okra with oil, then shut with its lid, set the fryer to 390°F, and cook for 10 minutes, stirring okra halfway through the frying. Serve straight away.

Nutrition: Calories: 249.6, Carbs: 37.5g, Fat: 8.6g, Protein: 3.6g, Fiber: 2g

309. Creamed Spinach

Preparation Time: 10 minutes
Servings: 2

Cooking Time: 15 minutes

Ingredients:
- *1/2 cup of chopped white onion*
- *10 ounces of frozen spinach, thawed*
- *1 teaspoon of salt*
- *1 teaspoon of ground black pepper*
- *2 teaspoons of minced garlic*
- *1/2 teaspoon of ground nutmeg*
- *4 ounces of cream cheese, reduced-fat, diced*
- *1/4 cup of shredded Parmesan cheese, reduced-fat*

Directions: Switch on the Air Fryer, insert fryer basket, grease it with olive oil, then shut with its lid, set the fryer at 350°F, and preheat for 5 minutes.
Meanwhile, take a 6-inches baking pan, grease it with oil, and set it aside.
Put spinach in a basin, add remaining ingredients (except for Parmesan cheese,) stir until well mixed and then add the mixture into a prepared baking pan.
Open the fryer, add pan in it, close with its lid and cook for 10 minutes until cooked and cheese has melted, stirring halfway through.
Then sprinkle Parmesan cheese on top of spinach and continue air frying for 5 minutes at 400°F. Serve straight away.

Nutrition: Calories: 272.5, Carbs: 7.5g, Fat: 22.6g, Protein: 8.6g, Fiber: 2g

310. Eggplant Parmesan

Preparation Time: 20 minutes
Servings: 4

Cooking Time: 10 minutes

Ingredients:
- *1/2 cup and 3 tablespoons almond flour, divided*
- *1.25-pound eggplant, ½-inch sliced*
- *1 tablespoon of chopped parsley*
- *1 teaspoon of Italian seasoning*
- *2 teaspoons of salt*
- *1 cup of marinara sauce*
- *1 egg, pastured*
- *1 tablespoon of water*
- *3 tablespoons of grated Parmesan cheese, reduced-fat*
- *1/4 cup of grated mozzarella cheese, reduced-fat*

Directions: Slice the eggplant into ½-inch pieces, place them in a colander, sprinkle with 1 ½ teaspoon salt on both sides, and let it rest for 15 minutes.
Meanwhile, place ½ cup flour in a bowl, add egg and water and whisk until blended.
Place remaining flour in a shallow dish, add Italian seasoning, remaining salt, and Parmesan cheese, and stir until mixed.
Switch on the Air Fryer and insert the basket. Grease with olive oil, then shut with its lid. Set the fryer to 360°F, and preheat for 5 minutes.
Meanwhile, drain the eggplant pieces, pat them dry, and then dip each slice into the egg mixture and coat with flour mixture.
Open the Air fryer, add coated eggplant slices in it in a single layer, close with its lid and cook for 8 minutes, flipping the eggplant slices halfway through the frying.
Then top each eggplant slice with a tablespoon of marinara sauce and some of the Mozzarella cheese and continue air frying for 2 minutes.
When the Air Fryer beeps, open its lid, transfer eggplants onto a serving plate, and keep them warm.
Cook the remaining eggplant slices the same way and serve.

Nutrition: Calories: 192.5, Carbs: 26.4g, Fat: 5.1g, Protein: 10.6g, Fiber: 6g

311. Cauliflower Rice

Preparation Time: 10 minutes
Servings: 3

Cooking Time: 22 minutes

Ingredients:
For the Tofu:
- *1 cup of diced carrot*
- *6 ounces of tofu, extra-firm, drained*
- *1/2 cup of diced white onion*
- *2 tablespoons of soy sauce*
- *1 teaspoon of turmeric*

For the Cauliflower:
- *1/2 cup of chopped broccoli*
- *3 cups of cauliflower rice*
- *1 tablespoon of minced garlic*
- *1/2 cup of frozen peas*
- *1 tablespoon of minced ginger*
- *2 tablespoons of soy sauce*
- *1 tablespoon of apple cider vinegar*
- *1 1/2 teaspoons of toasted sesame oil*

Directions: Switch on the Air Fryer, insert fryer pan, grease it with olive oil, then shut with its lid, set the fryer to 370°F, and preheat for 5 minutes.

Meanwhile, place tofu in a bowl, crumble it, then add remaining ingredients and stir until mixed.

Open the fryer, add tofu mixture in it, and spray with oil; close with its lid and cook for 10 minutes until crispy, stirring halfway through the frying.

Meanwhile, place all the ingredients for cauliflower in a bowl and toss until mixed.

When the Air Fryer beeps, open its lid, add cauliflower mixture, shake the pan to mix, and continue cooking for 12 minutes, shaking halfway through the frying. Serve straight away.

Nutrition: Calories: 257.6, Carbs: 20.1g, Fat: 12.6g, Protein: 18.8g, Fiber: 7g

312. Brussels sprouts

Preparation Time: 5 minutes **Cooking Time: 10 minutes**
Servings: 2

Ingredients:
- *2 cups of Brussels sprouts*
- *1/4 teaspoon of sea salt*
- *1 tablespoon of olive oil*
- *1 tablespoon of apple cider vinegar*

Directions: Switch on the Air Fryer, insert fryer basket, grease it with olive oil, then shut with its lid, set the fryer to 400 °F, and preheat for 5 minutes.

Meanwhile, cut the sprouts lengthwise into ¼-inch thick pieces, put them in a bowl, add remaining ingredients and toss until well coated.

Open the fryer, add sprouts in it, close with its lid and cook for 10 minutes until crispy and cooked, shaking halfway through the frying. When Air Fryer beeps, open its lid, transfer sprouts onto a serving plate and serve.

Nutrition: Calories: 87.5, Carbs: 10.5g, Fat: 4.1g, Protein: 4.6g, Fiber: 4g

313. Green Beans

Preparation Time: 5 minutes **Cooking Time: 8 minutes**
Servings: 4

Ingredients:
- *1-pound of green beans*
- *¾ teaspoon of garlic powder*
- *¾ teaspoon of ground black pepper*
- *1 ¼ teaspoon of salt*
- *½ teaspoon of paprika*

Directions: Switch on the Air Fryer, insert fryer basket, grease it with olive oil, then shut with its lid, set the fryer to 400°F, and preheat for 5 minutes.

Meanwhile, place the beans in a bowl, spray with olive oil, sprinkle with black pepper, garlic powder, salt, and paprika and toss until well coated.

Open the fryer, add green beans in it, close with its lid and cook for 8 minutes, shaking halfway through the frying.

When Air Fryer beeps, open its lid, transfer green beans onto a serving plate and serve.

Nutrition: Calories: 44.5, Carbs: 6.8g, Fat: 1g, Protein: 2.5g, Fiber: 3g

314. Fried Pickles

Preparation Time: 20 minutes **Cooking Time: 10 minutes**
Servings: 2

Ingredients:
- *1 egg, whisked*
- *2 tablespoons of buttermilk*
- *1/2 cup of fresh breadcrumbs*
- *1/4 cup of Romano cheese, grated*
- *1/2 teaspoon of onion powder*
- *1/2 teaspoon of garlic powder*
- *1 ½ cups of dill pickle chips, pressed dry with kitchen towels*

Mayo Sauce:
- 1/4 cup of mayonnaise
- 1/2 tablespoon of mustard
- 1/2 teaspoon of molasses
- 1 tablespoon of ketchup
- 1/4 teaspoon of ground black pepper

Directions: In a shallow bowl, whisk the egg with buttermilk.
In another bowl, mix the onion powder, cheese, breadcrumbs, and garlic powder.
Dip the pickle chips in the egg mixture, then, dredge with the mixture.
Cook in the preheated Air Fryer at 400°F for 5 minutes; shake the basket and cook for 5 minutes more.
Meanwhile, mix all the sauce ingredients until well combined. Serve the fried pickles with the mayo sauce for dipping.

Nutrition: Calories: 341.5, Fat: 28.1g, Carbs: 12.2g, Protein: 9.8g, Sugars: 4.2g

315. Green Beans with Pecorino Romano

Preparation Time: 15 minutes
Servings: 3

Cooking Time: 7 minutes

Ingredients:
- 2 tablespoons of buttermilk
- 1 egg
- 4 tablespoons of cornmeal
- 4 tablespoons of tortilla chips, crushed
- 4 tablespoons of Pecorino Romano cheese, finely grated
- Coarse salt and crushed black pepper, to taste
- 1 teaspoon of smoked paprika
- 12 ounces of green beans, trimmed

Directions: In a shallow bowl, whisk together the buttermilk and egg.
In a separate bowl, combine the tortilla chips, cornmeal, salt, black pepper, Pecorino Romano cheese, and paprika. Dip the green beans in the egg mixture, then, in the mixture. Place the green beans in the greased cooking basket.
Cook in the preheated Air Fryer at 390°F for 4 minutes. Shake the basket and cook for a further 3 minutes.

Nutrition: Calories: 339.5, Fat: 9.2g, Carbs: 50.1g, Protein: 13.7g, Sugars: 4.2g

316. Spicy Glazed Carrots

Preparation Time: 20 minutes
Servings: 3

Cooking Time: 15 minutes

Ingredients:
- 1 pound carrots, cut into matchsticks
- 2 tablespoons of peanut oil
- 1 tablespoon of agave syrup
- 1 jalapeño, seeded and minced
- 1/4 teaspoon of dill
- 1/2 teaspoon of basil
- Salt and white pepper to taste

Directions: Start by warming your Air Fryer to 380°F.
Toss all ingredients together and place them in the Air Fryer basket. Cook for 15 minutes, shaking the basket halfway through the Cooking Time.

Nutrition: Calories: 161.5, Fat: 9g, Carbs: 19.6g, Protein: 1.8g, Sugars: 12.8g

317. Roasted Broccoli with Sesame Seeds

Preparation Time: 15 minutes
Servings: 2

Cooking Time: 10 minutes

Ingredients:
- 1 pound broccoli florets
- 2 tablespoons of sesame oil
- 1/2 teaspoon of shallot powder
- 1/2 teaspoon of porcini powder
- 1 teaspoon of garlic powder
- Salt and pepper to taste
- 1/2 teaspoon of cumin powder
- 1/4 teaspoon of paprika
- 2 tablespoons of sesame seeds

Directions: Start by warming the Air Fryer to 400°F.
Blanch the broccoli in salted boiling water until al dente, about 4 minutes. Drain well and transfer to the lightly greased Air Fryer basket.
Add the shallot powder, porcini powder, sesame oil, cumin powder, garlic powder, salt, black pepper, paprika, and sesame seeds. Cook for 6 minutes, tossing them over halfway through the Cooking Time.

Nutrition: Calories: 266.5, Fat: 19.1g, Carbs: 19.6g, Protein: 9.6g, Sugars: 4.6g

318. Corn on the Cob with Herb Butter

Preparation Time: 15 minutes
Servings: 2

Cooking Time: 8 minutes

Ingredients:
- 2 ears new corn, shucked and cut into halves
- 2 tablespoons butter, room temperature
- 1 teaspoon granulated garlic
- 1/2 teaspoon fresh ginger, grated
- Sea salt and pepper, to taste
- 1 tablespoon fresh rosemary, chopped
- 1 tablespoon fresh basil, chopped
- 2 tablespoons fresh chives, roughly chopped

Directions: Spritz the corn with cooking spray. Cook at 395 degrees F for 6 minutes, turning them over halfway through the Cooking Time.
In the time being, mix the butter with the ginger, granulated garlic, rosemary, salt, black pepper, and basil.
Spread the butter mixture all over the corn on the cob. Cook in the preheated Air Fryer an additional 2 minutes.

Nutrition: Calories 238.7, Fat: 13.1g, Carbs: 30.2g, Protein: 5.8g, Sugars 5.1g

319. Rainbow Vegetable Fritters

Preparation Time: 20 minutes
Servings: 2

Cooking Time: 12 minutes

Ingredients:
- 1 zucchini, grated and squeezed
- 1 cup corn kernels
- 1/2 cup canned green peas
- 4 tablespoons all-purpose flour
- 2 tablespoons fresh shallots, minced
- 1 teaspoon fresh garlic, minced
- 1 tablespoon peanut oil
- Sea salt and pepper, to taste
- 1 teaspoon cayenne pepper

Directions: In a mixing bowl, combine all ingredients until everything is well incorporated.
Shape the mixture into patties. Spritz the Air Fryer carrier with cooking spray.
Cook in the preheated Air Fryer at 365 degrees F for 6 minutes. Fit them over and cook for a further 6 minutes.

Nutrition: Calories: 214.5, Fat: 8.1g, Carbs: 31.2g, Protein: 6.5g, Sugars: 3.8g

320. Mediterranean Vegetable Skewers

Preparation Time: 30 minutes
Servings: 4

Cooking Time: 13 minutes

Ingredients:
- 2 medium-sized zucchinis, cut into 1-inch pieces
- 2 red bell peppers, cut into 1-inch pieces
- 1 green bell pepper, cut into 1-inch pieces
- 1 red onion, cut into 1-inch pieces
- 2 tablespoons olive oil
- Sea salt, to taste
- 1/2 teaspoon black pepper, preferably freshly cracked
- 1/2 teaspoon red pepper flakes

Directions: Thread the vegetables on skewers; drizzle olive oil all over the vegetable skewers; sprinkle with spices.
Cook in the preheated Air Fryer at 400 degrees F for 13 minutes. Serve warm.

Nutrition: Calories: 137.6, Fat: 9.6g, Carbs: 9.5g, Protein: 2.8g, Sugars: 6.2g

321. Veggies with Yogurt-Tahini Sauce

Preparation Time: 20 minutes
Servings: 4

Cooking Time: 16 minutes

Ingredients:
- 1 pound Brussels sprouts
- 1 pound button mushrooms
- 2 tablespoons olive oil
- 1/2 teaspoon white pepper
- 1/2 teaspoon dried dill weed
- 1/2 teaspoon cayenne pepper
- 1/2 teaspoon celery seeds
- 1/2 teaspoon mustard seeds
- Salt, to taste

Yogurt Tahini Sauce:
- 1 cup plain yogurt
- 2 heaping tablespoons tahini paste
- 1 tablespoon lemon juice

112

- 1 tablespoon extra-virgin olive oil
- 1/2 teaspoon Aleppo pepper, minced

Directions: Toss the Brussels sprouts and mushrooms with olive oil and spices.
Preheat your Air Fryer to 380 degrees F. Add the Brussels sprouts to the cooking basket and cook for 10 minutes.
Add the mushrooms, turn the temperature to 390 degrees F and cook for 6 minutes more.
While the vegetables are cooking, make the sauce by whisking all ingredients. Serve the warm vegetables with the sauce on the side.

Nutrition: Calories: 253.6, Fat: 16.6g, Carbs: 19.1g, Protein: 11.8g, Sugars: 7.6g

322. Swiss Cheese & Vegetable Casserole

Preparation Time: 50 minutes   **Cooking Time: 50 minutes**
Servings: 4

Ingredients:
- 1-pound potatoes, peeled and sliced (1/4-inch thick
- 2 tablespoons olive oil
- 1/2 teaspoon red pepper flakes, crushed
- 1/2 teaspoon freshly ground black pepper
- Salt, to taste
- 3 bell peppers, thinly sliced
- 1 serrano pepper, thinly sliced
- 2 medium-sized tomatoes, sliced
- 1 leek, thinly sliced
- 2 garlic cloves, minced
- 1 cup Swiss cheese, shredded

Directions: Twitch by warming your Air Fryer to 350 degrees F. Spritz a casserole dish with cooking oil.
Place the potatoes in the casserole dish in an even layer; drizzle 1 tablespoon of olive oil over the top. Then swell the black pepper, red pepper, and salt.
Add 2 bell peppers and 1/2 of the leeks. Add the tomatoes and the remaining 1 tablespoon of olive oil.
Add the leeks, remaining peppers, and minced garlic. Top with cheese.
Cover the casserole with foil and bake for 32 minutes.
Remove the foil and increase the temperature to 400 degrees F; bake for additional 18 minutes.

Nutrition: Calories: 326.5, Fat: 16.1g, Carbs: 32.6g, Protein: 13.9g, Sugars 7.1g

323. American-Style Brussels Sprout Salad

Preparation Time: 35 minutes   **Cooking Time: 15 minutes**
Servings: 4

Ingredients:
- 1 pound Brussels sprouts
- 1 apple, cored and diced

Dressing:
- 1/4 cup olive oil
- 2 tablespoons champagne vinegar

- 1/2 cup mozzarella cheese, crumbled
- 1/2 cup pomegranate seeds

- 1 teaspoon Dijon mustard
- 1 teaspoon honey

- 1 small-sized red onion, chopped
- 4 eggs, hardboiled and sliced

- Sea salt and ground black pepper, to taste

Directions: Start by preheating your Air Fryer to 380 degrees F.
Add the Brussels sprouts to the cooking basket. Spritz with cooking spray and cook for 15 minutes. Let it cool to room temperature about 15 minutes.
Toss the Brussels sprouts with the apple, cheese, pomegranate seeds, and red onion.
Mix all ingredients for the dressing and toss to combine well. Serve topped with the hard-boiled eggs.

Nutrition: Calories: 318.7, Fat: 18.1g, Carbs: 26.5g, Protein: 15.2g, Sugars: 14.1g

324. Cauliflower Tater Tots

Preparation Time: 25 minutes   **Cooking Time: 20 minutes**
Servings: 4

Ingredients:
- 1 pound cauliflower florets
- 2 eggs
- 1 tablespoon olive oil
- 2 tablespoons scallions, chopped
- 1 garlic clove, minced
- 1 cup Colby cheese, shredded
- 1/2 cup breadcrumbs
- Sea salt and ground black pepper, to taste
- 1/4 teaspoon dried dill weed
- 1 teaspoon paprika

Directions: Blanch the cauliflower in salted boiling water about 3 to 4 minutes until al dente. Drain well and pulse in a food processor. Add the remaining ingredients; mix to combine well. Shape the cauliflower mixture into bite-sized tots.

Spritz the Air Fryer basket with cooking spray. Cook in the preheated Air Fryer at 375 degrees F for 16 minutes, shaking halfway through the Cooking Time. Serve with your favorite sauce for dipping.

Nutrition: Calories: 266.5, Fat: 18.6g, Carbs: 9.1g, Protein: 15.4g, Sugars: 2.2g

325. Three-Cheese Stuffed Mushrooms

Preparation Time: 15 minutes
Servings: 3

Cooking Time: 7 minutes

Ingredients:
- 9 large button mushrooms, stems removed
- 1 tablespoon olive oil
- Salt and ground black pepper, to taste
- 1/2 teaspoon dried rosemary
- 6 tablespoons Swiss cheese shredded
- 6 tablespoons Romano cheese, shredded
- 6 tablespoons cream cheese
- 1 teaspoon soy sauce
- 1 teaspoon garlic, minced
- 3 tablespoons green onion, minced

Directions: Brush the mushroom caps with olive oil; sprinkle with rosemary, salt, and pepper.
In a mixing bowl, thoroughly combine the remaining ingredients, combine it well, and divide the filling mixture among the mushroom caps. Cook in the preheated Air Fryer at 390 degrees F for 7 minutes.
Let the mushrooms cool slightly before serving.

Nutrition: Calories: 344.6, Fat: 27.6g, Carbs: 10.6g, Protein: 14.8g, Sugars: 7.6g

326. Sweet Corn Fritters with Avocado

Preparation Time: 20 minutes
Servings: 3

Cooking Time: 16 minutes

Ingredients:
- 2 cups sweet corn kernels
- 1 small-sized onion, chopped
- 1 garlic clove, minced
- 2 eggs, whisked
- 1 teaspoon baking powder
- 2 tablespoons fresh cilantro, chopped
- Sea salt and ground black pepper, to taste
- 1 avocado, peeled, pitted and diced
- 2 tablespoons sweet chili sauce

Directions: In a mixing bowl, thoroughly combine the eggs, onion, corn, cilantro, garlic, baking powder, salt, and black pepper. Shape the corn mixture into 6 patties and transfer them to the lightly greased Air Fryer basket.
Cook in the preheated Air Fry at 370 degrees for 8 minutes; turn them over and cook for 7 minutes longer.
Serve the cakes with the avocado and chili sauce.

Nutrition: Calories: 382.6, Fat: 20.8g, Carbs: 42.1g, Protein: 13g, Sugars: 8.6g

327. Greek-Style Vegetable Bake

Preparation Time: 35 minutes
Servings: 4

Cooking Time: 19 minutes

Ingredients:
- 1 eggplant, peeled and sliced
- 2 bell peppers, seeded and sliced
- 1 red onion, sliced
- 1 teaspoon fresh garlic, minced
- 4 tablespoons olive oil
- 1 teaspoon mustard
- 1 teaspoon dried oregano
- 1 teaspoon smoked paprika
- Salt and ground black pepper, to taste
- 1 tomato, sliced
- 6 ounces halloumi cheese, sliced lengthways

Directions: Start by preheating your Air Fryer to 370 degrees F. Spritz a baking pan with nonstick cooking spray. Place the eggplant, onion, peppers, and garlic on the baking pan's bottom. Add the mustard, olive oil, and spices. Transfer to the cooking basket and cook for 14 minutes.
Top with the tomatoes and cheese; increase the temperature to 390 degrees F and cook for 5 minutes. Let it sit on a cooling rack for 10 minutes before serving.

Nutrition: Calories: 295.6, Fat: 22.1g, Carbs: 15.6g, Protein: 9.8g, Sugars: 9.2g

328. Japanese Tempura Bowl

Preparation Time: 20 minutes
Servings: 3

Cooking Time: 10 minutes

Ingredients:
- 1 cup all-purpose flour
- Kosher salt and ground black pepper, to taste
- 1/2 teaspoon paprika
- 2 eggs

- 3 tablespoons soda water
- 1 cup panko crumbs
- 2 tablespoons olive oil
- 1 cup green beans
- 1 onion, cut into rings

- 1 zucchini, cut into slices
- 2 tablespoons soy sauce
- 1 tablespoon mirin
- 1 teaspoon dashi granules

Directions: In a shallow bowl, mix the flour, black pepper, salt, and paprika.
In a separate bowl, whisk the eggs and soda water.
In a third shallow bowl, combine the panko crumbs with olive oil.
Dip the vegetables in flour mixture, then in the egg mixture; lastly, roll over the panko mixture to coat evenly.
Cook in the preheated Air Fryer at 400 degrees F for 10 minutes, shaking the basket halfway through the Cooking Time. Work in batches until the vegetables are crispy and golden brown.
Then, make the sauce by whisking the mirin, soy sauce, and dashi granules.

Nutrition: Calories: 445.6, Fat: 14.2g, Carbs: 63.1g, Protein: 14.8g, Sugars: 3.2g

329. Balsamic Root Vegetables

Preparation Time: 25 minutes
Servings: 3

Cooking Time: 17 minutes

Ingredients:
- 2 potatoes, cut into 1 1/2-inch piece
- 2 carrots, cut into 1 1/2-inch piece
- 2 parsnips, cut into 1 1/2-inch piece

- 1 onion, cut into 1 1/2-inch piece
- Pink Himalayan salt and ground black pepper, to taste
- 1/4 teaspoon smoked paprika
- 1 teaspoon garlic powder

- 1/2 teaspoon dried thyme
- 1/2 teaspoon dried marjoram
- 2 tablespoons olive oil
- 2 tablespoons balsamic vinegar

Directions: Toss all ingredients in a large mixing dish.
Roast in the preheated Air Fryer at 400 degrees F for 10 minutes. Shake the basket and cook for 7 minutes more.

Nutrition: Calories: 404.6, Fat: 9.1g, Carbs: 74.1g, Protein: 8.3g, Sugars: 14.2g

330. Vegetable Braise

Preparation Time: 25 minutes
Servings: 2

Cooking Time: 20 minutes

Ingredients:
- 4 potatoes, peeled and cut into 1-inch pieces
- 1 celery root, peeled and cut into 1-inch pieces

- 1 cup winter squash
- 2 tablespoons unsalted butter, melted
- 1/2 cup chicken broth

- 1/4 cup tomato sauce
- 1 teaspoon parsley
- 1 teaspoon rosemary
- 1 teaspoon thyme

Directions: Start by preheating your Air Fryer to 370 degrees F.
Add all ingredients in a lightly greased casserole dish. Stir to combine well.
Bake in the Air Fryer for 10 minutes. Stir the vegetables with a large spoon and increase the temperature to 400 degrees F; cook for 10 minutes more.
Serve in individual bowls with a few drizzles of lemon juice.

Nutrition: Calories: 357.5, Fat: 12g, Carbs: 55.1g, Protein: 8.1g, Sugars: 7g

331. Family Vegetable Gratin

Preparation Time: 35 minutes
Servings: 4

Cooking Time: 30 minutes

Ingredients:
- 1-pound Chinese cabbage, roughly chopped
- 2 bell peppers, seeded and sliced
- 1 jalapeno pepper, seeded and sliced
- 1 onion, thickly sliced
- 2 garlic cloves, sliced
- 1/2 stick butter
- 4 tablespoons all-purpose flour
- 1 cup milk
- 1 cup cream cheese
- Sea salt and freshly ground black pepper, to taste
- 1/2 teaspoon cayenne pepper
- 1 cup Monterey Jack cheese, shredded

Directions: Heat a pan of salted water and bring to a boil. Boil the Chinese cabbage for 2 to 3 minutes. Transfer to cold water to stop the cooking process.

Place the cabbage in a lightly greased casserole dish. Add the onion, peppers, and garlic.

Next, melt the butter in a saucepan over moderate heat. Gradually add the flour and cook for 2 minutes to form a paste.

Slowly pour in the milk, stirring until a thick sauce form. Add the cream cheese.

Season with the black pepper, salt, and cayenne pepper. Add the mixture to the casserole dish.

Top with the shredded Monterey Jack cheese and bake in the preheated Air Fryer at 390 degrees F for 25 minutes.

332. Carrot and Oat Balls

Preparation Time: 25 minutes　　　　　　　　　　　　　　　　**Cooking Time: 15 minutes**
Servings: 3

Ingredients:
- 4 carrots, grated
- 1 cup rolled oats, ground
- 1 tablespoon butter, room temperature
- 1 tablespoon chia seeds
- 1/2 cup scallions, chopped
- 2 cloves garlic, minced
- 2 tablespoons tomato ketchup
- 1 teaspoon cayenne pepper
- 1/2 teaspoon sea salt
- 1/4 teaspoon ground black pepper
- 1/2 teaspoon ancho chili powder
- 1/4 cup fresh bread crumbs

Directions: Start by preheating your Air Fryer to 380 degrees F.

In a bowl, mix all ingredients until everything is well incorporated. Shape the batter into bite-sized balls.

Cook the balls for 15 minutes, shaking the basket halfway through the Cooking Time.

Nutrition: Calories: 341.6, Fat: 28.2g, Carbs: 12.1g, Protein: 9.7g, Sugars: 4.2g

333. Asparagus Salad

Preparation Time: 5 minutes　　　　　　　　　　　　　　　　**Cooking Time: 10 minutes**
Servings: 4

Ingredients:
- 1 cup baby arugula
- 1 bunch asparagus; trimmed
- 1 tbsp. balsamic vinegar
- 1 tbsp. cheddar cheese; grated
- A pinch of salt and black pepper
- Cooking spray

Directions: Put the asparagus in your air fryer's basket, grease with cooking spray, season with salt and pepper, and cook at 360°F for 10 minutes.

Take a bowl and mix the asparagus with the arugula and the vinegar, toss, divide between plates and serve hot with cheese sprinkled on top.

Nutrition: Calories: 199.5, Fat: 4.6g, Fiber: 1g, Carbs: 3.5g, Protein: 5.6g

334. Lettuce Salad with Beef Strips

Preparation Time: 10 minutes　　　　　　　　　　　　　　　　**Cooking Time: 12 minutes**
Servings: 5

Ingredients:
- 2 cup lettuce
- 10 oz. beef brisket
- 2 tbsp. sesame oil
- 1 tbsp. sunflower seeds
- 1 cucumber
- 1 tsp. ground black pepper
- 1 tsp. paprika
- 1 tsp. Italian spices
- 2 tsp. butter
- 1 tsp. dried dill
- 2 tbsp. coconut milk

Directions: Cut the beef brisket into strips.

Sprinkle the strips with the paprika, ground black pepper, and dried dill.

Preheat the air fryer to 365 F. Put the butter in the air fryer basket tray and melt it.

Then add the beef strips and cook them for 6 minutes on each side.

Meanwhile, tear the lettuce and toss it in a big salad bowl.
Crush the sunflower seeds and sprinkle over the lettuce. Chop the cucumber into the small cubes and add to the salad bowl. Then combine the sesame oil and Italian spices together. Stir the oil.
Combine the lettuce mixture with the coconut milk and stir it using 2 wooden spatulas.
When the meat is cooked – let it chill to room temperature. Add the beef strips to the salad bowl.
Stir it and sprinkle the salad with the sesame oil dressing.

Nutrition: Calories: 198.5, Fat: 12.1g, Fiber: 0.9g, Carbs: 3.1g, Protein 18.7g

Side Dishes

335. Air Fryer Buffalo Cauliflower

Preparation Time: 5 minutes
Servings: 4

Cooking Time: 15 minutes

Ingredients:
- Homemade buffalo sauce: 1/2 cup
- One head of cauliflower, cut bite-size pieces
- Butter melted: 1 tablespoon
- Olive oil
- Kosher salt & pepper, to taste

Directions: Spray cooking oil on the air fryer basket.
In a bowl, add melted butter, buffalo sauce, pepper, and salt. Mix well.
Put the cauliflower bits in the air fryer and spray the olive oil over it. Let it cook at 400 F for 7 minutes.
Remove the cauliflower from the air fryer and add it to the sauce. Coat the cauliflower well.
Put the sauce coated cauliflower back into the air fryer.
Cook at 400 F, for 7-8 minutes. Take out from the air fryer and serve with dipping sauce.

Nutrition: Calories: 100.8, Carbs: 3.7g, Protein: 3.5g, Fat: 6.5g

336. Mini Pizza

Preparation Time: 2 minutes
Servings: 1

Cooking Time: 5 minutes

Ingredients:
- Sliced olives: 1/4 cup
- One pita bread
- One tomato
- Shredded cheese: 1/2 cup

Directions: Let the air fryer preheat to 350 F.
Lay pita flat on a plate. Add cheese, slices of tomatoes, and olives.
Cook for five minutes at 350 F.

Nutrition: Calories: 343.8, Carbs: 36.7g, Protein: 18.5g, Fat: 12.7g

337. Air Fryer Egg Rolls

Preparation Time: 10 minutes
Servings: 3

Cooking Time: 20 minutes

Ingredients:
- Coleslaw mix: half bag
- Half onion
- Salt: 1/2 teaspoon
- Half cups of mushrooms
- Lean ground pork: 2 cups
- One stalk of celery
- Wrappers (egg roll)

Directions: Put a skillet over medium flame, add onion and ground pork and cook for 5-7 minutes.
Add mushrooms, coleslaw mixture, salt, and celery to skillet and cook for 5 minutes.
Lay egg roll wrapper flat and add filling (1/3 cup), roll it up, seal with water.
Spray with oil the rolls.
Put in the air fryer for 8 minutes at 400°F, flipping once halfway through.

Nutrition: Calories: 244.8, Fat: 9.5g, Carbs: 8.5g, Protein: 11.5g

338. Air Fryer Chicken Nuggets

Preparation Time: 15 minutes
Servings: 4

Cooking Time: 8 minutes

Ingredients:
- Olive oil spray
- Skinless boneless: 2 chicken breasts, cut into bite pieces
- Half tsp. of kosher salt & freshly ground black pepper to taste
- Grated parmesan cheese: 2 tablespoons

- *Italian seasoned breadcrumbs: 6 tablespoons (whole wheat)*
- *Whole wheat breadcrumbs: 2 tablespoons*
- *Olive oil: 2 teaspoons*

Directions: Let the air fryer preheat for 8 minutes, to 400°F.
In a mixing bowl, add parmesan cheese, panko, and breadcrumbs and mix well.
Sprinkle kosher salt, pepper, and olive oil on chicken, and mix well.
Take a few pieces of chicken, dunk them into breadcrumbs mixture.
Cook in an Air Fryer - sprayed with olive oil - for 8 minutes, turning halfway through.

Nutrition: Calories: 187.6, Carbs: 7.8g, Protein: 25.6g, Fat: 4.1g

339. Chicken Tenders

Preparation Time: 10 minutes
Servings: 3

Cooking Time: 15 minutes

Ingredients:
- *Chicken tenderloins: 4 cups*
- *Eggs: one*
- *Superfine Almond Flour: ½ cup*
- *Powdered Parmesan cheese: ½ cup*
- *Kosher Sea salt: ½ teaspoon*
- *(1-teaspoon) freshly ground black pepper*
- *(1/2 teaspoon) Cajun seasoning*

Directions: On a small plate, pour the beaten egg.
In a bowl, mix almond flour, powered Parmesan, salt, black pepper and seasoning.
Dip each tender in egg and then in flour mixture.
Using the fork to take out the tender and place it in your air fryer basket.
Spray the air fryer and tenders with oil spray.
Cook for 12 minutes at 350°F. Raise temperature to 400°F and continue to cook for 3 minutes.

Nutrition: Calories: 279.8, Proteins: 20.6g, Carbs: 5.4g, Fat: 9.8g, Fiber 5g

340. Kale & Celery Crackers

Preparation Time: 10 minutes
Servings: 6

Cooking Time: 20 minutes

Ingredients:
- *One cups flax seed, ground*
- *1 cups flax seed, soaked overnight and drained*
- *2 bunches kale, chopped*
- *1 bunch basil, chopped*
- *½ bunch celery, chopped*
- *2 garlic cloves, minced*
- *1/3 cup olive oil*

Directions: Mix the ground flaxseed with the basil, kale, celery, and garlic in your food processor and mix well.
Add the oil and soaked flaxseed, then mix again.
Scatter in the pan of your air fryer, break into medium crackers and cook for 20 minutes at 380 degrees F.

Nutrition: Calories: 142.7, Fat: 1g, Fiber: 2g, Carbs: 7.8g, Protein: 4.5g

341. Air Fryer Spanakopita Bites

Preparation Time: 10 minutes
Servings: 4

Cooking Time: 12 minutes

Ingredients:
- *4 sheets phyllo dough*
- *Baby spinach leaves: 2 cups*
- *Grated Parmesan cheese: 2 tablespoons*
- *Low-fat cottage cheese: 1/4 cup*
- *Dried oregano: 1 teaspoon*
- *Feta cheese: 6 tbsp. crumbled*
- *Water: 2 tablespoons*
- *One egg white only*
- *Lemon zest: 1 teaspoon*
- *Cayenne pepper: 1/8 teaspoon*
- *Olive oil: 1 tablespoon*
- *Kosher salt and freshly ground black pepper: 1/4 teaspoon, each*

Directions: In a pot over high heat, add water and spinach, cook until wilted.
Drain it and cool for ten minutes. Squeeze out excess moisture.
In a bowl, mix Parmesan cheese, cottage cheese, egg white, cayenne pepper, spinach, oregano, salt, black pepper, feta cheese, and zest. Mix it well.
Lay one phyllo sheet on a flat surface. Spray with oil. Add the second sheet of phyllo on top—spray oil. Add a total of 4 oiled sheets.
Form 16 strips from these four oiled sheets. Add one tbsp. of filling in one strip. Roll it around the filling.

Spray the air fryer basket with oil. Put eight bites in the basket and cook for 12 minutes at 375°F until golden brown. Flip halfway through.

Nutrition: Calories: 81.7, Fat: 3.8g, Protein: 3.6g, Carbs: 6.7g

342. Air Fryer Onion Rings

Preparation Time: 105 minutes   **Cooking Time: 10 minutes**
Servings: 4

Ingredients:
- 1 egg whisked
- One large onion
- Whole-wheat breadcrumbs: 1 and 1/2 cup
- Smoked paprika: 1 teaspoon
- Flour: 1 cup
- Garlic powder: 1 teaspoon
- Buttermilk: 1 cup
- Kosher salt and pepper to taste

Directions: Cut the stems of the onion. Then cut into half-inch-thick rounds.
In a bowl, add flour, paprika, garlic powder, pepper, and salt. Then add egg and buttermilk. Mix to combine.
In another bowl, add the breadcrumbs.
Coat the onions in buttermilk mix, then in breadcrumbs mix. Freeze these breaded onions for 15 minutes.
Spray the fryer basket with oil spray.
Put onions in the air fryer basket in one single layer. Spray the onion with cooking oil.
Cook at 370 degrees F for 10-12 minutes. Flip only, if necessary.

Nutrition: Calories: 204.8, Fat: 5.1g, Carbs: 7.2g, Protein: 18.5g

343. Air Fryer Squash

Preparation Time: 5 minutes   **Cooking Time: 10 minutes**
Servings: 2

Ingredients:
- Olive oil: 1/2 Tablespoon
- One delicata squash
- Salt: 1/2 teaspoon
- Rosemary: 1/2 teaspoon

Directions: Chop the squash in slices of 1/4 thickness. Discard the seeds.
In a bowl, add olive oil, rosemary, salt, with squash slices. Mix well.
Cook the squash for ten minutes at 400 F, flipping the squash halfway through.

Nutrition: Calories: 68.7, Fat: 3.7g, Carbs: 8.7g, Protein: 1.3g

344. Zucchini Parmesan Chips

Preparation Time: 10 minutes   **Cooking Time: 8 minutes**
Servings: 6

Ingredients:
- Seasoned, whole wheat Breadcrumbs: ½ cup
- Thinly slices of two zucchinis
- Parmesan Cheese: ½ cup (grated)
- 1 Egg whisked
- Kosher salt and pepper, to taste

Directions: Pat dry the zucchini slices so that no moisture remains.
In a bowl, whisk the egg with a few tsp. of water, pepper and salt.
In another bowl, mix the grated cheese and breadcrumbs.
Coat zucchini slices in egg mix then in breadcrumbs. Put all in a rack and spray with olive oil.
Add in the air fryer In a single layer, and cook for 8 minutes at 350 F.
Add salt and pepper on top if needed.

Nutrition: Calories: 100.3, Fat: 7.8g, Carbs: 5.4g, Protein: 10.8g

345. Air Fryer Roasted Corn

Preparation Time: 10 minutes   **Cooking Time: 10 minutes**
Servings: 4

120

Ingredients:
- 4 corn ears
- Olive oil: 2 to 3 teaspoons
- Kosher salt and pepper to taste

Directions: Clean the corn, wash, and pat dry. Fit in the basket of air fryer, cut if need to. Top with olive oil, kosher salt, and pepper. Cook for ten minutes at 400 F.

Nutrition: Calories: 27.5, Fat: 1.9g, Carbs: 0g, Protein: 7.2g

346. Air-Fried Spinach Frittata

Preparation Time: 5 minutes
Servings: 4
Cooking Time: 10 minutes

Ingredients:
- 1/3 cup of packed spinach
- One small chopped red onion
- Shredded mozzarella cheese
- Three eggs
- Salt, pepper
- Olive oil

Directions: Let the air fryer preheat to 375°F.
In a skillet over a medium flame, add oil and onion, and cook until translucent. Add spinach and sauté until half cooked.
Beat eggs and season with salt and pepper—mix spinach mixture in it.
Cook in the air fryer for 8 minutes.

Nutrition: Calories: 123.5, Fat: 11.2g, Carbs: 13.8g, Protein: 17.4g

347. Air Fryer Sweet Potato

Preparation Time: 5 minutes
Servings: 2
Cooking Time: 8 minutes

Ingredients:
- One sweet potato
- Pinch of kosher salt and freshly ground black pepper
- 1 tsp olive oil

Directions: Cut the peeled sweet potato in French fries. Coat with salt, pepper, and oil.
Cook in the air fryer for 8 minutes, at 400 degrees. Cook potatoes in batches, in single layers.
Shake once or twice. Serve with your favorite sauce.

Nutrition: Calories: 59.6, Carbs: 12.5g, Protein: 1.5g, Fat: 5.4g

348. Air Fryer Kale Chips

Preparation Time: 3 minutes
Servings: 2
Cooking Time: 5 minutes

Ingredients:
- One bunch of kale
- Half tsp. of garlic powder
- One tsp. of olive oil
- Half tsp. of salt

Directions: Let the air fryer preheat to 370 degrees F.
Cut the kale into small pieces without the stem.
In a bowl, add all ingredients with kale pieces.
Add kale to the air fryer and cook for three minutes. Toss it and cook for two minutes more.

Nutrition: Calories: 36.9, Carbs: 5.4g, Protein: 3.3g, Fat: 0.9g

349. Crispy Brussels sprouts

Preparation Time: 5 minutes
Servings: 4
Cooking Time: 15 minutes

Ingredients:
- Almonds sliced: 1/4 cup
- Brussel sprouts: 2 cups
- Kosher salt
- Parmesan cheese: 1/4 cup grated
- Olive oil: 2 Tablespoons
- Everything bagel seasoning: 2 Tablespoons

Directions: In a saucepan, add Brussel sprouts with two cups of water and let it cook over medium flame for ten minutes. Drain the sprouts and cut in half.

In a mixing bowl, add sliced brussel sprout with parmesan cheese, crushed almonds, oil, salt, and everything bagel seasoning. Completely coat the sprouts.

Cook in the air fryer for 12-15 minutes at 375 °F.

Nutrition: Calories: 154.5, Carbs: 2.7g, Protein: 5.8g, Fat: 2.7g

350. Vegetable Spring Rolls

Preparation Time: 10 minutes   **Cooking Time: 15 minutes**
Servings: 4

Ingredients:
- Toasted sesame seeds
- Large carrots – grated
- Spring roll wrappers
- One egg white
- Gluten-free soy sauce, a dash
- Half cabbage: sliced
- Olive oil: 2 tbsp.

Directions: In a pan over high flame heat, 2 tbsp. of oil and sauté the chopped vegetables. Then add soy sauce. Turn off the heat and add toasted sesame seeds.

Lay spring roll wrappers flat on a surface and add egg white with a brush on the sides.

Add some vegetable mix in the wrapper and fold.

Spray the spring rolls with oil spray and air fry for 8 minutes at 400°F. Serve with dipping sauce.

Nutrition: Calories: 128.2, Fat: 16.7g, Carbs: 7.8g, Protein: 12.4g

351. Zucchini Gratin

Preparation Time: 10 minutes   **Cooking Time: 15 minutes**
Servings: 4

Ingredient:
- Olive oil: 1 tablespoon
- Chopped fresh parsley: 1 tablespoon
- Whole wheat bread crumbs: 2 tablespoons
- Medium zucchini
- Freshly ground black pepper & kosher salt to taste
- Grated Parmesan cheese: 4 tablespoons

Directions: Let the air fryer preheat to 375°F.

Cut zucchini in half, and a further cut in eight pieces. Place in the air fryer, but do not start frying.

In a bowl, add cheese, parsley, black pepper, salt, bread crumbs, and oil. Mix well.

Add the mixture on top of the zucchini. Then cook the pieces for 15 minutes.

Nutrition: Calories: 80.9, Protein: 3.9g, Carbs: 5.8g, Fat: 4.9g

352. Air Fryer Bacon-Wrapped Jalapeno Poppers

Preparation Time: 10 minutes   **Cooking Time: 8 minutes**
Servings: 10

Ingredients:
- Cream cheese: 1/3 cup
- Ten jalapenos
- Thin bacon: 5 strips

Directions: Wash and pat dry the jalapenos. Cut them in half and take out the seeds.

Add the cream cheese in the middle.

Let the air fryer preheat to 370°F.

Cut the bacon strips in half. Wrap the cream cheese filled jalapenos with slices of bacon, securing with a toothpick.

Place the wrapped jalapenos in the air fryer, cook at 370°F and cook for 6-8 minutes.

Nutrition: Calories: 75.8, Carbs: 1g, Protein: 2.3g, Fat: 6.8g

353. Air Fryer Zucchini Chips

Preparation Time: 10 minutes
Servings: 2

Cooking Time: 10 minutes

Ingredients:
- Parmesan Cheese: 3 Tbsp.
- Garlic Powder: 1/4 tsp
- Zucchini: 1 Cup (thin slices)
- Corn Starch: 1/4 Cup
- Onion Powder: 1/4 tsp
- Salt: 1/4 tsp
- Whole wheat Bread Crumbs: 1/2 Cup
- 2 beaten eggs

Directions: Preheat the Air Fryer to 390°F.
Cut the zucchini into thin slices, like chips.
In a food processor bowl, mix garlic powder, parmesan cheese, bread crumbs, salt, and onion powder. Blend into finer pieces.
In three separate bowls, add corn starch in one, egg mix in another bowl, and breadcrumb mixture in the other bowl.
Coat zucchini chips into corn starch mix, in egg mix, then in bread crumbs.
Spray the air fryer basket with olive oil.
Add breaded zucchini chips in a single layer in the air fryer and spray with olive oil.
Air fry for ten minutes at preheated temperature.

Nutrition: Calories: 218.7, Fat: 27.1g, Carbs: 10.9g, Protein: 14.5g

354. Air Fryer Avocado Fries

Preparation Time: 10 minutes
Servings: 2

Cooking Time: 10 minutes

Ingredients:
- One avocado
- One egg
- Whole wheat bread crumbs: 1/2 cup
- Salt: 1/2 teaspoon

Directions: Cut the avocado into wedges.
In a bowl, beat egg with salt. In another bowl, add the bread crumbs.
Coat wedges in egg, then in crumbs.
Air fry them at 400°F for 8-10 minutes. Toss halfway through.

Nutrition: Calories: 250.5, Carbs: 18.7g, Protein: 6.5g, Fat: 16.5g

355. Avocado Egg Rolls

Preparation Time: 15 minutes
Servings: 10

Cooking Time: 6 minutes

Ingredients:
- Ten egg roll wrappers
- Diced sundried tomatoes: ¼ cup oil drained
- Avocados, cut in cube
- Red onion: 2/3 cup chopped
- 1/3 cup chopped cilantro
- Kosher salt and freshly ground black pepper
- Two small limes: juice

Directions: In a bowl, add pepper, sundried tomatoes, lime juice, cilantro, avocado, onion, and salt. Then mix well.
Lay egg roll wrapper flat on a surface, add ¼ cup of filling in the wrapper's bottom.
Seal with water and make it into a roll. Spray the rolls with olive oil.
Cook at 400°F in the air fryer for six minutes. Turn halfway through.

Nutrition: Calories: 159.6, Fat: 18.7g, Carbs: 5.1g, Protein: 19.8g

356. Cheesy Bell Pepper Eggs

Preparation Time: 10 minutes
Servings: 4

Cooking Time: 15 minutes

Ingredients:
- 4 medium green bell peppers
- 3 ounces cooked ham, chopped
- 1/4 medium onion, peeled and chopped
- 8 large eggs
- 1 cup mild Cheddar cheese

Directions: Cut each bell pepper from its tops. Pick the seeds with a small knife and the white membranes. Place onion and ham into each pepper.

Break two eggs into each chili pepper. Cover with 1/4 cup of peppered cheese. Put the basket into the air fryer.

Set the temperature to 390 ° F and change the timer for 15 minutes.

Peppers will be tender when fully fried, and the eggs will be solid. Serve hot.

Nutrition: Calories: 313.8, Protein: 25.2g, Fiber: 1.7g, Fat: 18.2g, Carbs: 5.9g

357. Air Fryer Egg Cups

Preparation Time: 10 minutes
Servings: 4

Cooking Time: 10 minutes

Ingredients:
- Toasted bread: 4 slices (whole-wheat)
- Cooking spray, nonstick
- Large eggs: 4
- Margarine: 1 and a half tbsp. (trans-fat free)
- Ham: 1 slice
- Salt: 1/8 tsp
- Black pepper: 1/8 tsp

Directions: Let the air fryer Preheat to 375°F, with the air fryer basket.

Take four ramekins, spray with cooking spray. Trim off the crusts from bread, add margarine to one side.

Put the bread down, into a ramekin, margarine-side in. Press it in the cup.

Cut the ham in strips, half-inch thick, and add on top of the bread.

Add one egg to the ramekins. Add salt and pepper.

Put the custard cups in the air fryer. Air fry at 375 F for 10 minutes.

Nutrition: Calories: 149.8, Fat: 7.8g, Carbs: 5.6g, Protein: 12.3g

358. Air Fryer Lemon-Garlic Tofu

Preparation Time: 20 minutes
Servings: 2

Cooking Time: 15 minutes

Ingredients:
- Cooked quinoa 2 cups
- Lemons: two zest and juice
- Sea salt & white pepper: to taste
- Tofu: one block - pressed and sliced into half pieces
- Garlic – minced: 2 cloves

Directions: Add the tofu into a deep dish.

In another small bowl, add the lemon zest, lemon juice, garlic, salt, and pepper.

Pour this marinade over tofu in the dish. Let it marinate for 15 minutes.

Add the tofu to the air fryer basket and air fry at 370°F for 15 minutes. Shake the basket after 8 minutes of cooking.

In a big deep bowl, add the cooked quinoa with the lemon-garlic tofu.

Nutrition: Calories: 186.8, Fat: 8.7g, Protein: 21.3g, Carbs: 7.7g

359. Sweet Potato Cauliflower Patties

Preparation Time: 20 minutes
Servings: 7

Cooking Time: 20 minutes

Ingredients:
- 1 green onion, chopped
- 1 large sweet potato, peeled
- 1 tsp. garlic, minced
- 1 cup cilantro leaves
- 2 cup cauliflower florets
- 1/4 tsp. ground black pepper
- 1/4 tsp. salt
- 1/4 cup sunflower seeds
- 1/4 tsp. cumin
- 1/4 cup ground flaxseed
- 1/2 tsp. red chili powder
- 2 tbsp. ranch seasoning mix
- 2 tbsp. arrowroot starch

Directions: Cut peeled sweet potato into small pieces, then place them in a food processor and pulse until pieces are broken up.

Then add the garlic, cauliflower florets, onion, and pulse; add the remaining ingredients and pulse more until well combined.

Tip the mixture into a bowl, shape it into 7 1 1/2-inch thick patties, each about 1/4 cup, then place them on a baking sheet and freeze for 10 minutes.

Switch on the air fryer, insert the fryer basket, and grease it with olive oil; close the lid, set the fryer at 400°F, and preheat for 10 minutes.
Open the fryer, add patties to it in a single layer, and cook for 20 minutes; flipping the patties halfway through the frying.
When the air fryer beeps, open the lid, transfer the patties onto a serving plate, and keep them warm.
Prepare the continuing patties in the same way and serve.

Nutrition: Calories: 84.5, Carbs: 8.7g, Fat: 2.8g, Protein: 3.2g, Fiber: 3.5g

360. Asparagus Avocado Soup

Preparation Time: 10 minutes   **Cooking Time: 15 minutes**
Servings: 4

Ingredients:
- *1 avocado, peeled, pitted, cubed*
- *12 oz. asparagus*
- *1/2 tsp. ground black pepper*
- *1 tsp. garlic powder*
- *1 tsp. sea salt*
- *2 tbsp. olive oil, divided*
- *1/2 lemon, juiced*
- *2 cups vegetable stock*

Directions: Set the fryer to 425°F, and preheat for 5 minutes.
Meanwhile, place the asparagus in a shallow dish, sprinkle with 1 tbsp. of oil, garlic powder, salt, and black pepper, and toss until mixed.
Open the fryer, add the asparagus, and cook for 10 minutes until roasted, shaking halfway through the frying.
Transfer asparagus to a food processor. Add the remaining ingredients into a food processor and pulse until well combined and smooth.
Tip the soup in a saucepan, pour in the water if it is too thick, and heat it over medium-low heat for 5 minutes until thoroughly heated. Ladle the soup into bowls and serve.

Nutrition: Calories: 207.8, Carbs: 12.8g, Fat: 15.4g, Protein: 6.3g, Fiber: 5g

Desserts

361. Tahini Oatmeal Chocolate Chunk Cookies

Preparation Time: 10 minutes
Servings: 8

Cooking Time: 5 minutes

Ingredients:
- 1/3 cup of tahini
- 1/4 cup of walnuts
- 1/4 cup of maple syrup
- 1/4 cup of Chocolate chunks
- 1/4 tsp of sea salt
- Two tablespoons of almond flour
- One teaspoon of vanilla
- 1 cup of gluten-free oat flakes
- One teaspoon of cinnamon

Directions: Let the air fryer Preheat to 350 F.
In a big bowl, add cinnamon, the tahini, maple syrup, salt, and vanilla. Mix well. Then add in the walnuts, oat flakes, and almond flour. Then fold the chocolate chunks.
Take a full tablespoon of mixture, separate into eight amounts.
Line the air fryer basket with parchment paper and place cookies in one single layer.
Let them cook for 5-6 minutes at 350°F.

Nutrition: Calories: 185, Protein: 12.5g, Carbs: 17.9g, Fat: 11.4g

362. Sugar-Free Carrot Cake

Preparation Time: 15 minutes
Servings: 8

Cooking Time: 30 minutes

Ingredients:
- All-Purpose Flour: 1 ¼ cups
- Pumpkin Pie Spice: 1 tsp
- Baking Powder: one teaspoon
- Splenda: 3/4 cup
- Carrots: 2 cups–grated
- 2 Eggs
- Baking Soda: half teaspoon
- Canola Oil: ¾ cup

Directions: Let the air fryer preheat to 350 F.
Spray the cake pan with oil spray, and add a pinch of flour over that. In a bowl, combine the flour, baking powder, pumpkin pie spice, and baking soda.
In another bowl, mix oil, the eggs, and Splenda. Now combine the dry to wet ingredients. Add in the grated carrots.
Add the cake batter to the greased cake pan. Place in the basket of the air fryer. Let it Air fry for half an hour.

Nutrition: Calories: 285.8, Fat: 20.8g, Carbs: 17.8g, Protein: 4.3g

363. Low Carb Peanut Butter Cookies

Preparation Time: 20 minutes
Servings: 24 cookies

Cooking Time: 40 minutes

Ingredients:
- All-natural 100% peanut butter: 1 cup
- One whisked egg
- Liquid stevia drops: 1 teaspoon
- Sugar alternative: 1 cup

Directions: Mix all the ingredients into a dough and make 24 balls.
On a cutting board, press the dough balls with the help of a fork to form a crisscross pattern.
Add six cookies to the basket of air fryer in a single layer. Make sure the cookies are separated from each other. Cook in batches.
Let them Air Fry, for 8-10 minutes, at 325°F.
Take the basket out from the air fryer and let the cookies cool for one minute, then with care, take the cookies out.
Keep baking the rest of the cookies in batches. Let them cool completely and serve.

Nutrition: Calories: 197.8, Protein: 9.8g, Carbs: 5.9g, Fat: 15.8g

364. Grain-free Lava Cakes in Air Fryer

Preparation Time: 5 minutes
Servings: 2

Cooking Time: 12 minutes

Ingredients:

- Two large eggs
- Half cup of dark chocolate chips
- 2 tbsp. of coconut flour
- Two tablespoons of sugar substitute
- A dash of sea salt
- Half teaspoon of baking soda
- Butter and cocoa powder for two small ramekins
- 1/4 cup of butter

Directions: Let the air fryer preheat to 370 degrees F.

Grease the ramekins with soft butter and sprinkle with cocoa powder. It will stick to the butter. Turn the ramekins upside down, so excess cocoa powder will fall out. Set it aside.

In a microwave, safe bowl, melt the butter and chocolate chips together, stir every 15 seconds. Make sure to mix well to combine.

In a large bowl, crack the eggs and whisk with sugar substitute, mix well. Add in the salt, baking soda, and coconut flour. Fold everything.

Add the melted chocolate chip and butter mixture. Mix well, so everything combines. Pour the batter in those two prepared ramekins.

Let them air fry for ten minutes. Then take them out from the air fryer and let it cool for 3-4 minutes.

Nutrition: Calories: 215.8, Protein: 10.2g, Carbs: 13.5g, Fat: 12.2g

365. Raspberry Cookies in Air Fryer

Preparation Time: 15 minutes
Servings: 10

Cooking Time: 7 minutes

Ingredients:

- One teaspoon of baking powder
- One cup of almond flour
- Three tablespoons of natural low-calorie sweetener
- One large egg
- Three and a half tablespoons raspberry (reduced-sugar) preserves
- Four tablespoons of softened cream cheese

Directions: In a large bowl, add egg, flour, sweetener, baking powder, and cream cheese, mix well until a dough wet forms. Chill the dough in the fridge for 20 minutes.

Let the air fryer preheat to 400°F, add the parchment paper to the air fryer basket.

Make ten balls from the dough and put them in the prepared air fryer basket.

With your clean hands, make an indentation from your thumb in the center of every cookie. Add one teaspoon of the raspberry preserve in the thumb hole.

Bake in the air fryer for seven minutes.

Let the cookies cool completely in the parchment paper for almost 15 minutes.

Nutrition: Calories: 110.2, Protein: 3.8g, Carbs: 8.3g, Fat: 8.8g

366. Banana Muffins in Air Fryer

Preparation Time: 10 minutes
Servings: 8

Cooking Time: 30 minutes

Ingredients:
Wet Mix:

- 3 tbsp. of milk
- Four Cavendish size, ripe bananas
- Half cup sugar alternative
- One teaspoon of vanilla essence
- Two large eggs

Dry Mix:

- One teaspoon of baking powder
- One and a 1/4 cup of whole wheat flour
- One teaspoon of baking soda
- One teaspoon of cinnamon
- 2 tbsp. of cocoa powder
- One teaspoon of salt

Directions: With the fork, in a bowl, mash up the bananas, add all the wet ingredients to it, and mix well.

Sift all the dry ingredients so they combine well. Add into the wet ingredients. Carefully fold both ingredients together. Then add in the chopped walnuts, and slices of dried up fruits.

Let the air fryer preheat to 260°F.

Spray muffin cups with oil, and add the batter into. Air fryer for at least half an hour.
Take out from the air fryer and let them cool down before serving.

Nutrition: Calories: 210.8, Protein: 12.5g, Carbs: 17.5g, Fat: 11.5g

367. Berry Cheesecake

Preparation Time: 10 minutes   **Cooking Time: 50 minutes**
Servings: 8

Ingredients:
- Half cup raspberries
- Two blocks of softened cream cheese, 8 ounce
- Vanilla extract: 1 teaspoon
- 1/4 cup of strawberries
- Two eggs
- 1/4 cup of blackberries
- One cup and 2 tbsp. of sweetener

Directions: In a big mixing bowl, whip the sweetener and cream cheese, mix with a whip until smooth and creamy. Then add vanilla extract and eggs, again mix well.
In a food processor, pulse the berries and fold into the cream cheese, mix with two extra tbsp. of sweetener.
Take a springform pan and spray the oil, pour in the mixture.
Put the pan in the air fryer, and let it cook for 50 minutes at 300°F.
Take out from the air fryer and cool a bit before chilling in the fridge. Keep in the fridge for 2-4 hours.

Nutrition: Calories: 223.8, Protein: 12.5g, Carbs: 16.5g, Fat: 15.4g

368. Air Fryer Brownies

Preparation Time: 10 minutes   **Cooking Time: 10 minutes**
Servings: 2

Ingredients:
- 2 tbsp. of Baking Chips
- 1/3 cup of Almond Flour
- One Egg
- Half teaspoon of Baking Powder
- 3 tbsp. of Powdered Sweetener
- 2 tbsp. of Cocoa Powder (Unsweetened)
- 2 tbsp. of chopped Pecans
- 4 tbsp. of melted Butter

Directions: Let the air fryer preheat to 350°F.
In a large bowl, add cocoa powder, powdered sweetener, almond flour, and baking powder, give it a good mix.
Add melted butter and crack in the egg in the dry ingredients. Mix well until combined and smooth.
Fold in the chopped pecans and baking chips.
Take two ramekins to grease them well with softened butter. Add the melted batter.
Bake for ten minutes in the Air Fryer, making sure to place them as far from the heat source from the top.
Take the brownies out from the air fryer and let them cool for five minutes.

Nutrition: Calories: 200.8, Protein: 8.3g, Carbs: 12,.8g, Fat: 9.8g

369. Eggless Cake

Preparation Time: 5 minutes   **Cooking Time: 10 minutes**
Servings: 8

Ingredients:
- Olive Oil: 2 Tbsp.
- All-Purpose Flour: 1/4 Cup
- Cocoa Powder: 2 Tbsp.
- Baking Soda: 1/8 Tsp
- Sugar substitute: 3 Tbsp.
- One tablespoon of Warm Water
- Milk: 3 Tbsp.
- Two Drops of Vanilla Extract
- 4 Raw Almonds for decoration – roughly chopped
- A Pinch of Salt

Directions: Let the air fryer preheat to 370°F for two minutes.
In a large bowl, add sugar substitute, some water, milk, and oil. Whisk until a smooth batter forms.
Then add salt, cocoa powder, all-purpose flour, and baking soda, sift them into wet ingredients, and mix to form a paste.
Spray a four-inch baking pan with oil and pour the batter into it. Then add in the chopped up almonds on top of it.
Put the baking pan in the preheated air fryer. And cook for ten minutes.
Take out from the air fryer and let it cool completely before slicing.

Nutrition: Calories: 120.5, Protein: 2.2g, Carbs: 18.2g, Fat: 7.3g

370. Air Fried Chocolate Soufflé

Preparation Time: 15 minutes
Servings: 2
Cooking Time: 15 minutes

Ingredients:

- Milk: 1/3 cup
- Butter soft to melted: 2 tbsp.
- Flour: 1 tbsp.
- Splenda: 2 tbsp.
- One Egg Yolk
- Sugar-Free Chocolate Chips: 1/4 cup
- Two egg whites
- Half teaspoon of cream of tartare
- Half teaspoon of Vanilla Extract

Directions: Grease the ramekins with softened butter. Sprinkle with Splenda, make sure to cover them.
Let the air fryer preheat to 325-330 F.
Melt the chocolate in a microwave-safe bowl. Mix every 30 seconds until fully melted.
Melt the one and a half tablespoons of butter over low-medium heat, in a small-sized skillet.
Once the butter has melted, then whisk in the flour. Keep whisking until thickened. Then turn the heat off.
Add the egg whites with cream of tartar, with the whisk attachment, in a stand mixer, mix until peaks forms.
Meanwhile, combine the ingredients in a melted chocolate bowl, add the flour mixture and melted butter to chocolate, and blend. Add in the egg yolks, vanilla extract, remaining Splenda.
Fold the egg white peaks with the ingredients into the bowl.
Add the mix into ramekins about 3/4 full of five-ounce ramekins.
Let it bake for 12-14 minutes.

Nutrition: Calories: 287.2, Protein: 6.2g, Carbs: 4.7g, Fat: 23.9g

371. Air Fryer Apple Fritter

Preparation Time: 10 minutes
Servings: 3
Cooking Time: 14 minutes

Ingredients:

- Half apple peeled, finely chopped
- Half cup of All-Purpose Flour
- One teaspoon of Baking Powder
- 1/4 teaspoon of Kosher Salt
- Half teaspoon of Ground Cinnamon
- 2 Tbsp. of sugar alternative
- 1/8 teaspoon of Ground Nutmeg
- 3 Tbsp. of Greek Yogurt (Fat-Free)
- One tablespoon of Butter

For the glaze:

- Two Tbsp. Of Powdered Sweetener
- Half tablespoon of Water

Directions: In a mixing bowl, add nutmeg, flour, baking powder, sugar alternative, cinnamon, and salt. Mix it well. With the help of a fork, slice the butter until crumbly.
Add the chopped apple and coat well, then add fat-free Greek yogurt.
Keep stirring until everything together, and a crumbly dough forms.
Put the dough on a clean surface and with your hands, knead it into a ball form.
Flatten the dough in an oval shape about a half-inch thick. It is okay, even if it's not the perfect size or shape.
Spray the basket of the air fryer with cooking spray generously. Put the dough in the air fryer for 12-14 minutes at 375ºF and cook until light golden brown.
For making the glaze mix, the ingredients, and with the help of a brush, pour over the apple fritter when it comes out from the air fryer. Slice and serve after cooling for 5 minutes.

Nutrition: Calories: 200.3, Protein: 9.8g, Carbs: 12.5g, Fat: 10.2g

372. Air Fryer Blueberry Muffins

Preparation Time: 10 minutes
Servings: 8
Cooking Time: 12 minutes

Ingredients:

- Half cup of sugar alternative
- One and 1/3 cup of flour
- 1/3 cup of oil
- Two teaspoons of baking powder
- 1/4 teaspoon of salt
- One egg
- Half cup of milk
- 2/3 cup of frozen and thawed blueberries, or fresh

Directions: Let the air fryer preheat to 330 F.
In a large bowl, sift together sugar alternative, baking powder, salt, and flour. Mix well.

In another bowl, add milk, oil, and egg. Mix it well.

Combine the dry ingredients to the egg mixture, and mix. Add the blueberries and pour the mixture into muffin paper cups.

Cook muffins for 12-14 minutes and let them cool before serving.

Nutrition: Calories: 210.5, Protein: 9.2g, Carbs: 12.8g, Fat: 9.8g

373. Air Fryer Sugar-Free Lemon Cookies

Preparation Time: 5 minutes   **Cooking Time: 5 minutes**
Servings: 24 cookies

Ingredients:
- *Half teaspoon of salt*
- *Half cup of coconut flour*
- *Half cup of unsalted butter softened*
- *Half teaspoon of liquid vanilla stevia*
- *Half cup of swerve granular sweetener*
- *One tablespoon lemon juice*
- *Two egg yolks*

For icing:
- *Three tsp of lemon juice*
- *2/3 cup of Swerve confectioner's sweetener*

Directions: In a stand mixer bowl, add coconut flour, salt and Swerve. Mix until well combined.

Then add the butter (softened) to the dry ingredients, and mix well. Add all the remaining ingredients but do not add in the yolks yet. Adjust the seasoning of lemon flavor and sweetness to your liking.

Add the yolks and combine well.

Lay a big piece of plastic wrap on a flat surface, put the batter in the center, roll around the dough and make it into a log form, for almost 12 inches. Keep this log in the fridge for 2-3 hours or overnight, if possible.

Let the oven preheat to 325°F. Spray the air fryer basket, and take the log out from plastic wrap.

Cut in 1/4 inch cookies, place them in the air fryer basket, but do not overcrowd the basket.

Bake for 3-5 minutes. Let it cool in the basket for two minutes, then take out.

Once all cookies are baked, pour the icing over.

Nutrition: Calories: 65.4, Protein: 1.3g, Carbs: 1.9g, Fat: 5.6g

374. Cheesecake Bites

Preparation Time: 40 minutes   **Cooking Time: 2 minutes**
Servings: 4

Ingredients:
- *½ cup almond flour*
- *½ cup and 2 tbsp. erythritol sweetener, divided*
- *4 oz. cream cheese, reduced-fat, softened*
- *½ tsp. vanilla extract, unsweetened*
- *2 tbsp. heavy cream, reduced-fat, divided*

Directions: Place the softened cream cheese in a bowl, add heavy cream, vanilla, and ½ cup sweetener, and whisk using an electric mixer until smooth.

Scoop the mixture on a baking sheet lined with a parchment sheet, then place it in the freezer for 30 minutes until firm.

Place flour in a small bowl and stir in the remaining sweetener.

Turn on the air fryer, insert the fryer basket, grease it with olive oil. Then close it with its lid, set the fryer at 350°F, and preheat for 5 minutes.

In the meantime, cut the cheesecake mix into bite-size pieces and coat it with almond flour mixture.

Open the fryer, add cheesecake bites, and cook for 2 minutes.

Serve straight away.

Nutrition: Calories: 197.8, Carbs: 5.6g, Fat: 17.9g, Protein: 3.3g, Fiber: 0g

375. Coconut Pie

Preparation Time: 5 minutes   **Cooking Time: 45 minutes**
Servings: 6

Ingredients:

- ½ cup coconut flour
- ½ cup erythritol sweetener
- 1 cup shredded coconut, unsweetened, divided
- ¼ cup butter, unsalted
- 1 ½ tsp. vanilla extract, unsweetened
- eggs, pastured
- 1 ½ cups milk, low-fat, unsweetened
- ¼ cup shredded coconut, toasted

Directions: Set the air fryer at 350°F, and preheat for 5 minutes.
Meanwhile, place all the ingredients in a bowl and whisk until blended and smooth batter comes together.
Take a 6-inches pie pan, grease with oil, then pour in the prepared batter and smooth the top.
Open the fryer, place the pie pan in it, and cook for 45 minutes until pie has set and inserted a toothpick into the pie slide out clean.
Let pie cool until garnish with toasted coconut Then cut into slices and serve.

Nutrition: Calories: 235.8, Carbs: 15.6g, Fat: 15.7g, Protein: 3.3g, Fiber: 2g

376. Crustless Cheesecake

Preparation Time: 5 minutes
Servings: 2

Cooking Time: 10 minutes

Ingredients:

- 16 oz. cream cheese, reduced-fat, softened
- 2 tbsp. sour cream, reduced-fat
- ¾ cup erythritol sweetener
- 1 tsp. vanilla extract, unsweetened
- 2 eggs, pastured
- ½ tsp. lemon juice

Directions: Set the air fryer at 350°F, and preheat for 5 minutes.
Take two 4 inches of springform pans, grease them with oil, and set them aside.
Crack the eggs in a bowl and then whisk in erythritol, lemon juice, and vanilla until smooth.
Whisk in cream cheese and sour cream until blended and then divide the mixture evenly between prepared pans.
Place springform pans in the air fryer and cook for 10 minutes.
Take out the cakes, and refrigerate for 3 hours before serving.

Nutrition: Calories: 317.9, Carbs: 0.9g, Fat: 29.1g, Protein: 12.1g, Fiber: 0g

377. Chocolate Cake

Preparation Time: 5 minutes
Servings: 6

Cooking Time: 15 minutes

Ingredients:

- ¼ cup coconut flour
- 1 tsp. baking powder
- ⅓ cup Truvia sweetener
- ¼ tsp. salt
- 2 tbsp. cocoa powder, unsweetened
- 1 tsp. vanilla extract, unsweetened
- 2 tbsp. butter, unsalted, melted
- eggs, pastured
- ½ cup heavy whipping cream, reduced-fat

Directions: Set the air fryer at 350°F, and preheat for 5 minutes.
Take a 6 cups muffin pan, grease it with oil, and set aside.
Place melted butter in a bowl, whisk in sweetener until blended, and then beat in eggs, vanilla, and heavy whipping cream until combined.
Add remaining ingredients, beat again until incorporated and smooth batter comes together. Then pour the mixture into the prepared pan.
Place the pan in the air fryer and cook for 10 minutes.
Let the cake cool and serve.

Nutrition: Calories: 191.9, Carbs: 7.8g, Fat: 15.8g, Protein: 4.3g, Fiber: 2g

378. Chocolate Brownies

Preparation Time: 10 minutes
Servings: 4

Cooking Time: 36 minutes

Ingredients:

- ½ cup chocolate chips, sugar-free
- 1 tsp. vanilla extract, unsweetened
- ¼ cup erythritol sweetener
- ½ cup butter, unsalted

- *eggs, pastured*

Directions: Set the air fryer at 350°F, and preheat for 10 minutes.
Place butter and chocolate in a heatproof bowl and microwave for 1 minute, stirring every 30 seconds.
Crack eggs in another bowl, beat in vanilla and sweetener until smooth, and then slowly beat in melted chocolate mixture until well incorporated.
Take a springform pan that fits into the air fryer, grease it with oil, and then pour in batter in it.
Place the pan in the air fryer, close with its lid, and cook for 35 minutes until cake is done.
When the air fryer beeps, open its lid, take out the pan and let the brownies cool in it.
Then take out the brownies, cut them into even pieces, and serve.

Nutrition: Calories: 223.7, Carbs: 2.8g, Fat: 22.9g, Protein: 4.2g, Fiber: 1g

379. Spiced Apples

Preparation Time: 5 minutes   **Cooking Time: 17 minutes**
Servings: 4

Ingredients:
- *4 small apples, cored, sliced*
- *2 tbsp. erythritol sweetener*
- *2 tsp. apple pie spice*
- *2 tbsp. olive oil*

Directions: Set the air fryer at 350°F, and preheat for 5 minutes.
Place apple slice in a bowl, sprinkle with sweetener and spice, and drizzle with oil. Stir until evenly coated.
Add apple slices in the air fryer, close with its lid and cook for 12 minutes, shaking halfway through the frying.
Serve straight away.

Nutrition: Calories: 89.2, Carbs: 21.2g, Fat: 1.8g, Protein: 0.8g, Fiber: 5.3g

380. Chocolate Lava Cake

Preparation Time: 5 minutes   **Cooking Time: 13 minutes**
Servings: 2

Ingredients:
- *1 tbsp. flax meal*
- *½ tsp. baking powder*
- *1 tbsp. cocoa powder, unsweetened*
- *½ tbsp. erythritol sweetener*
- *⅛ tsp. Stevia sweetener*
- *⅛ tsp. vanilla extract, unsweetened*
- *1 tbsp. olive oil*
- *2 tbsp. water*
- *1 egg, pastured*

Directions: Set the air fryer at 350°F, and preheat for 5 minutes.
Meanwhile, take two cups of the ramekin, grease it with oil, and set it aside.
Place all the ingredients in a bowl, whisk until incorporated, and pour the batter into the ramekin.
Open the fryer, place ramekin in it, close with its lid, and cook for 8 minutes until inserting a skewer into the cake slides out clean.
Let the cake cool before cutting into slices, and serve.

Nutrition: Calories: 362.1, Carbs: 3.2g, Fat: 32.9g, Protein: 12.1g, Fiber: 0.6g

Recipe Index

Recipes   Page

Bacon BBQ	36		Cheese and Egg Breakfast Sandwich	22
Bacon Chicken Breast	50		Cheese and Mushroom Frittata	24
Bacon-Wrapped Chicken	55		Cheese and Onion Nuggets	37
Bagel Crust Fish Fillets	104		Cheese Omelette	24
Bagels	24		Cheese Pork Chops	78
Baked Mini Quiche	22		Cheese Stuffed Mushrooms	107
Baked Parmesan Tilapia	103		Cheesecake Bites	130
Baked Salmon Patties	105		Cheesy Bell Pepper Eggs	123
Baked Tilapia	103		Cheesy Chicken Omelet	30
Balsamic Root Vegetables	115		Cheesy Chickpea and Zucchini Burgers	31
Banana Muffins in Air Fryer	127		Cheesy Pork Chops in Air Fryer	71
Basic BBQ Chicken	56		Cheesy Salmon Fillets	105
Beef and Ale Casserole	61		Chicken & Turkey Meatloaf	51
Beef Steak Kabobs with Vegetables	61		Chicken Bites in Air Fryer	43
Beef with Mushrooms	64		Chicken Casserole	53
Beef-Chicken Meatball Casserole	68		Chicken Cheese Quesadilla in Air Fryer	43
Bell Peppers Frittata	48		Chicken Coconut Poppers	49
Berry Cheesecake	128		Chicken Fillet	56
Blackened Chicken Breast	41		Chicken Fried Spring Rolls	52
Blueberry Buns	35		Chicken Goulash	51
Breaded Chicken Tenderloins	46		Chicken in Beer	56
Breaded Pork Chops	76		Chicken Mac and Cheese	54
Breakfast Cheese Bread Cups	20		Chicken Pie	41
Breakfast Cod Nuggets	20		Chicken Pot Pie	53
Breakfast Frittata	23		Chicken Tenders	119
Brine-Soaked Turkey	44		Chicken Thighs Smothered Style	43
Broccoli Chicken Casserole	54		Chicken Tikka Kebab	54
Brussels sprouts	110		Chicken with Lemon and Bahian Seasoning	56
Brussels Sprouts & Potatoes Dish	98		Chicken with Mixed Vegetables	43
Buffalo Cauliflower Wings	108		Chilean Sea Bass with Green Olive Relish	96
Butter Endives Recipe	97		Chili Beef Jerky	66
Butter Pork Chops	80		Chocolate Brownies	131
Buttermilk Chicken in Air-Fryer	42		Chocolate Cake	131
Buttery Cod	88		Chocolate Lava Cake	132
Cabbage Wedges	107		Cinnamon and Cheese Pancake	18
Cajun Salmon	89		Cinnamon Pancake	16
Carrot and Oat Balls	116		Coconut Pie	130
Catfish with Green Beans, in Southern Style	85		Coriander Chicken	51
Cauliflower Rice	109		Corn on the Cob with Herb Butter	112
Cauliflower Tater Tots	113		Corn Tortilla Chips	34
Cayenne Rib Eye Steak	68		Crab Cakes	89
Cheddar Chicken Drumsticks	50			

Crab Legs	88		Garlic Salmon Balls	36
Cream Buns with Strawberries	34		Garlic Tomatoes	37
Cream Cheese Stuffed Jalapeños	102		Garlic-Roasted Bell Peppers	97
Creamed Spinach	109		Ginger and Green Onion Fish	99
Creamy Chicken Thighs	55		Grain-free Lava Cakes in Air Fryer	127
Creamy Shrimp Nachos	91		Greek Lamb Pita Pockets	59
Crisp Egg Cups	27		Greek-Style Vegetable Bake	114
Crispy Air Fryer Fish	93		Green Beans	110
Crispy Breakfast Avocado Fries	21		Green Beans with Pecorino Romano	111
Crispy Brussels sprouts	121		Green Bell Peppers With Cauliflower Stuffing	31
Crispy Potatoes	28		Green Onions and Parmesan Tomatoes	30
Crunchy Cauliflower	97			
Crustless Cheesecake	131		Grilled Cheese Sandwiches	19
Diet Boiled Ribs	78		Grilled Salmon with Lemon	94
Dijon Tenderloin	75		Hamburgers	64
Dill Mashed Potato	98		Hard-Boiled Eggs	18
Easy Tuna Wraps	93		Herb Air Fried Chicken Thighs	57
Eggless Cake	128		Herbed Pork Ribs	74
Eggplant Fries	37		Herb-Marinated Chicken Thighs	40
Eggplant Parmesan	109		Homemade Flamingos	73
Eggs and Cocotte on Toast	22		Hot Dogs	65
Empanadas	62		Jamaican Pork with Jerk	70
Faire-Worthy Turkey Legs	57		Japanese Tempura Bowl	115
Family Vegetable Gratin	115		Juicy Pork Chops	78
Fennel Frittata	17		Kale & Celery Crackers	119
Fish Finger Sandwich	83		Ketogenic French Fries	38
Fish Tacos	100		Lamb Chops with Herb Butter	63
Flavored Pork Chops	72		Lean Lamb and Turkey Meatballs with Yogurt	59
Flavorful Egg Rolls	77			
Flavorful Meatballs	64		Lemon Garlic Shrimp in Air Fryer	82
French Toast in Sticks	35		Lemon Greek Beef and Vegetables	65
Fried Crawfish	92		Lemon Pepper Chicken	58
Fried Pickles	110		Lemon Pepper Chicken Breast	49
Garlic Beef Steak	67		Lemon Pepper Shrimp in Air Fryer	87
Garlic Cauliflower Nuggets	38		Lemon Pork Tenderloin	75
Garlic Green Tomatoes	38		Lemon Rosemary Chicken	46
Garlic Kale Chips	36		Lemon Scallops with Asparagus	99
Garlic Parmesan Chicken Tenders	44		Lemon Snapper with Fruit	100
Garlic Parmesan Roasted Shrimp	101		Lemon-Garlic Chicken	40
Garlic Parmesan Shrimp	91		Lemon-Garlic Tofu with Quinoa	27
Garlic Potatoes	32		Lettuce Salad with Beef Strips	116
Garlic Roasted Mushrooms	33		Lime Baked Salmon	88
Garlic Rosemary Grilled Prawns	95		Lime Trout and Shallots	88

Lime-Garlic Shrimp Kebabs	82		Pecan Crusted Fish Fillets	104
Low Carb Baked Eggs	29		Peppery and Lemony Haddock	92
Low Carb Peanut Butter Cookies	126		Pesto Scallops	105
Low-Carb White Egg and Spinach Frittata	18		Pistachio Crusted Salmon	92
Mango Shrimp Skewers	91		Popcorn Chicken in Air Fryer	40
Meatballs and Creamy Potatoes	65		Pork Almond Bites	79
Meatballs in Spicy Tomato Sauce	69		Pork Burgers with Red Cabbage Slaw	76
Meatballs in Tomato Sauce	66		Pork Chop with Broccoli	77
Meatloaf	62		Pork Chops	79
Mediterranean Vegetable Skewers	112		Pork Dumplings	77
Mini Meatloaf	63		Pork Head Chops With Vegetables	71
Mini Pizza	118		Pork Loin	74
Moist & Juicy Baked Cod	105		Pork Ribs	75
Monkey Bread	19		Pork Rind	73
Morning Mini Cheeseburger Sliders	23		Pork Satay	76
Muffins Sandwich	35		Pork Taquitos	77
Mushroom and Cheese Frittata	18		Pork Tenderloin with Mustard Glazed	70
Mushroom Cheese Salad	68		Pork Trinoza Wrapped in Ham	72
Mushroom Oatmeal	47		Pulled Pork	74
Mustard-Crusted Sole	93		Pumpkin Pie French Toast	20
No Frills Turkey Breast	57		Quick Shrimp Scampi	101
No-breaded Turkey Breast	46		Rainbow Vegetable Fritters	112
No-Breading Chicken Breast in Air Fryer	48		Ranch Chicken Wings	53
			Ranch Tilapia fillets	95
Okra	108		Raspberry Cookies in Air Fryer	127
Olive, Cheese, and Broccoli	32		Red Cabbage and Mushroom Stickers	32
Onion Bites	33		Ripe Plantains	39
Onion Rings	36		Roasted Bell Peppers	37
Orange Chicken Wings	41		Roasted Broccoli with Sesame Seeds	111
Oriental Omelet	21		Roasted Potatoes	99
Pandan Coconut Chicken	50		Roasted Red Snapper	89
Panko Coconut Shrimp	102		Roasted Salmon with Fennel Salad	82
Paprika Beef Tongue	68		Rolled Turkey Breast	55
Paprika Pulled Pork	70		Rosemary Beef Tips	67
Paprika Whole Chicken	49		Rosemary Lamb Chops	62
Parmesan Beef Slices	66		Salmon Fillets	94
Parmesan Broccoli and Asparagus	96		Salmon with Fennel and Carrot	94
Parmesan Cauliflower	33		Scallion Sandwich	19
Parmesan Chicken Meatballs	46		Scallops with Tomato Sauce	82
Parmesan French Fries	34		Scrambled Eggs	17
Parmesan Garlic Crusted Salmon	85		Sea Bass and Cauliflower	90
Peanut Butter and Banana Breakfast Sandwich	22		Sea Bass and Rice	90
			Sesame Seeds Fish Fillet	87

Shrimp and Okra	87		Tasty Hassel back Chicken	58
Shrimp Rolls in Air Fryer	81		Tasty Tuna Steaks	103
Shrimp Scampi	89		Tender Pork Chops	78
Skinny Pumpkin Chips	39		Teriyaki Hen Drumsticks	55
Southwest Chicken in Air Fryer	48		Three-Cheese Stuffed Mushrooms	114
Spiced Apples	132		Trout and Zucchinis	89
Spiced Nuts	38		Tuna Zoodle Casserole	90
Spiced Pork Chops	73		Turkey Breast with Mustard Glaze	45
Spicy Cajun Shrimp	101		Turkey Fajitas Platter in Air Fryer	44
Spicy Glazed Carrots	111		Turkey Juicy Breast Tenderloin	45
Spicy Jalapeno Hassel back Chicken	58		Turkey Meatballs with Dried Dill	52
Spicy Sweet Potatoes	31		Veg Buffalo Cauliflower	98
Spinach and Mushrooms Omelet	16		Vegan Mashed Potato	28
Spinach Beef Heart	67		Vegan Sandwich	28
Sriracha Calamari	81		Vegetable Braise	115
Steak Tips	66		Vegetable Egg Pancake	21
Strawberries Oatmeal	17		Vegetable Rolls	26
Stuffed Cabbage and Pork Loin Rolls	72		Vegetable Spring Rolls	122
Sugar-Free Carrot Cake	126		Vegetarian Omelet	25
Sweet & Sour Tuna	96		Veggie Air Fryer Eggs	29
Sweet Beets Salad	98		Veggie Mix	32
Sweet Corn Fritters with Avocado	114		Veggies with Yogurt-Tahini Sauce	112
Sweet Potato Cauliflower Patties	124		Whole Chicken with Italian Seasoning	52
Sweet Potato Fritters	107		Zucchini Crisps	39
Swiss Cheese & Vegetable Casserole	113		Zucchini Gratin	122
Swordfish Steaks and Tomatoes	87		Zucchini Parmesan Chips	120
Taco-Stuffed Peppers	63		Zucchini Turkey Burgers	45
Tahini Oatmeal Chocolate Chunk Cookies	126			

Made in United States
North Haven, CT
07 August 2023

40042783R00076